Philosophy of Life

Philosophy of Life

Modal Logic, Psychotherapy, and the Good Life

Aleksandar Fatić

ANTHEM PRESS

Anthem Press
An imprint of Wimbledon Publishing Company
www.anthempress.com

This edition first published in UK and USA 2026
75–76 Blackfriars Road, London SE1 8HA, UK
or PO Box 9779, London SW19 7ZG, UK
by ANTHEM PRESS
and
244 Madison Ave #116, New York, NY 10016, USA

British Library Cataloguing-in-Publication Data
A catalogue record for this book is available from the British Library.

Library of Congress Cataloging-in-Publication Data: 2026935548

ISBN-13: 978-1-83999-895-9
ISBN-10: 1-83999-895-4

Cover credit: Aleksandar Fatić

This title is also available as an eBook.

CONTENTS

INTRODUCTION

Originally, psychotherapy was a part of philosophy. This simple fact from the intellectual and everyday life history of our civilization is revived by the re-emergence of practical philosophy in the form of philosophical practice. There are a number of forms of philosophical practice, which today are primarily led by the American Philosophical Practitioners' Association and the iconic figure of its leader, Lou Marinoff, the author of the bestseller *Plato, Not Prozac*, and many other books that relate philosophy to psychotherapy and an array of practical counseling and related disciplines. A further development of this re-emergence of the awareness of the philosophical nature and methodological content of psychotherapy is Modal Integrative Psychotherapy (MIP), which is based on two important facets: philosophical practice as a conceptual foundation of all psychotherapy and the methodological reliance on modal logic, as opposed to the simple syllogistic logic that characterizes the piecemeal schools of "traditional" (in fact, quite recent) "schools" of psychotherapy (Fatić, 2025).

When I started developing MIP with my colleagues at the Institute for Practical Humanities in Belgrade, some years ago now, one of the key concerns that we faced practicing philosophical counseling and philosophical practice more generally was the one-sidedness of both psychotherapy and philosophical counseling. One of the persistent topics, which I found artificial, unconvincing, and fundamentally detrimental to the development of successful psychotherapy, was the insistence on "differences between psychotherapy and philosophical counseling." Various arguments were, and continue to be, put forward to "defend" the uniqueness of either: philosophical counseling was said to have to do with increasing the quality of life without recourse to pathology, while psychotherapy, among other differences, was seen as primarily "therapeutic." As I tested these assumptions in my practical work with clients, I grew increasingly convinced that the distinction was unsustainable. When people arrive for counseling, typically they do not care in the least whether the therapist is a philosophical counselor or psychotherapist, and if the latter is the case, what school of psychotherapy the therapist belongs to. These are self-identifications that serve only the therapist, not the client. What people seek is competent conversation and assistance in transforming their lives. The foundation of such transformation is a particular view of the world. Methodologically, such transformations are possible only through the application of a particular logic that structures the entire therapeutic relationship and the process of personal change of the client, but also of the therapist. It seemed to me that both philosophical counseling and traditional psychotherapy failed on this important account.

The initial confusion involved considerable misinterpretations. While philosophical practitioners were convinced that psychologists among the psychotherapists were insufficiently versed in philosophy and failed to understand the philosophical foundations of all psychotherapeutic theories and concepts, many psychologists working in psychotherapy were equally convinced that philosophers who were counselors and therapists lacked an understanding of psychological methodology, communication skills, and an understanding of standards of mental health and psychological disorders. In my experience, neither was true. The psychologists I had a chance to work with had a decent understanding of the philosophical origin and nature of the basic concepts they worked with and were, in fact, keen to become more involved in philosophical counseling. At the same time, the experienced philosophers who worked as therapists were familiar with the psychological schools and methods and were equally keen to learn more in that realm. It was clear that the best members of both "camps" sought convergence, while only those unsure of themselves and of their prowess in the field sought delineations and the solidification of barriers. The common shortcoming encountered in this composite helping activity appeared to be philosophical, however: traditional psychotherapy, irrespective of the underlying academic profile of the practitioners, was firmly based on a naïve, propositional logic, founded on the Aristotelian syllogistic inference and the assumption of the world as "real," as a "given" that the troubled person somehow needed to "metabolize" and adapt to. The world that hurts us and brings us to therapy, however, is neither so "real" and based on hard facts as naïve realism assumes, nor is it always subject to simple logic where beliefs and attitudes are either "true" or "untrue," either "justified" or "unjustified," either "useful" or "harmful." The world we live in is not just an environment that we need to adapt to. It is not simply a "given" in psychotherapy. Rather, the world that surrounds us is a *living organism that responds to us*. This is the crux of modal logic as the foundation of MIP, as opposed to the syllogistic logic that is the uncritical logic that traditional psychotherapy, often unwittingly, relies on.

Our world does not simply "exist," or even "evolve" around us. Evolutionary thinking, including evolutionary psychology, assumes that the changes in our world necessitate our adaptation, and where that adaptation fails, or misfires on the level of subjective experience, psychic problems arise. However, our world does not simply "evolve" and offer us demands to which we must respond: rather, our experiential reality shifts, bends, and warps, reflects our beliefs and responds to them, challenges us, talks back to us, and fundamentally, offers various contexts in which our beliefs, desires, hopes, and fears may be possible, more or less probable, or untenable. Traditional psychotherapy tends to be insufficiently radical in its hesitancy to shake the entire modal world of the client (and, sometimes, other people around the client, including the therapist himself). It so often hesitates to shake the current reality, to reshuffle the possibilities that are logically determined by each of the various possible worlds. The technical concept of "possible world" in modal logic is in fact a literal description of how the world works for us in psychotherapy and in life more generally. The reality we encounter and become attached to is only one possible world. There are, simultaneously, many other possible worlds hovering around, and each might be able to be called into the current reality, often through as little as a shift in attention (Galtung, 2009). *The technical terms of modal logic are in fact literal terms of psychotherapy.* Logical truths in their practical significance are both transformative and simple. This is how MIP was born.

The difference between MIP's understanding of our life-world, our experiential reality, and that of most traditional psychotherapeutic schools is reflected in the concept of "shaking the kaleidoscope," or "striking into the world."

If the world is a living subject that envelopes us, nurtures or depletes us, heals or sickens us, our relationship with the world must be active, rather than merely accepting. We must not be "realistic" in the sense of accepting the external "givens" and trying to shift our perceptions or framing of the life experience. Instead, one must strike into the living mass that surrounds us, causing it to coil, groan, contract, reposition, and change shape until the relationship with the world is changed and new possibilities emerge. In practice, this does not involve life struggle in the traditional sense: in fact, struggle in life is much more associated with the acceptance of the impossibilities that the "given" reality imposes on us than with shifting to, or calling into reality, an alternative modal world. Striking into the world, rather, involves causing the possible worlds to shift, expelling, as it were, one possible world from the determining structure of our life and calling into reality another, whereby the entire structure of possibility and impossibility transforms. For example, rather than fixing a relationship by changing tone and addressing the discrete inadequacies by seeking mutual "insight," MIP might suggest removing the entire context of a dysfunctional relationship: changing a place of living, selling real estate, taking a new job in a radically different environment, removing the various structures of expectations built into one's current structure and position in life that lock one out of key possibilities.

While the idea of striking into a live reality that surrounds our existence as a strategy to elicit change in the conditions of possibility or impossibility of certain choices, beliefs, desires, and values may suggest a radical approach that could be disproportionate to the degree of dysfunctionality or dissatisfaction one feels as a reason to enter counseling, the value and meaning of the strategy is, in fact, not exhausted in its radical nature. One may strike into contextual reality with radical force, but such a tactic may be therapeutically ineffective if the structure of modality, of the logical conditions that determine one's experiential reality, is unaddressed. The target of MIP interventions is not merely the set of facts that constitute the micro-existence of the client in their current life-world, but the underlying conditions that determine the *logical context* for the client's complaints. Sometimes, the underlying conditions will require anything but a radical shift. MIP works with meta-reality, namely with the logical presuppositions for what is the case (including the person's current problem), rather than focusing on addressing the problem within the existing propositional logical structure. The difference between the two approaches is comparable to that between healing a physical ailment or pathology through direct interventions, on the one hand, and eliminating them by changing the bodily, chemical, or environmental conditions that facilitate the pathology, on the other. Metalogical thinking shifts the structure, rather than the manifestation of that structure that is one's immediate complaint. The shifts may indeed be radical, but they may also be minuscule; the sheer volume of the change does not necessarily affect its nature: one may conduct a micro-change that is structural, and at the same time one may conduct major changes that are epiphenomenal, behavioral, and remain within the existing logical structure of one's life.

Let me share two very simple examples of how this structural/logical approach functions from the perspective of operating a counseling practice. The first example is the selection of clients. We can fairly accurately assess whether a person is a suitable client for us already from the first few interactions, without ever seeing them in person, based on a structural and methodological analysis of their communications. I was recently approached by a woman, highly articulate in her presentation, who "begged" for an appointment because she had an "unbearable life" of not having contact with her 47-year-old son, who had "cut her out" of his life and "would not reconsider his mistakes." Although I was not taking new clients at the time, I offered her an in-person appointment. She cancelled on the day of the appointment, citing a headache, but asked whether we could talk on the phone, which I ignored. In the following days, she kept contacting me repeatedly, asking for another appointment. As she was extremely persistent, I offered her one online, knowing that she would probably not show up. She agreed, but immediately asked for a follow-up appointment in-person. I ignored that request. On the day of the appointment, she failed to pay the fee and did not show up, citing difficulties in connecting online, and she immediately asked for another in-person appointment. A few minutes later, she sent the message: "Alas, it was not meant to be."

The described, common and simple situation is a structural presentation of a modal world adopted by the client that shows no prospect of improvement. In fact, her manipulative actions offer an interesting prima facie account of the probable reasons she is rejected by her son. The foreseeable logical and methodological conditions of working with such a client tell the observant therapist everything they need to know, without even having to see the client. Logic precedes the phenomenological presentation.

The second example is that of payments for therapy. Unlike in other contexts, in psychotherapy payment is an integral tool for relationship-building. Money, here, is not merely a remuneration for service—it is a statement of value and commitment that solidifies a sense of direction, primarily within the client, but also in the therapist. That is why observing the regularity of payment, and willingness of the client to pay for therapy (all other relevant conditions obtaining, such as the client's actual ability to pay for therapy), are important markers of the very meaningfulness and steadiness of the therapeutic process in the client. Even if the money paid for therapy were to go to someone else, other than the therapist (humanitarian, social or other causes), it is essential that the client regularly pays for therapy and shows an internal "accounting" efficiency, where he or she follows the agreed rhythm of payment of his or her own accord. Payment in therapy is the attitude, or more precisely, a reliable presentation of one's attitude towards therapy. It is a structural feature of therapy, just like the client's showing up on time, not missing sessions and preparing for them adequately.

In his economistic philosophy of law, Richard Posner, a Chicago judge and legal theorist, advances a theory that, potentially, even criminal law could be reduced to the law of torts, based on the principle that all values (including, controversially, that of justice) eventually end up in the hands of those who value them the most (or, in a simplified phrase, who are willing to pay the most for those goods) (Posner, 1985: 1195–1196 and 1205, 1986: 204–205). While this principle is somewhat oversimplified when it is cast upon the therapeutic process, its underlying dynamics is at the core of how payment operates in therapy.

Both examples are so simple and frequent that they seem almost banal. However, they clearly illustrate how structural features of one's presentation allow an assessment of the effectiveness of an interpersonal interaction without ever having to actually engage in that interaction or face the phenomenological content of what the relationship would actually have to deal with.

Practical Differences Between Emphases on Modal and Propositional Logic

Traditionally, most conventional methods of psychotherapy tend to rely on propositional logic in their therapeutic reasoning. The crux of the difference between a reliance on syllogistic logic and the psychotherapeutic thinking based on modal logic is in the perception and treatment of "reality," both existential and psychic. Syllogistic logic rests on conclusions that are based on valid truths, namely on premises that, when extended into the psychotherapeutic realm, usually resonate with the precepts that one ought to be "realistic" and work within the given circumstances to overcome one's psychic difficulties in processing the experience of that reality. Thus, one of the most common ideas in traditional schools of psychotherapy is that psychotherapy is primarily concerned with a change in one's perceptions of reality and circumstances, and an increase in one's *subjective* capacities to address and overcome the negative and traumatizing experience of that reality.

The above horizon of intervention is included in MIP, but it is insufficient to speak to a plethora of issues that a person typically encounters when feeling stuck in one's life and, as a result, seeking psychotherapeutic help. Modal logic, contrary to strictly syllogistic logic, works with logical operators such as "possible" or modal worlds, namely the different sets of circumstances that are, in a way, clustered up as closely associated possibilities, where only one set is actual, or "real," while all the other possibilities are "irreal" to use the term coined by Johan Galtung. They are not real in the sense that they do not actually obtain where one actually finds oneself in life, however, they could become real almost in an instant, if one's attention and related action were to shift in a way that would call such possible worlds (again, the term refers merely to a different set of circumstances) into the actuality, or reality, of one's current existential situation (Galtung, 2009).

Consider an example. A client, in his early 30s, arrives for counseling with a complaint related to a romantic relationship. He has been in a 10-year-long relationship with a woman who exhibits a pattern of what seems like classic narcissistic abuse: she offers him some short-term warmth and love, only to follow on by devaluing and disparaging him, to eventually discard him. She regularly blocks him on social networks and makes contact difficult for months at a time. Once he becomes used to the distance between them, she contacts him again and begins the "hoovering" process of "sucking him back in," into the relationship, which, again, leads to a repeated cycle of devaluing, discarding, hoovering, and so on (Kernberg, 1975). The client is emotionally exhausted, but "hooked" to this pattern, to such an extent that he describes a precise timetable of the four phases of the narcissistic abuse: the "nice part" of the relationship (the hoovering) usually takes place between May and September each year. The devaluation occurs roughly between September and November, while the discarding takes place from November to next May. This cycle has repeated itself for a decade. Thus, the client is a victim of active abuse about two-thirds of the year, while the rest is a highly manipulative relationship. He says that he cannot live without this person and believes that she gives him something that increases his value and symbolizes for him a social "stepping up" from his current circumstances. He sees her as superior and more socially valuable than he is.

The client is a calm, apparently well-composed young man who had had a gambling problem; however, he went to work abroad, to a distant country and culture, to earn enough to pay his gambling debts, and he returned "clean" from his addiction and with some savings. He is now renovating his house and has managed to constructively manage very difficult family relationships and events with his parents (mother's psychosis and hospitalization, father's re-marriage, and his and his brother's cohabitation with the father's new family, with a small child, in the same house, while continuing to help his mother through an acute psychosis and subsequently covering her living costs and maintaining almost daily visits).

Previously, the client underwent a psychotherapy with which he was dissatisfied. He sees this therapy as having focused primarily on locating his inadequacies. His desire is for the therapy to help him re-engage with the elusive woman. While the emotional suffering is obvious, the person obviously has the openness and strength of character required to grapple with the difficult "actuality." What does MIP suggest in such a case?

The client's current situation is one of narcissistic abuse (Fatić, 2023a, 2023b; Pies, 2023; Amir, 2023). His horizon of perceived solutions is within his immediate specter of circumstances. He seeks (or craves) a reconnection with his romantic partner in the existing context of his life.

D's therapy starts with a focus on reducing the tension in the client. For the first several weeks, his erratic and uncontrollable attempts to connect with the manipulating partner are brought in check by disciplined and precisely timed, brief and non-intrusive communications, to which he receives no response. As the treatment unfolds, each week he extends the periods of non-communication. Within several weeks, the client is able to discuss the need to change his career and find employment in a different, more satisfying, and socially dynamic setting. Only a minor part of the sessions remains devoted to his romantic issue. His attention shifts to what things would feel like if he were able to buy an apartment for his mother, who now lives in inadequate circumstances. He makes a decision to decline an invitation to go abroad for work again, as this makes him feel isolated and unhappy. In the subsequent sessions, D is given the therapeutic task to apply for one job every day: positions that would allow him to address his sense of inadequacy and meet new people, while at the same time making him financially more stable.

After several sessions, the client notes that the therapy helps him and that "he should have taken therapy long ago," as that way he would "not have lost so much time of his life." He is still engaged in the abusive relationship; however, the therapy does not focus on solving that relationship; rather, it is driven by a need for the client to make a "jump" from the current modal world into a different one, where he as a person would feel empowered and more in control regardless of his romantic issue. He notices that he is increasingly "displaced" from the circumstances that had determined his life for a decade. His new idea is to enroll in a language school to remedy his sense of "shame" for not speaking English (although the client speaks fluent Russian and has lived and been fully functional in Russia). He further considers investment options and potential independent business avenues. His romantic problem, still unsolved, remains in his orbit, however, it occupies an increasingly marginal space. D is on the way to changing his modal worlds.

The circumstances where D now operates, only weeks into therapy, were "not real" for him when he started therapy: his normative and psychic environment has changed because he has moved from his initial situation into a new situation. This is not just a change of perceptions or of his pattern of reactions to the "given" or "real." It is a change of objective circumstances, which the client has called into reality by shifting his attention. He notes this difference between his current thought process and the one he experienced before. Earlier in counseling, before we met, he had been kept in the immediate, daunting proximity of his initial problem and encouraged to "face" it and "outgrow" it, with defeating results. The difficulty here is that one does not "face" or "outgrow" advanced narcissistic abuse. The cure for this situation is only a modal shift, or pivot: one changes one's circumstances alongside an adjustment of one's values. One starts thinking about something else, calling into one's experience a different modal world of intentions, ideas, and structured plans, while *abandoning* the previous modal world and the initial problem within it. The difference here seems subtle, but it is decisive. It is, logically, a difference between continuity and discontinuity. Reinterpreting, reframing, and metabolizing a failed relationship in order to integrate it into one's overall life script is a therapeutic goal of continuity. Abandoning an unresolved (and unresolvable) relationship issue and focusing on completely different life goals is a seemingly related, but logically different, therapeutic goal. In the first perspective, the life script as a whole is seen as linear. In the latter, it is presented as a set of transformations and changes of direction. The former paradigm is characteristic of propositional logic-based psychotherapy. The latter is characteristic of modal psychotherapeutic thinking.

After the initial paradigm switch, one stage, the client operates in a different modal world: he now sees emotional partnership and romantic encounter as merely an addition to his main preoccupation in life, which is to contribute to others, to one's own well-being and a sense of self-realization through engagement with work and sociality. This change is not "reframing," because the focus is not on the unresolved issue. It is not a change of the frame of the issue, but a completely different painting, where the old painting is left in the corner of the atelier of one's life plan. That is not limited to romantic relationships. The initial problem remains unsolved, but it is, in a sense, "dissolved": it is no longer relevant in the different modal world.

What is impossible in one modal world (in this case, self-empowerment and re-engagement with life) is possible in another modal world, and one that is only a hand's reach away, although momentarily "irreal." In the first six months of therapy, D did not resolve his romantic problem, but he found a well-paid job, regained his vitality, created all kinds of new problems for himself, and is now in the process of dealing with them. The old painting of life is still there, eliciting the occasional melancholy, but it is gathering dust and losing appeal by the day. The old modal world has been left.

The above-described example is what one might consider a fairly everyday, ordinary issue in psychotherapy, where the methodological difference in approach compared to "traditional" psychotherapy is at once obvious and relatively common, nondramatic, and straightforward to implement.

Deep Engagement

Another defining aspect of MIP is the deep engagement of the therapist with the client. MIP does not, generally, condone a "neutrality" in the therapist's relationship with the client, whether it is a value neutrality or a positional neutrality regarding the client's goals. While the main intent of therapy is to empower the client to address their difficulties more or less on their own, constructively, because this is the way for them to develop skills that will be useful in advancing their overall quality of life across the span of issues that they face in life, the MIP practitioner does not shy away from actively helping the client shift the objective circumstances and achieve a different strategy vis-à-vis the others and the client's overall living reality. This, then, changes the person's vision of their specific issues that they seek to address through counseling.

Paula was a university lecturer with issues of workplace conflict with her director. She arrived for counseling with symptoms of serious burnout. Paula could not concentrate; she rarely slept more than 5 hours and would typically find herself waking up while "hugging her computer," having fallen asleep while (ineffectively) working. Her academic title was expiring shortly, and she needed to apply either for reinstatement at the same rank or for promotion, but was unable to fulfil the conditions for either because, as she saw it, she was being "mobbed" at work. A researcher with a doctorate, she was forced to work a nine-to-five job at her university, doing administrative tasks, writing projects for others, filing financial reports for activities she did not participate in, and even driving her superior to and from work. Paula was even forced to illegally use her personal bank account transactions where she would nominally receive payments for the services she provided as a part of her regular job, and then she would have to withdraw these funds and give them to her director to pay for technical services not included in the project budget. For years, she was unable to break away from this cycle of abuse. As a result, she was under such stress that she was unable to become pregnant, despite all the medical checks being in perfect order, and was panicking that, at the age of 40, she would not be able to have the family she desired. At one time, Paula was hospitalized for potentially serious oncological surgery. Eventually, this turned out well for her, with a benign outcome. However, during the post-surgery recovery, while she was still in hospital, she had to continue working online to meet the administrative deadlines imposed on her by her director. When she arrived for counseling, she was disoriented, suffered from a crisis of self-confidence ("I cannot write anything of any quality, it is all high school-level description. I am lucky that nobody reads my work. I don't believe in any significance of what I do as a researcher.").

Paula was extremely articulate. She was a mellow, sophisticated woman who cared for the emotions and interests of others, and she found herself in what she described as a "shark pond" with individuals who simply used her in the most professionally reckless ways. Her position in her institution was unenviable, and she was unable to shift the balance of power and protect herself. She sought advice on how to "reframe the experience" so as to "physically and mentally survive." In the initial counseling session, Paula mentioned leaving her career "to save her life."

My MIP approach to Paula involved an initial evaluation of the modal world she was in, and the identification, in conversation with Paula, of the potential modal changes in her circumstances that would place her differently within the strategic situation that she found herself in.

The first thing Paula did after commencing counseling was to go on sick leave for three months. During this sick leave, she used the legally protected time she had to complete one of the important papers for publication that she needed for her promotion, and she concentrated on developing resilience and skills to fend off the onslaught of demands by her boss while she was legally absent from work. The intervention that had led to this strategy by Paula was predicated upon her conclusion that her promotion would objectively position her in a more resilient situation within the institution, allowing her at the same time to seek a different academic job more effectively. Thus, it was essential for Paula to focus on calling into her actuality a different objective set of circumstances that would change her "fighting capacity" to protect herself. Paula was so articulate that little space was left to work with her on modifying her subjective perceptions of her situation. She already understood everything. The difficulties were simply so threatening to her well-being that she needed help to switch "objective" modal worlds quickly and very strategically.

While working with Paula, I engaged with her issues at work outside the therapeutic framework. I was lucky to understand Paula's work environment well and I had contacts in her institution. I coached Paula to set a rhythm for the completion of her written work, put her in contact with journal editors, and asked a colleague at her institution to help with organizing the technicalities for her promotion (assist her with finding a graduate student to supervise, "having her back" at meetings where she was mobbed, etc.). Paula rose from psychological ashes like a Phoenix. At the time of writing this book, roughly two years later, Paula is the mother of a little girl she conceived naturally, after a prolonged stress of trying in vitro fertilization during her troubles at work. She is able again to pursue her passion, archery. Paula is a veteran, top-notch archer and an archery umpire. Her burnout is now gone. While she still appears at sessions reeling from continuous emotional assaults launched at her at her workplace, she is far more resilient and exhibits high energy levels. There is still a fight ahead of Paula; she now operates in a different modal world: all her administrative tasks have vanished (she described this as "miraculous"). She has simply "jumped" to another modality and is now fighting for her academic goals. She is so firm in meetings with her director that she (the director) insists on taping the meetings because she is "afraid" of Paula. This is the same person that, two years earlier, served as her director's driver. Paula no longer identifies with the victimhood she perceived as her primary condition when she started counseling.

Note that in neither of the two examples described above did we work primarily on a subjective reinterpretation of the client's experience. The first client, D, was so emotionally abused and fixated on his abuser that he needed to leave the hellish paradigm completely and jump to another modality or modal world. This changed him, while at the same time reducing the significance of the (unsolved) emotional situation within his newly found circumstances and priorities. The second client, Paula, was able to challenge her institutional (and, as a result, psychic) situation by actually developing a new skill to say "no" and by no longer lingering in the modal world of administration and challenges of being mobbed; she decided to simply leave that modal world and call another into existence by working on different tasks and, correspondingly, by refusing to work on the previous tasks. To do this without losing her job, she needed *objective* help outside the counseling process itself: help with publishing, finding allies, and so on.

The described type of intervention is controversial in traditional psychotherapy because it extends beyond the counseling room. It is a deep, living engagement with the client. This entails a different relationship between the therapist and the client that is broader and more comprehensive than the mere professional therapeutic alliance. Such "going beyond," or transcendence, of the therapeutic relationship alone has, indeed, characterized many fathers of psychotherapy, including Freud, who befriended his patients, contrary to his recommendations to other psychotherapists to remain "clinical," even "surgical" in mentality. The mature Freud violated many prescriptions for psychoanalytic therapy given by the young Freud, including the precept not to embark on the psychoanalysis of close persons and family members. In fact, Freud analysed his own daughter, who later became a psychoanalyst. Jung became intimate with his female patients. One of the fathers of modern existential psychotherapy, Irvin D. Yalom, describes in his book entitled *Lying on the Couch* how a therapist engages his clients outside the therapeutic process and faces his own demons, frustrations, and shame in the process (Yalom, 2014).

The above examples illustrate the need, even for conservative psychotherapy, to transcend the customary, self-imposed boundaries. Such situations are, in a sense, incidents, or violations of the otherwise unquestioned rules of therapy, however, they suggest that something is insufficient in those rules. MIP does not violate rules by engaging with the client outside the therapeutic process: such engagement, when appropriate and practicable, is a part of the very modal logic that MIP rests on. Not everything can be solved by working on changing a person's perceptions of the given reality; many times, clients in psychotherapy, who tend to be intelligent, articulate, and sensitive individuals ("a brute cannot suffer a personality disorganization"—goes a saying among psychotherapists), have tried, on their own, everything that could be done to address their problem. Once they arrive at a counseling room, in many cases, modal logic requires a move to address the circumstances themselves, and thus to position the person differently *vis-à-vis* the initial problem. Just like a person standing in one spot may not see an object in the same way and from the same angle as when they stand in a different spot, experiencing a psychic or existential problem from one vantage point may not be the same as viewing it from a different objective vantage point. However, to acquire a different vantage point sometimes requires more than changing one's perception; it requires an actual moving from one point, for example, one where the proverbial water is up to the person's neck and rising quickly, to an elevated point that allows both an escape route and maneuvering room to try to stop the flood. To move to that different position will require action that is seemingly outside the therapeutic process, like with Paula, whose struggle to climb to a different level of power structure in her institution needed to be helped "objectively," and this translated into her "subjective" revitalization. The MIP counselor will not shy away from engaging in such a process that has traditionally been seen as a "heresy" in conventional, piecemeal psychotherapeutic schools.

For 15 years prior to the writing of this book, the Institute for Practical Humanities (www.iph.edu.rs) has offered training in MIP. Our experience in the application of this approach and methodology is growing and showing that philosophical integration of psychotherapy is a credible way forward for psychotherapy. Most experienced psychotherapists and psychiatrists recognize this logic of evolution of their disciplines. This is witnessed in the very titles of the dominant journals and publications that command professional attention in philosophically informed psychotherapy today. An increasing number of serious systematic academic studies focus on the philosophical integration of psychotherapy that was initially pioneered by the Philosophical Practice and Philosophical Counseling movement, and that is more strictly psychotherapeutically articulated by the modern MIP.

MIP arises from a broader philosophy of life that is founded on a modal logic-focused understanding of ways not just to heal dysfunction, but to achieve a wider frame of what could be called "the good life."

References

Amir, Lydia (2023). "Narcissism: A focal point for examining the interrelatedness of psychology and philosophy." *Philosophy, Psychiatry, and Psychology*, Vol. 30, No. 2: 169–172. https://doi.org/10.1353/ppp.2023.a899947.

Fatić, Aleksandar (2023a). "Narcissism as a moral incompetence." *Philosophy, Psychiatry and Psychology*, Vol. 30, No. 2: 159–167.

Fatić, Aleksandar (2023b). "Why narcissists are morally responsible." *Philosophy, Psychiatry and Psychology*, Vol. 30, No. 2: 177–180.

Fatić, Aleksandar (2025). *Modal integrative psychotherapy: A logical integration of psychotherapy.* New York: Palgrave Macmillan. https://link.springer.com/book/9783031919336.

Galtung, Johan (2009). *Theories of conflict: Definitions, dimensions, negations, formations.* Oslo: Transcend. www.transcend.org.

Kernberg, Otto (1975). *Borderline conditions and pathological narcissism.* New York: Jason Aronson.

Pies, Ronald W. (2023). "Narcissism, empathy and moral responsibility." *Philosophy, Psychiatry, and Psychology*, Vol. 30, No. 2: 173–176. https://doi.org/10.1353/ppp.2023.a899948.

Posner, Richard A. (1985). "An economic theory of the criminal law." *Columbia Law Review*, Vol. 85: 1193–1231.

Posner, Richard A. (1986). *Economic analysis of law.* 3rd ed. Boston: Little Brown.

Yalom, Irvin (2014). *Lying on the couch.* New York: Basic Books.

Chapter 1

CONCEPT OF THE GOOD LIFE AND THE PRACTICAL INTERVENTIONS OF PHILOSOPHY

A Martial Arts Metaphor for Modal Logic in Practical Life

An important logic-grounded aspect of philosophical interventions in practical life (including in the helping contexts such as counseling and psychotherapy) is based on the shifting of modalities, or the circumstances within which certain options are possible and others are unattainable. Such a shift is often achieved by as little as a systematic redirection of focus. This simple principle generates profound differences in insight, interpretation, and approach to solving problems, making decisions, conducting negotiations, and other relational activities. One particularly easy way to illustrate how this operates is by comparing it to the Japanese martial-arts concept of *Nagashi*. The strategy of *Nagashi* is the embodied equivalent of the switching of modal worlds characteristic of interventions grounded in modal logic.

Nagashi is an art form, yet also a simple move. In Japanese Karate and other Japanese martial arts, *Nagashi* is used to minimize damage from an incoming attack, reduce the chance of being hit, and dramatically increase the range of counterattacks and other martial moves available to the practitioner. In practice, *Nagashi* is a simple step forward and sideways, away from an incoming attack, accompanied by a pivot of the body to the side while maintaining balance. Rather than meeting the incoming punch, push, or other strike by the opponent head-on, the *Nagashi* practitioner pivots about 45 degrees relative to the incoming attack. He is still there, close and engaged with the opponent, still within range of the attack—close to the opponent's arms, legs, and face. The opponent remains within his reach, yet the force and direction of his actions are no longer met directly. *Nagashi* positions the practitioner at such an angle that most of the attack's force deflects sideways, past the practitioner, while the attacker's flank and vulnerable points are exposed to the *Nagashi* practitioner.

An opponent who attacks in a linear motion begins with an advantage: in martial arts, the first attacker always holds a temporal advantage. This advantage is explained by the OODA Loop, a concept grounded in strategic science. OODA stands for the four cycles of orientation in combat or in any complex, high-stakes situation: Observation, Orientation, Decision, and Action. Every action follows this cycle. The attacker has an advantage because he is by definition further along in the OODA Loop than the defender: he is already in the Action phase, while the defender is still in the Observation phase, after which they must orient, decide, and only afterward act. By the time the defender completes the OODA Loop and is ready to act, the attacker has already initiated the next loop with the follow-up attacks. In principle, martial training focused solely on self-defense is generally insufficient, because it is almost destined to fail. When, on rare occasions, it is successful, it is because of the exceptional mastery, demonstrated in the practitioner's ability to "condense" the OODA Loop, thereby assuming the offensive role (Enck, 2012; Ryder and Downs, 2022). Initially the concept of OODA Loop was attributed to retired U.S. Air Force Colonel John Boyd and has since been applied across multiple domains of human activity, including conflict management and counseling.

The concept of OODA Loop quickly reveals a key challenge: under trying circumstances, one must condense the loop to gain an advantage in the mental process that runs the whole situation. *Nagashi* is a straightforward way to achieve this, adapted to combat scenarios. While the opponent is busy running the loops associated with his offensive actions in a given direction, the defender simply pivots to a different modality. He now perceives the attacker in a way significantly different from a direct confrontation. The range of options in the *Nagashi* modality is transformed. Stepping off the line of a stressful event or situation (in combat, a sudden attack) can easily condense the OODA Loop and, if executed decisively and with proper training, allow the person to prevail. In psychotherapy, *Nagashi* represents a condensed practical application of modal logic within Modal Integrative Psychotherapy (MIP). It is based on switching "possible worlds" or modal worlds. Such "worlds" are in fact sets of circumstances that seem difficult to attain, yet, once perceived in modal logical terms, are often just a grasp or shift of attention away from the current state of affairs.

Nagashi is not just a reinterpretation of the situation. It is an objective change in the situation, a different modal world, achieved with apparent ease through a slight shift in position. This shift alters what is possible and what is not, determining the difference between prevailing and succumbing in a life situation. In this sense, *Nagashi* is a paradigm for a practical philosophy of life that is manifested, among other areas, in psychotherapy and counseling. It implies that to face adversity, one must cultivate strategic thinking, so that strategic positioning becomes second nature, overriding the immediate instincts to face the problem head-on or to flee from the problem. Neither instinct is appropriate.

A key aspect of *Nagashi*'s effect on a situation involves emotions. Once the reality appears differently to us, we respond with different emotions. As a result, our dispositions to act, our agility, and our ability to address our difficulties change in response. Emotions are the primary drivers of our actions. They are triggered by our other faculties, including cognition, but ultimately our emotional dispositions drive our significant actions and fuel motivation.

An often-overlooked aspect of emotions is their ethical foundation: emotions are associated with values, and the latter are adopted through more or less conscious choices. Thus, psychotherapy inevitably boils down to ethical considerations. Philippe Pinel recognized this in his clinical practice and established it as the founding principle of his affective psychopathology (Weiner, 1992). The change of the facts that we seek through a modal shift of possible worlds, rooted in a modal logic-based understanding of psychotherapeutic intervention, treats emotions themselves as facts—elements of the possible worlds factored in the change. This emotional structure rests on the ethical reception of values; in fact, the moral emotions in particular (emotions such as solidarity, loyalty, and trust) specifically arise from the interplay between affect and value. That interplay renders them actionable, rather than mere impressions of the world. The emotional side of the value–affect interface drives active solidarity rather than passive empathy, active trusting action rather than non-actionable generalized trust.

Once the practitioner in martial arts executes a *Nagashi*, both their physical and emotional states change. He sees his opponent from an angle that allows previously unattainable actions and reduces the opponent's ability to proceed in the direction initiated. At the same time, *Nagashi* allows the practitioner to perceive the opportunities; it facilitates a sense of internal empowerment and motivation to act, particularly in the context of the OODA Loop discussed above. People who come for counseling are similarly falling behind in the OODA Loops of their lives: they have been attacked, cornered, or exhausted by situations they cannot resolve or process. A change of modal worlds, like the small *Nagashi* step, transforms everything because it places them in the position of offense, rather than defense. They turn their emotions of fear, depression, or helplessness into the actionable, morally engaged emotions of self-affirmation.

I shall start my discussion of the philosophy of life in light of the role of ethics and moral judgment more broadly in addressing personal difficulties in the more traditional psychotherapeutic context, specifically with the logical integration framework for psychotherapy represented by MIP (Modal Integrative Psychotherapy—Fatić, 2025). This discussion will show how logical and ethical considerations intertwine in the embodied methods of MIP intervention that have originated in philosophical counseling.

Tasks for Dreaming: The Somatic Cognition of Emotions in Moral Judgment[1]

The two model MIP interventions described here are based on somatized, embodied emotions as key informative blocks of moral decision-making. Theoretically, the model rests on a broadly sentimentalist virtue ethics. Practically, it connects the ideas of sentimentalism (based on the assumption that emotions govern our moral life and decision-making as much as rational arguments do) with everyday bodily movements and practices. The approach presented here attempts to use the everyday motions and exercises to elucidate the connections between our authentic emotions about moral dilemmas and our conscious narrative that determines our concrete decision-making with regard to these dilemmas. The assumption behind the interventions is that most situations in psychotherapy contain a moral layer, that much of the drama that proves exhausting and distressing to individuals who seek counseling arises from moral controversies (Woods and Carlson, 1961).

The Sentimentalist Perspective on Virtue Ethics

Sentimentalism in ethics is a general approach where certain emotions are taken to be the ethical standards for what types of choices are morally sound. Its significance for psychotherapy, and especially for MIP, is massive, because it accords the emotions a normative role in addressing experiential difficulties which contain significant moral texture.

By our lights, sentimentalism in ethics is best understood when it is contrasted with Kantianism in ethics. Where Kantianism is a sort of "rationalist extremism" as we would call it, sentimentalism is a more holistic approach that tries to realistically interpret the way we make moral judgments and moral decisions. To do this, sentimentalism tends to discuss first of all ordinary, everyday situations and moral challenges. In this it differs starkly from Kantianism, which, because of its extremism and intuitive problems when applied to ordinary situations, tends to base its arguments on extreme examples (Kant, *Metaphysics of Morals* 6:331a; Kant, *Metaphysics of Morals Vigilantius,*

1 The first section of this chapter draws significantly on the text of Fatić (2015). Gratitude is due to LIT and the volume editor for permission to use that text.

27: 552–553).[2] Where Kantianism insists on the ethics of duty which is ultimately grounded in what are essentially anthropological views about human nature (man as a moral creature whose "essence" is compromised when the categorical moral principles are forsaken), sentimentalism favors an ethics of virtue that arises from developing a propensity to act morally correctly based on one's personal sensibility. The sentimentalist context involves both rational and emotional aspects to moral normativity. A propensity to act in a certain way arises from one's values and emotions, from the dynamic factors that constitute one's overall structure of motivation. This suggests that with a proper sensibility one can (and ideally would) have a high quality of life based on virtuous choices, because one enjoys those choices—they make the person happy. We have said something about this in the previous chapter, when we discussed *eudaimonia* in the context of psychotherapy.

While for Kant and the Kantians it is fundamentally irrelevant whether or not one finds joy in acting morally correctly (in fact for Kant himself acting morally rightly in situations where this brings pleasure or satisfaction to the agent is "less noble" than doing so at the cost of suffering and sacrifice), for the moral sentimentalist it is essential that acting rightly comes from the heart as much as from the mind: the perfectly moral actor is one who both does the right thing and enjoys it. While discipline and repetition may be required to cultivate the sensibilities that will later give rise to pleasure when certain virtues are exercised, just as discipline and repetition do in physical training until the training itself becomes a source of pleasure, the ultimate measure of the virtue is *spontaneous action* that is morally correct. Hume, as arguably the first moral sentimentalist in the Western philosophical tradition, for his part, believed that training the virtuous sensibility was possible for anyone with a "tolerably virtuous character" to start with (Hume, 1963: 174).

This type of sentimentalist perspective is broader than the most influential accounts of sentimentalism today, which insist on the moral significance of particular emotional capacities or qualities for the judgment of actions and decisions. For example, Michael Slote's sentimentalism rests heavily on the normative value of *empathy*, and other accounts emphasize the emotional and volitional disposition of *care* as the foundations for the moral justification of actions and the constitution of respective virtues (Slote, 2010; Gilligan, 1982).

---

2 References to Kant are given here as per the Prussian Academy edition to ensure easy location of the appropriate text across the various subsequent editions that use the Prussian Academy markings in addition to their own pagination. The cumulative list of references at the end of the book cites more contemporary editions that are more easily available.

While these types of sentimentalism share the same opposition to Kantian apriorism and essentialism in ethics (moral duty as fundamentally constitutive of "the universal mind" and, in a sense, the very human nature), they focus on particular "sentiments" as the normative criteria for the justification of actions.

The sentimentalism that we propose here is more general in the sense that it focuses on sentiments in general, in addition to rational considerations, as necessary conditions for the moral justification of actions. The concept of virtue that we propose is thus one that is reconcilable with *eudaimonistic* ethics: the possession of virtue that leads to morally proper action also entails the capacity to lead a good life. Since the fullness of virtue is acquired only when one's sentiments follow one's rational views of virtue, namely when one's spontaneity associated with joy, pleasure, or satisfaction (the generally positive and fulfilling feelings) is triggered by morally proper action, this comprehensive sentimentalist view *rules out the possibility of moral justification of actions that deteriorate the good life of the person* as far as most ordinary moral challenges are concerned.

Ideally, the moral sentimentalism hinted at here would entail that the highest achievement in moral development would coincide with discovering a good life in acting morally properly. In other words, it would lead to individual happiness through moral action, something that seems utopian.

The reality of such moral improvement is, of course, more complicated. One will need to exercise "moral self-interruption" in Hume's phrase, along much of the road leading up to the moral perfection described by a virtual coextensiveness between happiness and moral action. During this often arduous progress in moral education, sacrifice and discomfort are one's regular companions. Thus, the overall picture of virtue and its achievement is far from being entirely rosy. However, the fundamental difference between this reality of sentimentalist moral development and the Kantian ethics of duty is that for the former the suffering and self-deprivation associated with acting morally rightly while one's sentiments are still pulling one in a different direction mark the imperfection of virtue, thus also a moral imperfection. For Kant, the sacrifice and discomfort in performing the moral duty add nobility to one's moral profile, just as any coincidence between an action in accordance with moral duty and any pleasure arising from such an action detracts from such moral nobility. This is where the ethics of sentimentalism is congruent with ethics of the good life, while Kantian essentialism militates against any association of the good life with moral propriety. Customarily, Kant is particularly clear on this distinction when he discusses the morality of punishment, thus the relationship between moral duty and guilt: Kant makes it very clear what he means by categorical retribution: "Woe unto him who crawls through the windings of eudaimonism in order to discover something that releases the criminal from punishment" (Kant, *Metaphysics of morals* 6:331a).

The price that moral sentimentalism pays for the rather convenient convergence between a practical quest for the good life and the moral justification of actions based on virtue, in theoretical terms, is that it is intended for, but also limited to, "ordinary situations." It is not a universalist moral doctrine that is capable of supporting moral decisions in extreme situations, such as those in warfare, in contexts of dramatically divided loyalties with grave consequences attached to one's actions, or in life-or-death situations generally. In such situations the issue of the good life typically does not even arise: pressures of time and practical exigency usually require moral judgments that are based on a sense of justice and duty. This is the favorable practical terrain for Kantianism, of course. When Kantians discuss the role of "the universal mind" in morally justifying a decision to conduct a military intervention against another country, in order to address the social practice of raping young girls or the sale of children, which takes place in that country that they believe ought to be invaded, the intuitive moral demands arising from the extreme moral challenge appear to rule out any *eudaimonistic* element for the person who makes the decision. These are situations that readily invite considerations of moral duty as opposed to harmonic virtue; they invite a sense of responsibility, moral rights and individual rights as they attach to various subjects in the constellation at hand. All these categories allow moral decision-making to unfold in the direction of duty ethics and a course of action based on simple, universally applicable and aprioristic maxims translated into the specific circumstances of the case.

The above limitation of sentimentalist ethics may be significant from a theoretical perspective; however, for the purposes of counseling and psychotherapy, and indeed in large part for the practical purposes of everyday life, it is of limited relevance. What virtue ethics is after is a sense of moral propriety that is built into personality traits that make morally justified actions as spontaneous as possible and moral choices as clear as possible, in as many everyday situations as possible.

The Body as an Instrument of Cognition

While the traditional view in Western philosophy has been that cognition is exclusively a matter for "the mind," a result of the interplay between perception and intelligent processes, at least since Richard Shusterman's work on pragmatist aesthetics the role of the body as an instrument of cognition has recently started to become recognized (Shusterman, 2012). Philosophers have become more sensitive to what on closer observation becomes obvious as "embodied cognition": although perception and mental processing of the perceptual information play a crucial part in cognition, the actual behavioral "engraining" of various types of knowledge, including the "know-how," usually involves the body in one way or another.

Embodied cognition is particularly obvious in physical skills, where the learning of a skill often requires rational planning, systematic repetition, and simulation of adequate external circumstances, all of which create a learned habit that reveals itself when triggers for action occur.

Soldiers and fighters typically start their training with highly unusual physical movements which, at first, impair their balance and coordination, because they are "unnatural." However, with an increasing understanding of their design and practical use, and with frequent repetition, they become "second nature"; a learned response to challenges on the battlefield, just like driving a car, while initially a cumbersome set of mutually distracting moves (the clutch, the gas, the gear shift, the steering wheel.) grows into a subconsciously coordinated "second nature" so that one is able to drive long distances, respond to challenges on the road, and at the same time maintain a meaningful conversation. Learning how to fight or how to drive a car involves the reception of perceptual and theoretical information and its integration with the development of a new set of physical skills. In fact, structurally, learning either of these two things is more complex than any type of mere theoretical learning, for the latter includes only the processing of information and its structuring in a way that allows symbolic or imaginary applications (e.g., mathematics, most cases of medical diagnostics, the writing of philosophy articles).

The learning of complex sports, such as the martial arts, is a particularly good example of the integration of the mind and body in the process of holistic cognition. Just learning a simple throw requires a legion of detailed information about body mechanics, distribution of weight, sequence of moves, required direction of movement, and the precise coordination of all this knowledge with the visual, audio, and tactile perception during a wrestling match. While someone might have all the information required for a successful throw, the quality of the knowledge is suboptimal until it is adequately embodied so that a throw can be accomplished.

The difference between wrestling and theoretical physics is primarily in the ultimate intention of the exercise vis-à-vis the embodiment of knowledge. In wrestling or boxing, the embodied knowledge serves the execution of a physical skill, which is the goal of the learning process. One learns everything that one needs to know about a throw in order to execute the throw at a particular moment and under particular circumstances (e.g., in competition). In theoretical physics, the goal is not directly physical: the intent of the research and/or learning might be to shed light on the relationship between physical and temporal change, or between temperature and energy or speed of moving objects. Ultimately, however, the knowledge gained in theoretical physics will be embodied, directly or indirectly, through applied science and its inventions and innovations; the goal of theoretical medicine will (hopefully) be an embodied change in the quality of human life; the goal of theoretical philosopher is perhaps more obscure, but it likely leads to an embodied outcome, either in those who read the philosopher's work or for the philosopher herself, in the very act of writing and expressing her thoughts.

At this stage we are not suggesting that all knowledge is embodied or strives for embodiment. It is sufficient for us to work with the conclusion that knowledge tends to be embodied in most ordinary situations. Thus we are not proposing a strong theoretical thesis; merely an empirical observation that we see as uncontroversial regardless of one's theoretical outlook.

The embodiment of cognitive insights is equally obvious in counseling. While cognition is clearly crucial in counseling work toward a perspective that will allow the development of problem-solving and/or coping skills, the success of counseling is typically shown much more in embodied reactions than in merely mental representations and rational conclusions. A counselee might declare that she has gained a crucial perspective on her problem, yet this will mean little unless the insight manifests itself through behavioral change, such as increased tranquility, self-confidence, workplace functionality, personal satisfaction leading to better health and a healthier lifestyle. In fact, a large part of the initial "diagnosis" in psychodiagnostics rests on embodied manifestations of mood and values; the observation of the counselee's behavior during the first session is considered equally important as listening to what he says.

Assuming that moral dilemmas are made up of cognitive and emotional building blocks (the starting point of sentimentalism as it has been briefly described here), and that both cognition and emotional reactions tend to be embodied, the body reveals itself as a powerful tool for generating feedback about the inner archaeology of our feelings and thoughts.

In order to resolve a moral issue, sometimes a rational discussion along philosophical grounds will be sufficient; sometimes a stringent logical analysis of the statements that express the dilemma will do the trick. This is the case in situations where a confusion of meaning generates dilemmas relating to real-life choices. However, this is only a small minority of cases that are relatively easily dealt with. The more difficult and challenging for the counselor are cases where any distortions or confusion of insights into the problem generate severe emotional consequences. These are the overwhelmingly dominant cases characterized by anxiety, insomnia, depression, relationship issues, inability to work, and inhibitions in enjoying and actively pursuing life that arise from a sense of purposelessness.

Uncovering the Register of Emotions on Moral Dilemmas

Sometimes the identity and intensity of the emotions that drive our moral dilemmas is foreign to us. Discovering the register of emotions that create the cacophony of a moral problem is thus an important step toward stripping the moral conflict naked of any rationally imposed additions and facing the core issue of the moral dilemma with a full awareness of one's authentic emotions, as well as one's values that are involved. However, the rationalization that follows a moral dilemma: the early onset of the question of "what should I do here" obscures the emotional content that creates tension within the moral issue and gives it a dramatic appearance. The pressure of "what should I do" is a powerful screen that shields our emotions from being confronted in their fullness. Once the emotions are fully comprehended, the drama of the dilemma tends to fade away. The register of emotions, once complete, often provides a clear way toward the solution, because the very identity of the emotions tends to clarify our relationships with others and the priorities in our own lives vis-à-vis these relationships, so that the options for action are no longer the same.

A good example of the above is the emotion of hatred. We live in a society that educates us that hatred is a socially unacceptable emotion, however natural it might be. Societies sanction "crimes of hatred" more severely and attach a greater stigma to them than "ordinary crimes." "Hate mongering" is considered subversive whether it occurs between ethnic communities or between groups of schoolchildren. "Hate language" is so highly politically incorrect that its use might prevent someone from gaining public office or even land a person in prison in some countries. Hate, in other words, is an almost taboo word in our modern culture. Unfortunately, as with most taboo words, this does not only mean that we learn not to hate, but often, more likely, we learn not to recognize hate when we feel it, and not to admit that we hate when we do recognize it. There are strong socially generated incentives for all of us not to consider hate as a possible authentic emotion, not to work with it, and not to express it almost under any circumstances. The more enhanced our social image is, the more reluctant and, consequently, unable we tend to become to recognize or express hate. Yet, however strange this might sound at first, hate, just like any other emotion, may be the solution to some of our moral dilemmas.

A moral obligation that is felt toward someone whom we hate loses its force once we recognize the hate. This applies, for example, to people we used to be closely emotionally tied with, such as former partners, friends, or business associates. Societal expectations may require someone who has just split up with a partner to assist the partner in coping with career or family difficulties; they might place pressure on the former spouse to provide support to the ex-partner in ways that cause anxiety in the spouse and generate strong psychological and somatic resistance. One might be forced to be nice to someone in ways that militate against one's own well-being.

The sense of moral obligation that is superimposed by society, the projected image of a benevolent person that we are taught to strive to become, can actually seriously debilitate one's sense of satisfaction with one's life and may endanger the very prospect of achieving the good life. The duties that are imposed on us, most of them internalized as our own apparent values, are the cause of much of the neurosis of modern day. While people are often taught by psychotherapists that they should "release" the frustration in various ways and try to achieve a situation where the duties no longer trouble them, often this does not work. Realizing that we hate someone might be an emancipatory feeling, just as understanding that we suffer from an allergy to an external factor might save us from hospital treatment or premature death. To do this we need to be able to access our register of emotions in an effective and reliable way that is sufficiently unhinged from the politically correct values that dominate our rational projections of value.

The same is the case with passions of physical attraction, fear, or a sense of personal inadequacy. Any emotion, if it makes up the core of our authentic relationship to a moral issue, if it is clouded or masked for whatever reason, has the capacity to block the resolution of that issue and, when made explicit, it has the capacity to unblock it. Given that emotions that we feel in the face of moral issues, at least according to the sentimentalist account of virtues, point to the presence of absence of virtue, the ability to confront such emotions, especially when they are the negative emotions such as hatred, requires the same sincerity and realism that are required of us to be accurate judges of our own character.

In fact, the tension between the idea that unpleasant and "negative" emotions, even socially and politically "incorrect" ones, must be allowed to exist and recognized just like any other emotions, on the one hand, and the idea that the development of virtue requires a systematic cultivation of sensibilities through active self-coercion to do the right thing under the right circumstances is only a surface, prima facie tension. When one considers more closely how the process of moral self-improvement operates, it becomes clear that, in order to plan and exert the effort to become a better person through self-discipline, one must first be able to properly appraise one's own virtue status. While one might desire to become a highly disciplined athlete, one's ability to progress toward that goal first depends on one's ability to confront the fact that one is neither disciplined nor an athlete. If one's current situation causes problems to one that impair one's well-being, this, just like any other challenge, requires one first to adequately appraise one's moral, emotional, psychological, and physical status. Unless one is able to be aware of oneself, one is in a suboptimal position to proceed with resolving any serious "internal" problem, whether it is a difficult decision to be made with conflicting priorities and loyalties, or a moral dilemma with regard to family, friends, society at large, or oneself. As a moral sentimentalist, one is obliged not to stay with the mere recognition of one's suboptimal moral status; one's task is to work on the cultivation of virtues that constitute capacities for a good life as one sees it, and at the same time for doing the right thing by others in as many different situations as possible. This does not mean that, simply because one has internalized the goal that one should become a benevolent person, one should not be able to recognize the fact that at any point in time one is (still) not a fully benevolent person. In other words, the fact that as a moral sentimentalist one believes that the ideal of moral virtue toward which one strives is that where one would no longer feel hatred, and would in fact find joy even in the making of sacrifices or suffering injustice (as is the case in Christian ethics), does not, nor should, prevent one from seeking to understand the hatred that one (still) feels in a situation where this might be the core feeling that blocks one in the tracks in attempts to resolve a psychological or moral dilemma. A person may not allow himself to act fully as hatred commands him to, but he will hardly be able to understand his own moral or psychological predicament unless he is able and willing to recognize his hatred. In this sense, synchronically, hatred might liberate a person, while diachronically, as a moral sentimentalist, one may not remain with hatred. In other words, hatred may be incompatible with someone's moral goals in character development, yet it may not only exist in him, but also be the key to his being able to progress in addressing any specific moral situation that he might become stuck in during his life of self-development. The same is the case with any other emotion, positive or negative. After all, this is a familiar thing in psychotherapy: the presupposed "moral neutrality" of psychotherapy is predicated exactly upon this insight, namely that a person suffering from unresolved issues might only be able to be helped if the moral judgment of her expression of the truth about her feelings is suspended.

The suspension of moral judgment is temporary and serves to assist the process of negotiating an existential crisis and/or giving expression to true emotions. Once such emotions are brought into the open, they are subjected to moral critique in the context of the overall sentimentalist paradigm of moral improvement and self-development. Thus, there is no contradiction in principle between adopting moral sentimentalism and arguing for techniques that suspend moral judgment, in order to facilitate the expression of blocked emotions.

Exercise 1: Tasks for Dreaming

One of the best ways for uncovering the authentic emotions that we harbor vis-à-vis certain existentially challenging situations, including moral dilemmas, is to allow our subconscious mind to manifest itself by loosening conscious controls at the edges of sleep. This means that the otherwise suppressed emotions are likely to surface when conscious controls weaken just before we fall asleep, and even more so just as we wake up. Sometimes, the early morning thoughts and feelings are the most direct manifestations of our authentic emotions and attitudes regarding things that preoccupy us.

This is an individual exercise which lasts at least a week, while preparations take another week. The exercise takes place after the counseling process has advanced to the point where the moral dilemma or similar problem has been clearly defined and articulated, and it has become clear that a rational approach to the issue at hand (specifically, a dilemma) alone is insufficient to break the action impasse in the counselee.

Typically, Tasks for Dreaming will be scheduled several months into the counseling process, after both the counselor and the counselee are satisfied that the core problem has been identified in a sufficiently articulate way. The counselor will have established the basic facts about the counselee's personal circumstances in order to make an informed decision about the use of the Tasks for Dreaming exercise: if the counselee has small children, for example, looks after an elderly or frail family member, or has responsibilities that require her constant availability to others, then Tasks for Dreaming would not be the method of choice.

For those counselees who can organize themselves to spend a week alone, without disturbances and off work, and whose core issue or dilemma suggests that the release of blocked emotions might create inroads into the problem, Tasks for Dreaming is the right choice.

The exercise starts with a preparatory week when the counselor will schedule two or three sessions to inform the client about the exercise and to help her clear up her agenda for the following week to free as much time as possible for meditation, contemplation, and relaxation (staying at home, off work, preferably alone). At the conclusion of the final session in the preparatory week, the counselee should start the exercise immediately, which means that the final session in the week before the exercise should be scheduled the day before or on the day the exercise is planned to begin. The counselee will focus on writing a diary of emotions and thoughts that concern the core problem whenever they arise (or become conscious) during the day; however, each morning immediately after waking up and each evening immediately before going to sleep, the counselee will consciously concentrate on the problem at hand and write whatever ideas or emotions one has or experiences at that time. The counselee will organize her week to try to maximize sleep without the aid of any medication. After a week of such regimen, the counselee returns to the counseling session immediately (the very following day of the conclusion of the exercise week) with the diary prepared during the exercise.

If the initial week is insufficient—the counselee suffers disturbances, has problems concentrating, or just can't fall asleep—the exercise is attempted the following month, and again until the goal is reached.

The task for the counselee is to articulate any emotions that arise in relation to the problem in a state of relaxation, particularly in the early mornings, to write these emotions and/or thoughts down, and thus compile a register of emotions that may well represent a broad spectrum of mutually contradictory feelings and ideas. These are the ideas that may well be quite different from the ones that arise in the short and intensely filled time spans of counseling sessions where a rational exchange dominates the discourse between the counselor and the client.

Once the register of emotions is compiled, counseling sessions will resume and focus on the considerations of specific emotions and thoughts found in the register. Solutions are sought in the counselee's attitudes to the results of the week spent in dreaming and contemplation. Experience has shown that people tend to change their behavior and approach to the problem after such intense periods of meditative searching inside, as deeply suppressed "solutions" that prima facie seem socially or personally acceptable tend to resurface. Typically, these are changes that manifest themselves in relationship issues, in a decision to break a relationship or to simply accept things that seemed to be the main hurdles to the relationship in ways that were previously unlikely, even inconceivable to the client. The reason for such changes is that the real emotions toward something that may be rationally defined in a very different way, requiring a different solution, tend to surface and color the entire mindscape of the counselee's decision-making on the issue, often leaving little real doubt as to what one should do, in ways that, considered strictly rationally, before these emotions have resurfaced, would have been unimaginable.

One counselee who was subjected to the "Tasks of Dreaming" method had suffered several years from an unresolved relationship with her husband. They had a child whom they both loved dearly and did all in their power to protect him from the typical consequences of a divorce. The woman was unable to fully "let go" of the ex-husband, although she did not want a renewed relationship with him because she was strongly repelled by his apparent values and what she saw as a complete lack of emotional, even personal integrity. She was also deeply put off by the company the husband was keeping and his affairs. The husband had been involved in a criminal culture and much of his pre-married life had to do with serious crime and serious criminals on all levels of his personal life. Yet he had deceived her into believing that he had been a typical middle-class technocrat in search of a traditional family. Their relationship was thus a source of deep ambivalence for the counselee. She was trying to "understand" the ex-husband by attempting to relate his actions and apparent values associated with such actions to her own, and this always landed her in even greater bewilderment and chronic stress. Years of counseling had facilitated only periods of temporary relief. The problem appeared to be truly chronic.

After the counselee had undergone the Tasks of Dreaming week, she came back to counseling unusually calm and decisive. "I think I have articulated what I feel for John. I simply hate him. I wish he would die suffering. He does not deserve to be alive." She made it very clear that she did not consider this to be in line with her Christian values but was happy to formulate an emotional self-diagnosis. She discontinued the practice of seeing her ex-husband every day, decreased telephone and messaging communication with him, and reduced time spent with their son (who was living with his father) to twice per week. She regained her interests, started on the way of regaining her health by returning to physical activity, and increased her productive work hours (as opposed to emailing and internet surfing). The problem and the conflict between the two ex-spouses remained; however, the moral conflict within the counselee was resolved in a way few would consider recommendable: she discovered that she hated him and modeled her life according to this fact. She did not do anything to harm him, but the articulation of her negative emotions toward him helped her draw boundaries that allowed a healthier and more productive life for her. She was free to embark on her own way of self-development and, even more importantly, to continue her own emotional life. She soon lowered the intensity of the counseling and within a few months she asked for the sessions to end as she felt that she no longer needed them. This came in the fourth year of acute suffering and intensive counseling with various therapists.

Exercise 2: Physical Exhaustion (What Can U.S. Marine Corps Training Teach Us About Authenticity)

One of the basic tactics to mentally "engrain" learned fighting techniques which require a combination of naturally programmed responses to threat, on the one hand, and rationally constructed movements, on the other, is simulating the conditions that bring the mind and body outside "the zone" of optimal functioning by creating perceptual, physical and mental exhaustion. These are the physiological conditions that most closely resemble the physiology of body and mind under stress, when large quantities of adrenaline are "dumped" into the bloodstream, resulting in a narrowing of vision, auditory exclusion and a "fight or flight" state that makes only the basic movements by large muscle groups available to the brain. In military training, stressing the body through physical exertions simulates the fight or flight state that the body enters in an actual life-threatening situation of combat, where, for example, small muscle movements such as those of fingers, hands, or feet are simply cut off. The aim of military training is twofold. First, it is to reduce the actual effects of the fight or flight state for soldiers by exposing them to physical and mental conditions characteristic of an actual fight so often that their bodies and brains become accustomed to them. As small muscle movements are crucial in military battle (such as pulling a trigger), and the fight or flight state is known to seriously damage the eye-hand coordination (critical for aiming with a firearm), the military finds it imperative to develop techniques for soldiers to cope with the adrenaline rush. This aim is not directly relevant for dealing with emotions in our technique of Physical Exhaustion. However, the second and related aim in military training is directly relevant to our goal here.

The second goal of training is to help answer the question of which fighting techniques are most compatible with the naturally programmed physical actions in the human being when under the stress of combat. This question is critical for two reasons. First, the more a fighting technique is in line with what the body would tend to do anyway, the less likely it is that the hundreds of hours spent learning this technique will be in vain, because in the real situation of threat the body will revert to its own "innate" responses and simply "shut off" any learned skills that are not supported by these innate reflexes. Secondly, the more compatibility there is between the natural and the learned skills, the less time, energy, and effort is required to develop and maintain these combat skills. Thus, both reasons are entirely practical. The common assumption in both rationales for a combination of natural and learned reactions is that when the body is brought to a suboptimal level of functionality through exhaustion, it reveals things about what is "natural" and in a sense "authentic" that are far less obvious when the body is well fed, well rested, and exercising in safe conditions.

For example, a soldier practicing a martial art in a sports club will without hesitation execute high kicks, sometimes with considerable success, even under the stress of competition. However, if the same soldier, in a real battlefield, wearing a helmet, 30 kilograms of equipment in the backpack, heavy boots, and strapped with hard and awkwardly shaped weapons, on uneven or muddy terrain, attempts a high kick, this will pretty much spell his death or serious injury. An accomplished martial artist under the comfortable and regulated conditions of training in everyday life, if faced with real combat with suboptimal lighting, balance, or information, is most likely to become a victim. This marks the difference between martial arts and combat training. In combat training, only physical skills that are realistic in suboptimal conditions—physically, mentally, and environmentally—are learned. These skills may be completely useless in a martial-arts competition, just as the competitive skills may be fatally useless in real combat.

The same logic applied by the military holds for emotions when we are faced with serious crises. Such crises drain our energy gradually, but when we are rested and energized, we are usually able to manage and control the emotions that give rise to such issues. However, when we reach the breaking point after long periods of containing such emotions, and this usually coincides with compromised physical health, the emotions erupt with all their force and may overwhelm our personal coping skills and resources.

The exercise Physical Exhaustion consists of the counselee's exposure to intensive physical effort (running, doing repetitive strength exercises, lifting weights, or punching a heavy bag) for repetitive albeit brief periods ("bursts" of activity), such as, for example, 2 minutes of intensive running or hitting a heavy bag, followed by one minute rest, followed by 3 minutes of abdominal crunches, followed by one minute rest, followed by 4 minutes of riding a stationary bicycle.

The exercise is performed in the presence of a counselor, for two reasons. First, the counselor must be there to "take the anamnesis" from the counselee immediately after the exercise, because the counselee by herself would not be able to concentrate on the moral dilemma or emotional issue at hand, articulate her thoughts and emotions, or write them down under the stress of the exercise. Secondly, the counselor is there to appraise the value of the emotions expressed and the actual evaluation of the problem by the counselee when she is out of breath, low on energy, and undergoes a triple or quadruple the resting heart rate. The assumption of the exercise is that the "base" response by the person stripped of the coping resources she has under the everyday circumstances will shed light on the "naturally programmed" emotional responses of that person to the problem, of which she is likely unaware under ordinary conditions. Again, the emotional register uncovered through the exercise is discussed in regular counseling sessions later. Unlike the Tasks for Dreaming, Physical Exhaustion tends to reveal relatively few emotions, which, very often, include the emotions of "letting go" or indifference to things that might seriously upset the person under regular conditions. The counseling process tends to take some time after this exercise, because the final form in which the person is likely to accept the core emotions expressed through the exercise tends to differ from their barren form during the exercise; some refinement is usually required through additional counseling. For example, one who, during the exigencies of physical exhaustion, decides to give up on previously important personal matters, will not feel exactly the same after the straining exercise, although one will remember why one felt the way one did. One will, however, usually be able to process and inculcate one's new feeling in one's decision once the raw emotion experienced during the exhaustion episode is adequately discussed in an ordinary session. In this sense, Physical Exhaustion sometimes provides less direct solutions to the dilemma than the Tasks for Dreaming; however, it is easier to organize and conduct, because it requires fewer prerequisites and much less time.

Reconstructing the Moral Narrative Based on the Emotional Register

On a practical level, Tasks for Dreaming and Physical Exhaustion provide tools to address intractable emotional and volitional problems that concern an array of life issues, including serious moral dilemmas that may impair the person's overall emotional and physical well-being. The exercises are administered only when regular counseling sessions have helped clearly articulate the problem but seem to fail to help the counselee move toward breaking the impasse of ambivalence or to "see the way ahead." Hence, for the counselor who is concerned only with crisis intervention, the exercises themselves are sufficient to create conditions under which the counselee is likely to change perspective on the problem.

On a more strategic level, however, the moral register uncovered through these and similar exercises reveals what could be considered an "emotional narrative," or emotional sensibility of the counselee and might assist the overarching goals of philosophical counseling based on a moral sentimentalism. If the counselor and the counselee can both agree to adopt, at least temporarily and heuristically, a sentimentalist ethics and work to develop certain virtues and emotional capacities in the counselee that might help the counselee reach what she would consider a "better life" and a "better self," then the uncovering of the core emotional register is a natural first step in this direction. They are both "archaeological" tools to dig for deep or core emotions and attitudes in situations of blocked decision-making. At the same time, they are powerful diagnostic tools to appraise one's current emotional profile vis-à-vis one's key dilemmas, problems, and issues in life, and plan a strategy of self-development accordingly. This strategy must correspond to the actual emotional narrative if it is to be effective in sentimentalist terms, that is, if it is to help the counselee develop moral views and propensities and associate positive emotions toward affirmative moral choices.

The embodied emotional and moral narrative that drives our self-revelation through the described methods conforms to its own logic. The various modal worlds in this in-depth self-exploration are not clustered around the person's choices, decisions, and life predicaments, as they were presented in the Introduction. There, I described a standard decision-making scenario based on modal thinking, where one simply makes decisive shifts between modal worlds, abandoning the current one for an alternative one, where the conditions of possibility and the truthfulness of various beliefs, assumptions, and the propositional content of different attitudes are all altered. However, the "clustered up," relatively linear alignment of modal worlds is not the only modal structure possible. While it is characteristic of modal logic-grounded decision-making, it does not fully apply in-depth counseling and therapy that are more focused on self-exploration.

In-depth psychotherapy, the logic of modality is structurally different: the modal worlds are contained in one another, like the Russian babushka dolls: opening one doll reveals another one inside it, and so on. The challenge in therapy is to unlock the present modal world, so that it can release a deeper, enclosed one. This is achieved by the use of boundary-states such as dream-like states and the state of physical exhaustion. The structures of embodiment and psychic compartmentalization or intertwining correspond to the structures of modality: the horizontal clustering together of modal worlds (characteristic of decision-making), and the structure of progressive self-enclosure is traced back in-depth psychotherapy as the corresponding self-disclosure. Especially the latter logical structure, and the interventions that rest on it, can lead to internally conflicted processes of self-revelation that reveal another unconventional view in MIP, namely its relative acceptance of conflict, not just as a transient and spontaneous feature of our internal processes and external relationships, but as a personal and social strategy, as well.

While, in the linear, decision-making structure of clustered-up modal worlds that one shifts between, the relationship between these worlds, or sets of circumstances that determine possibilities and the truthfulness of beliefs can be described as competition, in the self-enclosed structure of modal worlds their relationship is more tense and can be described as strife. Each confined, enclosed modal world requires energy to be kept confined (somewhat similar, but not identical, to the familiar dynamics of repression, from Freud). Likewise, opening the logical and emotional box within which it is confined also requires strife and struggle. Once it is released, again, it is questioned, placed under pressure, and "squeezed" to open and release what is within it. Such a dynamic is highly conflictual and requires a degree of psychic violence to be exerted on one's own internal structures through the self-exploration process. That is why analytic processes can be highly unpleasant, while decision-making, however initially scary it might appear, can quickly feel emancipatory.

This conflictual dynamic of the dialectic of enclosure-disclosure makes the corresponding modality of thinking and action paradigmatic for one's overall personal "style." One's approach to, or strategy for, uncovering and disclosing meanings and relationships that are not obvious might be seen as confrontational and challenging by other people, yet it is a form of truth-seeking that is as philosophical as the calm contemplation that is typically portrayed as the general philosophical stance. Underlying logical structures determine not just our inference and judgment, but also our personal mentality and a strategic approach to others and to life in general. Such mentalities, predicated on the various structures of modality in thinking, come across as "personality" and "character." The relationship between practical modal logic and personality is layered and mediated through a range of phenomena that manifest themselves in psychotherapy. This interplay between modality and personality is the subject of the following chapter.

References

Enck, Robert E. (2012). "The OODA Loop." *Home Health Care Management & Practice*, Vol. 24, No. 3: 123–124. https://doi.org/10.1177/1084822312439314.

Fatić, Aleksandar (2015). "Tasks for dreaming: The somatic cognition of emotions in moral judgement." In *Socratic Handbook,* edited by Michael Noah Weiss, 67–82. Vienna: LIT Publishers.

Fatić, Aleksandar (2025). *Modal integrative psychotherapy: A logical integration of psychotherapy.* New York: Palgrave Macmillan.

Gilligan, Carol (1982). *In a different voice: Psychological theory and women's development.* Cambridge, MA: Harvard University Press.

Hume, David (1963). *An enquiry concerning the principles of morals.* La Salle: Open Court.

Ryder, Mike and Downs, Carolyn (2022). "Rethinking reflective practice: John Boyd's OODA LOOP as an alternative to Kolb." *The International Journal of Management Education*, Vol. 20, No. 3. Online edition. https://doi.org/10.1016/j.ijme.2022.100703.

Shusterman, Richard (2012). *Thinking through the Body: Essays in somaesthetics.* Cambridge: Cambridge University Press.

Slote, Michael (2010). *Moral sentimentalism.* Oxford: Oxford University Press.

Weiner, Dora B. (1992). "Philippe Pinel's 'Memoir on Madness' of December 11, 1794: A fundamental text of modern psychiatry." *The American Journal of Psychiatry*, Vol. 149, No. 6: 725–732. https://doi.org/10.1176/ajp.149.6.725.

Chapter 2

MODAL LOGIC AND PROPOSITIONAL LOGIC: PRINCIPLED DIFFERENCES AND PRACTICAL SIGNIFICANCE

Modality Versus Fixed Logical Values

One of the key characteristics of integrative thinking in general, and of integrative humanities as a social and theoretic application of this type of thinking, is the use of modal logical thinking as opposed to conventional binary logic, which is predicated upon certain very naive, and very deceitful, assumptions about reality, about our relationship to it, and about our ability to influence, cause events, or, speaking in terms of Galtung's modal rhetoric, "call them into reality."

Modality is a pervasive context of our existence and our relationships. The fundamental principle of modality is that almost any current state of affairs, "what is actually the case," is just one possible "world," which coexists, almost at the same level of reality, with all the other possible worlds, or potential states of affairs. The latter could often be realized, or "called into reality," by very minute changes in our thinking and decision-making.

In this context, a fixation on the present state of affairs as "the real" in the hard, ontologically strong sense is both "unrealistic" and unproductive: the flux of states of affairs is facilitated by the way we reason about events, especially if we don't consider only the actual as the only real. Galtung's idea that "the irreal" that is possible is not so far from "the real" in the sense that "real" is the actual state of affairs, and the "irreal" is a state of affairs that could, sometimes very easily, become actual, or replace the actual state of affairs, is key to modal thinking. We live in a variety of modal or possible worlds, where each possible world is just one possible state of affairs. (I use the term *modal world* instead, because it is more precise and less arbitrary, for "possible world" can be interpreted in all kinds of ways characteristic of folk psychology.)

Treating a situation, such as an interpersonal relationship, in terms of fixed realities can be detrimental to the potential development of that relationship.

For example, people who have a mutual interest in developing a relationship in a romantic or friendly direction often run into initial difficulties because of the misjudgments of mutual expectations. Frequently, this results in conflict, and sometimes that conflict leads to a cut in communication, because one or both participants in the relationship feel vulnerable and fear further hurt that might result from continued communication. Ceasing communication "freezes" the relationship at an early stage of development. Especially in light of the politically correct values that are promoted in modern Western culture, including the culture that "a no is a no," which has been taken from sexual ethics into all kinds of human relationships, for many people a statement "I don't want to communicate with you" seals a reality that remains unchangeable and unmovable in any direction.

The above situation is very common in counseling. It is an actual relationship with its own dynamism, which is frozen by one person's decisions. It thus becomes a still record in time, the dead script of an otherwise living and changing environment of a personal relationship. Can this situation change?

The answer largely depends on the way we think about the relationship. If broken communication is the best one person is capable of in terms of relating to another person, then little can be done. However, the perception of the relationship and the actions we take with regard to the broken communication might be crucial in overcoming the immaturity that characterizes many of such situations. One way to approach the broken communication channel is to try to address the reasons for cutting off communication. Such questioning tests the other's reasons for making the decision and rarely produces good results because it mobilizes the person's defenses.

Another way is to approach the situation as transient and to challenge the other person to growth and courage. This is often a better approach because it causes the interlocutor to self-examine and to try and show virtue: "I am not afraid, it is just that I have decided to cut the communication, but I can communicate and will demonstrate it; afterwards I can cut the communication off again."

A third approach would be to focus on the community as the healing factor. The faces of the organic community are manifold. Such a community can include a group of friends or coworkers, if they are close and intimate. Alternatively, it can include just the participants in the frozen relationship and one or more counselors. In any case, the community-based approach will attempt to immerse the person in a social environment that is relaxing and safe, stimulating and accepting, and thus empower them to reconsider the rudimentary models of behavior that one resorts to.

Individuals seek validation of their behavior in the eyes of close ones, and no suboptimal behavior would last long if the community were there to correct it. It is the influence of the community that resolves blockages in communication, just as the community can heal trauma and facilitate greater initiative in its members. Hence the ancient habit of resolving interpersonal, and sometimes even political conflicts, by third-party mediation and involvement of the tribe, the whole society, or an international organization in a regional, political, or military conflict. This principle is too often overlooked in individualistic cultures, where it is mistakenly believed that each person is responsible for resolving their own personal difficulties, more or less by themselves, possibly with "professional help."

The help the counselor offers in personal issues is closely connected with the counselor's ability to constitute a mini organic community with the client. It is the same kind of assistance that would be offered much more effectively by a larger community, which encompasses the members of the same family or group who share with the affected individual important elements of collective identity.

One of the key conceptual preconditions for a successful intervention in such relatively difficult situations where communication is severed and information can no longer be exchanged is an understanding of the current situation as merely one of a variety of possible situations, where the varying of certain attitudes and influences may just as well bring about a different modal world into actuality.

Conversely, a fixed, binary thinking that sees a person's "decision" to sever communication with others as definitive, as their right and, consequently, something that must be respected by everybody else, factually deprives the participants in the relationship, including the one who has severed communication, of the healing influence of the community. Modal thinking is "softer" in that it does not take spoken words as legal norms, nor does it focus on the present decisions without considering their context and the potential for change in the course of time.

One of the problems with modal thinking is that it runs contrary to many of the norms of political correctness that tend to define modern societal relationships. The trade-off for this potential risk of running into conflict with the accepted norms of communication is the ability of modal thinking to go deep and resolve underlying issues. Such problems are often masked by the norms of social and political correctness. The described example of political correctness in accepting a "no" to continued communication between people who are at a critical stage of their relationships again serves well to illustrate the point here. It is true that "a no is a no" when a person is asked to engage in sexual intercourse, because any different interpretation would open the room for sexual violence. This is the context wherefrom the general norm "a no is a no" has spread into all kinds of social relationships, including what is now not only the right to, but also a fashion of, severing communication in otherwise developing relationships, which, then, brings people to counseling in order to either achieve "closure" of the prematurely and violently ended relationship, or to try to continue communication and potentially the relationship, either in the prior form, or in a changed and transformed way.

In modal thinking, "a no" is not always "a no." Sometimes it is "a not yet yes." In many situations, individuals make decisions just because deciding appears to empower them and give them a sense of control; however, these decisions are deeply detrimental both to others and to themselves. Thus, counseling must involve the possibility of changing the detrimental decisions, or at least seriously re-examining them in the interest of constructive human relationships and the preservation of communities.

Modal logic assumes that various possible states of affairs coexist at the same time, and that as little as a change of focus or perspective on one or more of them can bring them into reality, or alter the current "reality," in fact merely actuality. Whether somebody will pay attention to us or not is an example of a situation where we have two possible states of affairs, two modal worlds, one of which is actual, or "real." The fact that somebody, let's say, does not pay attention to me in a particular situation is, indeed, perhaps "real" as opposed to the possibility that they do pay attention to me being "not real," however the difference is slight, because both states of affairs are possible. If I raise my voice, do something unexpected, or start to walk away from the conversation, the person will likely immediately pay attention to me. However, if I take it as a cemented fact that this person is not interested in me and in what I have to say, my ego may cause me to simply give up trying to get their attention. Actualities are indeed somewhat more "real" than potentialities, but this difference, in modal logic, is far less significant than in ordinary binary logical thinking, based on "is" and "is not" as the ultimate measure of the truth.

Modal logic is particularly obvious in interpersonal relationships with a dimension of romantic partnership. Many clients in psychotherapy suffer because of problems in getting someone's attention, and one of the ways in which they try to get that attention (which may be absent for a variety of reasons) is to try and force themselves in front of the other person, whether physically, or more commonly these days, "electronically," through their "virtual self" (social networks, mobile messages, etc.). The result is often a further alienation of the other person because attempts to attract their attention do not yield results. The actual state of affairs, where there is a deficit of attention, is additionally worsened by attempts to get the attention in unproductive ways. This is also a change in the modal worlds.

Where once there was some lukewarm communication, now all communication ceases, because the person loses that little interest that she had had for the interlocutor. The fact that this is an undesirable change of modal worlds does not change the logical fact that it is still a change that was brought about by a slight amendment to the first person's strategy in communication. In many similar cases, the opposite strategy would also yield a change in modal worlds, however one that is more desirable. Should the person who is ignored cease all communication and establish a different kind of perspective on the person who ignores them, that other person would likely sense a loss of attention and would perhaps try to establish contact, which then would also represent a change in the modal worlds. However, the third scenario is also possible. The modal worlds constantly change as the actuality changes, and taking a particular point in time and the actuality of that specific moment as a fixed reality is detrimental to constructive human relationships. We must think about current realities in our interactions as elements of a flow of actualities, where looking at any current actuality from a different angle may present it in a different way, in different colors and with a different glow, and this may allow us to simply wait out the next stage in the flow where we might experience the relationship differently.

Changes in relationships occur for a variety of reasons, at least one of which is ontological: modal worlds as logical categories are not stable independently of the way in which we think of them. They are subject to flow and may become more fixed or more changeable depending on the way in which we perceive them. This again is obvious in the example described. My perception of the modal world whereby somebody ignores me becomes part of that modal world, namely it is a part of my relationship with the person who ignores me. Thus, my waiting it out until the current modal world changes and the person reaches out for me is the immediate result of my thinking about the relative significance of the current modal world, and at the same time it becomes part of the actual state of affairs: the other person's attitude to me is met by my attitude to the modal world whereby she ignores me, and my perception, and corresponding behavior, become part of the very actual modal world. This world is less sustainable in the longer term than a world where I would try to capture the attention of the other person by taking various actions that would provide gratification to that person, while at the same time discouraging her from taking any initiative herself. Our perceptions of social relationships feed those relationships various content, and this content helps determine the fate of the actual modal world. There is thus a meta-perspective on relationships that is logical and may influence their deep structure more profoundly than a binary logic-based, action-oriented approach that is so common.

We alter our relationships primarily by the way we conceptualize and reconceptualize them. A particular view of a relationship might lead to certain states of affairs, and a changed view might entirely change the nature of the same relationship, leading to completely different modal worlds occurring within the relationship. Our patterns of understanding and perceiving our structural realities, our relationships with others, are inextricable parts of those very relationships, and they not only lead to corresponding behaviors within the relationship, which can change the relationship; the perceptions and conceptualizations of the relationship are elements of the relationship itself, and their change automatically changes the relationship.

The way in which we think of another person largely determines the relationship we will have with that person, not only on the level where our way of thinking causes us to act in certain ways toward that person, but also in the sense that the other person's perception of our perception of them will constitute a separate level of our relationship, which is almost independent of our behavior. It is possible to appreciate someone and love them, while at the same time acting in critical and not particularly pleasant ways. However, if the feeling and perception are strong, in many cases the other person senses that, and pays little attention even to behaviors. Correspondingly, an absence of love and respect can be felt even when the behavior is exemplary.

Many marriages have fallen apart because one or both spouses *felt* a lack of genuine affection, despite careful and caring mutual behavior that many observers would have witnessed. It is possible to push someone away on a strictly mental level by thinking badly or unappreciatively of them, while at the same time exhibiting extremely accepting behavior and being nice and polite to that person. Similarly, it ought to be possible to attract someone by thinking warmly and intimately about that person, even when there are few opportunities to communicate with them explicitly.

Freud has written extensively about dreams and how they compensate for our repressed ideation and desires (Freud, 2010, e.g., 153 and in numerous other places). Jung described dreams in more ambitious ways, as manifestations of the collective subconscious, where dreams were able to capture aspects of reality that would otherwise be inaccessible to us. He writes about a dream he had in July 1914, which he interpreted as a message from the subconscious warning him that a war in Europe was about to erupt (Jung, 1989: 201–202). Richard Shusterman, the author of "somaesthetics," believes, with William James and others, that all our feelings are ultimately bodily sensations, and that dreams, as well as fantasies and emotional projections of desires built into daydreaming and proper dreaming, are in fact cognitive tools on a par with our senses and rational faculties (Shusterman, 2008).

There is only a step from the above arguments to the quantum-physics-informed counseling world, where dreams, emotions, and thoughts are considered as energies that not only help understand the various modal realities but, more proactively, can help us shift from one modal world to another, or even create new modal worlds, which can then be brought into actuality, into our present here-and-now. Whether or not we can "think things into reality" is not an esoteric question: it is an empirical one. It is the experience of many people that they have been able to think one modal world (the key attribute here is "possible" world, not a dreamed-up impossible state of affairs) into actuality instead of a different, currently actual modal world, without much physical or social action. Our thoughts are instruments of our action on a different, but no less real, level than our physical or social movements.

Assuming that modality governs our practical logic, the ways in which one ventures into the different structures of modal worlds described in the previous chapter and at the beginning of this one determine not only the decisions that one takes and one's ability to dive deep into one's own identity but also one's beliefs. I hope that the previous section illustrates how adopting modal thinking allows beliefs about what is possible and what is not possible that would otherwise be rejected if the person's prevailing logical horizon was that of propositional logic. There is a subtle but crucial difference here between strictly formal logic and its practical application. This is the reason I repeatedly refer to "practical logic" in this book. Things that seem one way on the level of formal logic may manifest quite differently when such a logic is applied in an existentially tense situation. For example, formally speaking, propositional logic is just one of the possible modal logics. Existentially, practically, thinking based on propositional logic is a world away from thinking and decision-making focusing on modal logic, and this includes the range of acceptable beliefs about the world and about oneself. For example, if it is possible that I will get in touch with a particular person, and the current modal world is that we do not communicate as much as I would like us to, I may choose to call that person or contact them in some other way to see if I can establish a line of communication. However, I may also choose to "draw" that person out of silence by thinking about her in a way that is welcoming, accepting, and which portrays that person as a part of my social world. While this is not a rationalistic action and cannot be explained rationally, a situation where after "drawing" that person into my social reality they call me, or appear somewhere in my social circle, or start to communicate regularly with me, is no less real just because it cannot be explained by reference to something "concrete" that I have done, such as calling that person. The result is the same, and such events in the experience of many people occur with a regularity and frequency that defy the idea that they are "coincidence." Lou

Marinoff writes about this illustratively, describing it as the phenomenon of synchronicity (Marinoff, 2009).

Synchronicity

In his "Black book no. 2," Jung writes about psychology and psychotherapy and describes them as "certainly not a science." He practices psychotherapy as an art. This is likely the most accurate description of psychology in its utmost value for humankind: it is an art of understanding and interpretation of psychic processes which, ideally, ought to result in decisions that concern important aspects of our lives. Reducing psychology to a science, trying to reinvent it as an intellectual endeavor where measurements and exactness are the rule, means degrading psychology to a quasi-science, with very little value for the most important problem-solving issues that we face in psychotherapy, specifically the questions of meaning, language, subliminality, and synchronicity.

The concept of synchronicity refers to situations where certain material events occur in conjunction with thoughts or dreams, without a clear material causality. The example described by Marinoff (Marinoff, 2009) is the appearance of a snake (a python) on the bookshelf of a psychotherapist working with a client who had been obsessed with snakes. Similar synchronicities appear in all kinds of life contexts, such as hearing from a person we think about very intensely or dreaming about events that occur the next day or within a short time span after the dream.

When there is no external causality to explain such events (e.g., we have not heard from a person we think about very intensely for many months or years, and then they contact us after we have thought about hearing from them), the events are described as synchronicity. Quantum physics may provide a contribution to the scientific explanation of synchronicity based on an exchange of energies, some of which are mental and may call into existence some of the possible states of affairs or events that are not actual. Perhaps the most direct explanation of synchronicity is modal logic.

Jung's experiments with "switching off consciousness" by deliberately entering a state of fantasy and then engaging with it as within a dream, or by using dreams to access the subconscious, illustrate how modal worlds operate: depending on our state of consciousness, the fact that we are part of the modal world we are engaged with, the modal world itself will change. Thus, accessing a subconscious dynamic will change the actual dynamics of the modal world which represent our actual state of affairs, our current condition. This condition will respond to what we experience, consciously or subconsciously. The quality of our modal world, that is our actuality, will change.

When writing about his subconscious experiences, or simply when noting ideas for working with the subconscious, Jung thought of this as *writing letters to his Anima*, to his archetypal soul. He believed that through accessing the subconscious, he was able to return to his soul which he had partly abandoned by choosing to pursue the science of medicine (Sonu Shamdasani's introduction to the *Red Book*—Jung, 1989: 200).

Jung's concept of Anima invites us to move deeper beyond the rational Persona that we present to the world and consider deeper sources of authenticity, fears, frustrations, and ambitions. While Jung's description of Anima is very different from, say, Shusterman's account of the role of intuition and emotions as fundamentally bodily functions, the general strategy vis-à-vis the rational Self is the same: a more intimate knowledge of ourselves and the world, and correspondingly a more intricate capacity to influence events and relationships subliminally and subconsciously, requires moving beyond the common and the conventional. They require an exploration of what facilitates synchronicity.

In fact, the beginning of Jung's own programmatic statement with which he opens his *Red Book*, reads:

> The years, of which I have spoken to you, when I pursued the inner images, were the most important time of my life. Everything else is to be derived from this.

This inward direction, based on looking for knowledge in the already assembled, already available in the individual and collective subconscious, through collective experience, takes one away from binary logic and brings us closer to fully appreciating the role of modal logic in dealing with everyday decision-making. In more than one way, synchronicity is a phenomenon that, experientially, does not conform to the binary logic of truth values, of things "being the case" or "not being the case." For example, contrary to the rational, causally oriented way of thinking about how to "bring about" certain outcomes and to think about various decisions that one must make in the course of everyday life, synchronicity usually occurs when one least "tries" and when our focus is not on causal action, but on accessing the particular situation, event, or person on the level of thoughts.

Jung himself explains his own ability to access knowledge about events which, as it turned out, were to happen soon after he had dreamed of them, as irrational, something that robbed him of his freedom and, in a sense, canceled out the scientist in him, calling him to more primal and fundamental, intuitive forms of knowledge. He describes his transformation from a conventional psychiatrist into a therapist focused on introspection and symbolic interpretation as a brutal influence of "the spirit of the depth." This spirit does not leave him any liberty to choose to be a scientist, a rational psychoanalyst, and psychiatrist: it draws him into the murky depths of his own and collective unconscious, forces him to focus on his dreams and visions, causes him to doubt his own sanity, only to reassure him when worldly events conform to his dreams. The synchronicities caused him to doubt himself countless times, yet they are now accepted as a well-known phenomenon for which there is no rational explanation, but it is so evident and so widely present that it is simply taken as a fact.

The work of this "spirit of the deep" that stands behind synchronicities is obvious when we decide to resolve situations which we have faced many times in our lives and have always been unsuccessful in resolving them rationally. This particularly concerns interpersonal relationships. Sometimes, the voice of the spirit of the deep, or the unconscious, teaches us to go in directions which, rationally, we would never choose, and yet they yield results. When looked back upon, these solutions again do not appear rational: sometimes it is even difficult to rationally understand how they could possibly have worked, yet they did. There thus appears to exist a logic of the deep, a particular set of laws that govern the subconscious, which we simply cannot access from our ordinary state of mind when we reason about our experiences and the decisions we make.

The occurrence of synchronicity is often connected with the experience of action upon intuition, as opposed to acting rationally, based on clearly explicable reasons. This is experienced differently and described as "going with the flow" of things, "listening to the gut," "following the wisdom of the body," or obeying one's "inner drive" or "impulse." All these descriptions suggest an acquiescence in a sort of spontaneity that is not formally structured by reason, but by feeling. Thus, a focus on feeling (as something different from emotions) appears to relate to the experience of synchronicities. The feeling at stake here is the sort of mental and bodily state which we experience when we have a strong sense not to go down a dark alley, even though we might have passed there at night thousands of times, or when we get the urge not to get on that plane, or when we have a sense that in some social interactions, we are about to walk into a trap that might turn against us.

A modal logic perspective on feeling as a precursor to synchronicity involves a difference between two existential quantifiers, namely the quantifier of necessity and that of possibility. A modal logical principle that the statement "A is necessarily the case" immediately translates into the statement "A is the case," while "A is possibly the case" does not translate into "A is the case" is associated with the difference between a rational and an intuitive perspective on events and states of affairs. Namely, "A is necessarily the case" is associated with the rational understanding that A must be the case in the sense that it would be rationally inconceivable for A not to be the case. For example, me being identical to myself or the a priori mathematical truths, such as equations, are considered necessarily true, because they rest on logical principles which are the very foundations of our rational reasoning and, if they were not automatically true, our entire logical structure of thought would be shaken. However, the statements which are possibly true, and states of affairs that they describe which, consequently, are possibly the case, or may be the case, are subject to other types of considerations. A serpent showing up on my bookshelf (the example Marinoff uses for synchronicity) is, of course, not a necessary state of affairs, nor even a likely one, but nevertheless it is possible, and it has, as we have seen from Marinoff, actually happened to his fellow therapist.

Things that we long for sometimes occur without a clear, rationally explicable line of causation between our external actions and those events. When they occur frequently enough, without such external causation, we can speculate, rationally speaking, about some other, rationally inexplicable types of causation, because we assume that there must exist some type of causation to bring these events about.

The modal logic of possibility brings us closer to the idea that what we consider necessity is merely based on a causation which we rationally understand, or more precisely, which we have invented. Synchronicities are a manifestation of what might be such a causation, and the fact that today synchronicities are a well-recognized phenomenon in psychic life, and in life generally speaking, merely shows that our traditional understandings of Newtonian physics and the seemingly clear-cut deductive logic may not be all that there is to logic.

Modal logic, while not immediately militating against the binary deductive logic, makes us more aware of these softer perspectives on causation and logic in general, if we become sufficiently accustomed to thinking about psychic life, and again, about life in general (for psychotherapy is about life issues in general, not just about psychic phenomena), in terms of the categories of modal logic.

It is important, for the readers' sake, to distinguish between the phenomenon of synchronicity in its meaning which is closely associated with modal logic-based thinking, and the coincidences which, through their frequency and suggestive contextual dimensions, appear to have been intended, planned events or actions.

There is a popular saying that "there are no coincidences," in the sense that most situations which we perceive as accidental are either intentionally caused by someone else, or have a deeper meaning which one must analyze and use to orient one's future actions. However, this meaning of coincidence is completely different from the concept of synchronicity. An example here might be in order.

During the writing of this book, I was active in the media against the political regime in my country. This was (and likely still is, at the time of publication of the book) a government composed of former radically nationalist politicians combined with former communists, and their manner of government was a strange mixture of populism, collective bribery (payment of money taken from international loans to poor pensioners and the general population just before elections), and a massive amount of involvement in organized crime, including the industrial cultivation of narcotics. During the current regime, several of its outspoken critics had been murdered, some have ended up drowned in rivers under suspicious circumstances, and the amount of repression against the media and the critics of the government has been so terrible that even children have been taken away from some of the critics. I was one of those whose child had been illegally taken by corrupt institutions and as a result of that I had little to lose and was particularly sharp in my media articles and critique of the government.

After an initial Open Letter to the President, which I had published along with a colleague, my car was vandalized in broad daylight, in front of surveillance cameras at the parking lot of the building where I lived. Following a second Open Letter, I received threats of arrest in written form, and shortly afterward also indirect threats that I would be removed from my job in the University if I continued to publish against the president (Petković, 2021). As I did not allow these threats to stop me, and in fact I intensified my media appearances and critique, in the summer of 2021 I was suddenly surrounded by several attractive women who appeared to have emerged "from nowhere" (from a social circle which until then had been only marginal among my acquaintances), and these women started to communicate with me very closely and even traveled with me on two occasions. I had a sense of strangeness about the new acquaintances and on at least one occasion I directly refused to become more closely involved in that circle, because I suspected that something out of the ordinary might have been behind afoot.

At the same time, for some reason, a former colleague of mine who I knew worked for the government invited me to "discuss politics" in his apartment and was obviously recording our conversation, using a remote control pretending to put the radio on and off each time we discussed something of interest to the government. This "onslaught" continued for several months, and I was forced to cut off all communication and social links to the persons whom I felt were involved in this social maneuver of experiment with me, in particular with one person whom I believed to be the organizer of the whole process.

After I had cut off these connections, suddenly, one morning in November 2021, two police inspectors from the Department for Organized Crime (the most elite police department in the country) showed up at my door. To make things bizarrely amusing, one of them turned out to be my former student. They entered my apartment and gave me a summons to appear at their headquarters the next day to be interrogated about my media appearances. Their demeanor was polite and unaggressive; however, the format of their approach appeared to convey a clear threat: they could have called me on the phone, or sent me a summons through a uniformed police officer or even by post, but instead they chose to appear at my door unannounced. I felt that the intention was to intimidate me, but at the same time not to go too far in intimidation so that I do not react with anger and again intensify my media appearances.

The same night, while I was getting ready to be interrogated the next morning, I received a message from the same person I had suspected had been at the center of the previous maneuver to disturb me, with the women who had been trying to take my attention away from political actions and writing. This person had not been in touch with me for a while, and the message she sent, in the middle of the night, read: "Sasha, is everything allright?"

I ignored the message and appeared at the police headquarters the next day, where, to my surprise, they met me very warmly, offered me coffee and water, and insisted that they wanted to "help me deal with the general issues that I had been voicing in the media." They transferred me to a different section of this police department, in charge of anti-corruption policy, and tried to co-opt me and reassure me that they were merely acting conscientiously. When I decided to cut through the obvious sham and asked the police inspector why they had vandalized my car, he responded, with a smile: "We didn't do that, but of course we know who did." This escalation transpired immediately after my colleague and I had published a third open letter, this time to an American Undersecretary of State, calling for the Serbian president to be indicted before the International Criminal Court for a variety of crimes and abuses of power against the opponents of the regime.

Following these events, even those of my colleagues and friends who had previously believed that the demolition of my car, threats by arrest and by sacking, and finally the women who had suddenly appeared around me, had all been coincidences, became gravely convinced that all of this had been a part of the intent to distract, and then to silence me in public. Interestingly, while I was giving a statement at the police headquarters, the police officer who played the "good cop" role said to me, suddenly: "You do know that there is no such thing as a coincidence, don't you?"

This is the sort of sequence of events which, while they could all be coincidental in terms of modal logic (these events are not *necessarily* parts of a particular strategy), strongly suggests that there is a pattern and consequently also an intention behind all these actions taken by the various actors, some of whom are obviously direct exponents of the state. This is the sort of "coincidences" that is often discussed and described as "suggestive synchronicities," while in fact it has little to do with the phenomenon of synchronicity that I am concerned with in this book. In other words, such events are often seen as synchronicities, but they are *not synchronicites.*

Synchronicity is the occurrence in the actual state of affairs of something that preoccupies us in our thoughts, without a clear causation between those events and our external actions.

The events that had happened to me during the writing of the book could be coincidences because there was no necessary, rational connection between them that would be irrefutable; there was no necessity in the conclusion that this was all government strategy to exert pressure on me to silence me in the media. However, they were not synchronicities because there were *clear potential causal connections between my external actions and the events which had transpired for me.* I had not criticized the president and the government in my thoughts, but very openly, by my actions, and through my newspaper articles, which had been numerous. Thus, the events with the police, which were the culmination of a sequence of other suspicious events apparently engineered by the government to silence me, had not been caused by my thoughts and feelings: the state of affairs where the police showed up at my door had not been called into actuality as a modal world becoming the actual world by my psychological actions; it was a physical event that had arisen from my other physical actions, namely by my open public critique of the government and the president, and this causality was actually confirmed by the police who said that this was why they were going to interrogate me. Thus, one might conclude, it seems to me with a high degree of probability, that I had been targeted by the government to frighten, disturb, distract, and finally openly caution me to stop calling for the president's indictment before the international criminal judiciary, thus that these events had not in fact been coincidences (in line with the policemen's remark that "there is no such thing as a coincidence"); however, the events were not synchronicities.

A synchronicity is when I dream about the ideal postgraduate student who has philosophical qualifications and who is interested in philosophical psychotherapy to supervise their postgraduate thesis and cultivate someone who will carry on my work in the particular university department where I teach this subject, and this actually occurs. Another synchronicity is when I am gravely ill and face a bad medical prognosis of the outcome, and I have a strong mental conviction that, contrary to all medical reasons, I would actually fully recover, to the extent that I refuse even to go to hospital, and what I had pictured in my mind occurs and I make a full recovery. The recovery is not the result of my specific actions (I had, after all, refused to go to hospital), but it is the actualization of a modal world which, through my strong emotion and conviction, I appear to have "called into reality." This is not to say that I or anybody else should make this strategy a habit, because it can result in a fatal outcome, however this particular instance might be in line with the concept of synchronicity (though there are also other potential explanations, such as the causal actions of my convictions on my physical processes, but again it is unclear to what extent the causal actions of our thoughts and mental states are generally involved in all synchronicities).

Ideas as Modal Worlds

Perhaps the surest way to alter the actuality by calling another modal world into it is the clear and vivid formulation and experience of an idea. This is a phenomenon that is connected with synchronicities, although it does not exhaust itself in the very concept of synchronicity. Namely, the occurrence of a particularly clear and elaborate idea about a situation, problem, or desire (the way to bring the desire to actuality) is a first step to the actual change of modal worlds. Often the stalemate we find ourselves in with regard to particular life situations is first and foremost characterized by the absence of an articulate idea about how to approach the problem. Thus, the thought process is clearly pivotal in changing modal worlds in situations where we experience the absence of ideas, and this stifles any potential action to resolve the issue at hand.

Individuals in counseling often experience the development, or emergence, of an idea with regard to a problem as an exceptionally empowering mental state: they almost feel, and sometimes they say, that they "have resolved" the problem by the very fact that they now have an idea as to how to approach it. Obviously, having an idea is not enough; however, in personal experience, it is often "almost enough," that is how much power the thought of a solution gives to our emotional self and our self-esteem. This change of self-perception from that of a powerless victim to circumstance to that of an agent with considerable power to address the situation is a change of modal worlds in itself: the existential situation characterized by the former feeling is fundamentally different from the situation characterized by the latter feeling, not just in the quality of life and experience, but in its potential to effect a change in external circumstances. Even in situations when, for whatever reason, an external change does not happen, the internal change initiated by the onset of an idea is sufficient to alter the experience of life and thus the modal world in which we exist at a particular time and in a particular place.

From the point of view of modal logic, ideas are modal worlds. The closer they are to us, namely the more clearly and elaborately we are able to adopt them and develop them, own them as our own and be prepared to act on them, the more fully the modal world is called into reality and factually becomes our actuality. Numerous people throughout history have lived and died for an idea: sometimes these ideas were brought into actuality by those same people, but in most cases they were either actualized by someone else, after many of their protagonists had perished, or they never actualized in the form and to the extent that those laying their lives for the idea had hoped for or had been convinced the ideas would unfold. Some ideas had even been perverted in their actualization and had resulted in states of affairs that the protagonists of the idea would have abhorred and would certainly have disowned. Consider political ideologies, such as communism, various forms of nationalism, and so on. However, does the fact that in many situations the ideas one had fought for have failed or backfired in actuality change the fact that these ideas had changed the modal worlds of life of those individuals, that they had shaped their lives in ways which, without them adopting the idea, would likely have been very different?

An idea has not only the capacity to change our current existential experience, it also holds great therapeutic potential. Developing an idea with regard to a particular situation in life means developing a structural vision of the situation which allows that experience to be processed mentally without excessive damage. Whether any action based on an idea is successful or not, the very structured decision-making and attempts to alter the physical circumstances externally will likely additionally organize our psychological structures in ways that will make us more resilient and more effective in problem-solving in the future. Failing to act, and meandering around a life problem without a clear idea, on the other hand, serves as a disempowering experience that reduces both the ability to act in the future and resilience to defeat. Thus a certain savviness in developing and manipulating ideas and in making decisions, ranging from micro- to macro-decisions, goes a long way toward the development of personal tools to address a broad variety of challenges, as well as to act self-therapeutically in situations of personal crisis.

The emergence of an idea is the self-presentation of a modal world which, from that moment on, coexists on a level of possibility with a number of other modal worlds, including the actual state of affairs. The emergence of an idea thus increases the number of modal worlds which might be called into reality. Thus, ideation is a form of action, and the ability to theoretically conceptualize solutions and potential strategies to address seemingly frozen life issues is the same as the creation of new practical possibilities. The difference between theory and practice, between ideation and action, is in fact very slight; it is nowhere near as major or important as we are conventionally taught to think and believe.

Sometimes an idea will involve a complete and clear strategy to address a problem with its structural features, namely the relationships with significant others involved; on other occasions, the idea will simply contain an intuitive inkling, a suggestion as to where to go and from what angle to approach a situation, without a clear rationale of why the idea has that particular shape. Ideas can be rational and intuitive, and in most cases, they are both when they are productive. This means that an idea, to drive us to act, must possess the necessary dynamism, the emotional, and thus bodily, dimension, and will ideally develop through a rational elaboration of what exactly to do and how to act on the fundamentally intuitive directions which we develop through bodily cognition. Such are ideas with regard to solving interpersonal problems, where after a period of unsuccessful rational deliberation as to whether and how to act, a sudden resolution comes from the deep, an idea emerges from the subconscious, which then branches out into elaboration through rational analysis and results in specific actions or reactions which cause a change of modal worlds.

The inspiration for new ideas with regard to problems that had hitherto seemed rationally difficult to solve appears to arise from deep structures that Jung describes as "spirit of the deep." More importantly, the appearance and consequences of acquiescing in the teachings and messages of the spirit of the deep force us to cast out our pride, our dignity, and to embrace what Jung describes as a melting of the reasonable and the paradoxical (Jung, 1989: 229). He describes the emergence of an idea in this way as a sacrifice of our Persona as a rational person, and our inevitable agreeing to be drawn into irrational discourse, where paradox is the foundation of what he calls "supreme meaning." The connection between supreme meaning, namely the intuitive interpretation that brings together various seemingly paradoxical (contradictory in terms of binary logic) elements and insights, on the one hand, and God on the other hand, is experienced as an image. This image is an archetype, and it is fundamentally an image of God (Jung, loc. cit.). It is the image that is capable of elucidating the future, even forecasting it, at least in a sense: it is not the experience or image of God yet, but the anticipation of the image of God to come, where God is the truth and at the same time an image: the archetypal image of the truth is the knowledge which God offers; however, this knowledge is partly mysterious and can neither be accessed nor fully interpreted by rational means only (loc. cit.).

The reason Jung is so important in our understanding of the root and well of ideas that appear irrational and emerge from the depths of our subconscious is perhaps contained in a single sentence in his *Red Book*: "Hence I had to speak to my soul as to something far off and unknown, which did not exist through me, but through whom I existed" (Jung, 1989: 232).

Jung's idea about "returning to his soul," which he had abandoned through his rational pursuit of medicine, the acquisition of worldly reputation, power and wealth, and the practice of psychiatry, draws on the assumption of a generalized collective unconscious that underlies all our conscious efforts and articulations. It is this realm of the unconscious that is primal and that nurtures our original soul (in Jung's terms, *Anima*) that is also the root of most of the ideas that arise seemingly without connection to our rational arguments or the information about the states of affairs in which we find ourselves, which we are explicitly aware of.

The very idea of the unconscious, as a vast ocean underneath the seemingly solid ground of the conscious that we stand on and that we consider the foundation of our reasoning, challenges the binary logical modality and draws us into the more subtle and more ambiguous realms of thinking based on modal logic. If we understand an idea not as a construction springing straight from the explicit facts that we are consciously aware of concerning a particular situation, or modal world, but as an emergence of a deeper wisdom from the unconscious, which is awakened by our powerlessness to deal with the problem "above ground," then the concept of idea becomes more intricate and potentially much more powerful.

The context of the unconscious, especially in Jung's interpretation, portrays an idea as a spark, or a structure which arises from the interplay of the rational and the irrational, from the conscious and the unconscious, from the above ground and the psychic underground about which we can only speculate and where many of our hopes about knowing the future and guessing our fate are vested. The conscious thus appears as a continent amid the oceans of the unconscious, and the assumption is that just as life has emerged from the ocean, all of the important secrets about our rationally unfathomable truths of existence and future lie in the ocean, in what Jung calls the collective unconscious.

Given this general picture of the relationship between the conscious and the unconscious, an idea—that is, the very concept of an idea—is a sort *of announcement of the unconscious in a way acceptable to the conscious*; it is something in between the two extremes of solely rational interpretation, on the one hand, and the freer and more radical esoteric understanding of the unconscious, on the other. To fully illustrate this "middle of the ground" nature of the idea, which in a sense mediates between the conscious and the unconscious, it is perhaps useful to first briefly discuss the other extreme, namely the psychological reception of the esoteric interpretation of the unconscious, again primarily with reference to Jung, who was by far the most explicit of all psychoanalysts with regard to this particular interpretation.

The Esoteric Receptions of the Collective Unconscious in Jung

In Jung's interpretation of man's relationship to the desirability and beauty of the world and worldly experiences, what we see in the so-called reality is a *projection of our soul, or the exteriorization of our desire.* The psychoanalytic concept of desire as driver (later taken on by Lacan in a different application of the unconscious) is fundamental to questions about identity, and Jung is true to this tradition. He argues that our desire speaks about our soul, and consequently, the person who "possesses" his desire can "lay a hand" on his soul because "his desire is the image and expression of his soul" (Jung, 1989: 232).

The beauty of the experiences, of other people, and of material things in the world is also a projection of the values that make up our deeper identity, our soul. Thus, depending on who we are, we will experience events differently because our souls are different; our sensibilities differ, and they are ultimately what decides whether we will enjoy or suffer the people and events we encounter in our lives.

Lacan takes over this idea to develop the concept of "*jouissance*," namely the idea of satisfaction which is the affective indicator of personality that is key in psychodiagnostics: looking at where one's *jouissance* lies allows the diagnostician to locate the personality (Lacan, 1998: 64–77 and 51–63). Jung insists that our perception of the world, and the quality of our experience of it, depends on the image we have of the world, thus his repeated statement that "he who possesses the image of the world, possesses half the world [...]" (Jung, 1989: 232). This is a key point which he also elaborates elsewhere, in his *Transformations and Symbols of the Libido*, etc. The psychoanalytic interpretation that he develops is that our libido, our desire for life, projects the positive attributes of life, such as beauty and desirability, to objects and people, and thus the more our libido is active and the stronger it is, the more beauty and desirability we will see in the world, in our everyday experience. Conversely, depression as a crisis of the libido is reflected in a dulling of enjoyment in the life-related positive reception of the world.

This perspective leads directly to the perspective of our various projections, which found the qualities of external experience based on the strength of our libido, being able to actually influence not only our immediate experience and quality of life (thus switching our various modal worlds in important life situations), but also influencing the similar perceptions and projections by others, which are also connected to and fundamentally arise from their libido. This means that our perception of reality is predicated on what we expect from reality, or as Jung calls it, on our "longing," and the longing is more a quality of the soul than something triggered by the external world. This conceptualization of longing is applicable, for example, to falling in love. The very phenomenon of falling in love, often without knowing the other person sufficiently, involves considerable projections of the qualities we long for; as a result of these projections, we start to long for the other person, whom we don't actually know, that is we don't really know whether or not that person really possesses the qualities we long for. This is one of the paradoxes that fall into the context of what Jung describes in his *Red Book*: we long for something in someone where we are rationally aware that we don't have any reliable knowledge whether that quality, which is the object of our longing, even exists in the person we long for. The result is that falling in love, more often than not, shows itself to be a misguided perception after we have come to know the other person, and quite frequently we find out that the person we had fallen in love with is not a person we can actually love, because they are "nothing like we believed them to be," where in fact they have no responsibility for our misperception. This phenomenon is simply the result of a projection of the libido, which adorns the external experiences and events, including people, with the qualities that our soul values and desires. The fact that we have found that a particular person we had fallen in love with is not in fact the sort of person we imagined (rather than believed) them to be when we had fallen in love does not change the quality of our experience of having been in love. Thus, many people at later stages of their lives declare in therapy that "they only want to fall in love one last time."

They already know that falling in love is not the same as loving someone, that falling in love is a projection of the libido which usually ends in our realization that the object of the projection does not adequately correlate with the values projected onto them; however, the satisfaction, what Lacan calls *jouissance*, the application of the libido, is arousing and mobilizing to the extent that people who fear old age, death, and solitude sometimes desire falling in love more than an actual partnership.

The beauty and the longing are in the soul, and they influence our experience perhaps more strongly than any actual realization of a relationship, or actual actions by other people who are significant to us.

The idea that longing is inextricably connected to an image, and that the image of the world is what drives us, distantly relates Jung to Wittgenstein and his understanding of the role of language as a picture of the world. However, in Jung's interpretation, the image is not just a picture of reality which we see in one way, and some other person in another way, where the distortions from what the actual states of affairs are "really" like are due to our individual differences. Rather, in Jung's psychology, the image is more primordial than might seem at first sight; it is more universal and paradigmatic, and the way in which we tend to capture reality through images is more common between us than we would care to recognize in most cases.

In his esoteric work, Jung was particularly interested in the visual images used for fortune telling in various cultures. His main interest was the Chinese "Book of Change," the *I Ching*; however, he was almost obsessed with paintings of archetypal images and, in addition to painting such images himself in *The Red Book* itself, he was aware of the traditions of forecasting the future by the drawing of images, which he considered to be universal and closely connected to archetypes of the collective unconscious. One such practice was the Tarot. At one stage in his 1933 lecture Jung mentioned that the pictures depicted on the Tarot cards were a sort of playing with the unconscious, and he explicitly linked the Tarot to the Chinese *I Ching*, suggesting that they "at least" had a value in helping us understand the present moment. The similarity in colors and some of the representation style between the Tarot and Jung's own drawings and paintings in *The Red Book* are obvious, and thus the implicit suggestion that he would have considered the Tarot images as pictorial representations of the archetypes of the collective unconscious.

Jung's preoccupation with dreams was obvious in his work, including in the titles of his writings, and in his 1933 lecture he comments on the Tarot image of the Devil, as a hermaphroditic creature that seems to represent a paradoxical union of the opposites. He further comments on the similarities between the Tarot and *I Ching*'s hexagrams and interprets both as pictorial interpretations of the mutual interaction of the opposite forces and the flowing movements of reality, which we may not be able to rationally or perceptually comprehend.

The dialectic in the esoteric reception of the unconscious such as Jung's reflects a way of thinking that is more specifically tied to modal than to binary logic, where the merging of contradictory information and meanings is seen as a play of the subconscious in which the truth, which is never simple and one-sided, reveals itself to us. To grasp this truth, especially when it is relational, namely when it has to do with human inter-relationships, it is not sufficient to use the conventional perceptual and rational faculties; one must also rely on bodily reactions, on feelings and on spontaneous interpretations of the archetypal content that surfaces in visions, dreams and daydreaming, as well as in artistic representations, for those who engage especially in the visual arts.

Many of Jung's seemingly "esoteric" interpretations have been incorporated in what are now considered very standard and conservative methods of psychological assessment, psychodiagnostics, and therapeutic interventions. For example, the projective techniques in psychological assessments and diagnostics are based on a standardized interpretation of images, some of which, even graphically, resemble Jung's drawings and paintings of archetypal content from his visions, and some bear a striking resemblance to images depicted on the Tarot cards. In fact, one wonders whether Jung himself, if he had been involved in the use of modern projective techniques, would rather have used some other images, including those on the Tarot cards, or those in his own *Red Book*.

Similarly, the psychotherapeutic interpretation today draws on many of Jung's symbols of archetypes which he had derived from his introspective investigations and his visions. In fact, it appears that the main reason some of Jung's research can be seen as esoteric is the fact that he had drawn his conclusions from a free interpretation of his own and the experiences of others based on speculation about the symbolism of some elements of those experiences. However, the same, then, could be said of Freud, whose interpretation of dreams, for example, although it is seen as a classic in psychoanalysis, and is in no way treated as esoteric, is also based on what would today be considered wild speculation.

It is the subsequent experience and the actual confirmation of the symbolic meanings of the content originally depicted by Freud, and likewise, by Jung, that has turned those wild speculations into standard psychological knowledge. In fact, it seems that there is no other way to innovate in psychology and psychological interpretation than to follow sources such as dreams, intuitions, and visions, as well as to interpret the experiences of clients and one's own experiences in light of the ideas that arise from our own subconscious, and may be part of the wealth of what Jung considered to be the collective unconscious.

When Jung writes that "dreams are the guiding words of the soul," he says the same as Freud, however in more directly introspective terms, because he connects the dreams with the knowledge of the unconscious and makes it explicit that he considers the inklings and suggestions of the unconscious as more valuable and more practical knowledge than the rational and restrictive norms of knowledge imposed by the "spirit of this world" (Jung, 1989: 233). He goes as far as to say that "The spirit of the deep even taught me to consider my action and my decision as dependent on dreams" (Jung, loc. cit.). This clearly suggests Jung's *practical application* of the borderline cognitive experiences, such as dreams, as inroads into gaining knowledge of the unconscious. For him, using the Tarot cards or the *I Ching* to consider the meaning of "at least the present moment," as he says, and possibly to inform his actions and decisions, might well have been of the same level of cognitive assurance as the more conventional interpretation of dreams in psychodiagnostics and psychotherapy. In fact, there is no principled reason why this should not be the case, and this casts a general and wide shadow over our suspicion of the so-called esoteric practice in seeking to understand a variety of life situations.

One of the issues here is why we are used to thinking about modal worlds with suspicion just because they are not the actual world, and why the ways that do not conform with the "waking" practices of rational and deductive thinking, although they are often confirmed in our everyday experience as valid and actually produce useful conclusions, are described as esoteric.

If it is reasonable to assume that much of our learning occurs through actual experience, where the accompanying emotions and bodily sensations make the memory sufficiently vivid to remember, rather than through strictly rational or perceptual, "cognitive" channels which can be rationally understood, and if one agrees that visual representation is an important, if not the crucial, aspect of our ideation in general, then it is unclear why Jung's ideas about the visual presentation of archetypal content and their use in practical psychotherapy and in making decisions in life are considered unconventional.

Visualization has been so obviously and remarkably a foundation of our ideation that throughout history people have recorded their important collective experiences through the visual arts. Today some of this art, such as the Aboriginal paintings found in caves throughout Australia, are accorded not only the highest artistic esteem but also an exquisite cultural relevance and the meaning of condensed statements of important and long collective experience. The symbolism of visuality is a language of our subconscious and, as Jung believed, of the collective unconscious. Our subconscious relates to the collective unconscious in that it derives from that deeper well of collective experience and informs our decisions in ways which are only accessible to us if we actually pay attention to dreams, archetypal representations, and our own bodily reactions to situations, where even registering such reactions requires training and special attention because we have gradually been alienated from our awareness of our own body.

If all our reactions can ultimately be traced to our body, then the fact that we learn most effectively through vivid experience that contains emotional reactions means that in fact we learn through the body (Shusterman, 2012: 91–111).

One reason why the archetypal content is more universal than one would perhaps expect of spontaneous visual representations of what is a deeply personal experience of life may be that certain shapes and structures of symbolic processing of experience are shared between all or most of us, in much the same time as the fundamental value-laden concepts such as good and evil are shared between all people. Everybody understands the existence and at least a practical difference between good and evil; however, any particular culture might actually influence the specifics of whether certain choices, actions, or events are considered good or evil. Similarly, it appears that the archetypal images such as those in the Tarot, including "Temperance," "The Emperor,"

"Death," or "Devil," are meanings that describe the experience, expectations, and values of all people in ways that allow a rich interpretation to take place regarding concrete life dilemmas.

An example of a particularly important Tarot symbol analyzed by Jung is the symbol of a child, portrayed on the Tarot card "The Sun." The card depicts a naked, joyful child on a white horse with a red flag by his side and a serious, powerful sun overhead. The child has flowers in his hair and is surrounded by yellow flowers. Its appearance suggests a promise of development, of fulfillment, and of happiness and beneficial change. It is an image of a promising new modal world that is almost there, a promise almost come true, an encouragement on a road to change and improvement.

In his 1940 paper "On the psychology of the child archetype," Jung describes the symbol of the child as that which opens a vision of self-development; he argues that the typical events that can befall a child symbolize the events of one's self-improvement (Jung, 1953–1983, 9: 1). In paragraph 278, Jung specifically mentions that *the essential feature of the symbol of the child is the future*, a call of the future, of the move to another modal world.

Similarly, "esoteric" and equally futuristic is the concept of hope in Christianity. It is a normative expectation for a Christian never to lose hope, even in situations that appear hopeless. This insistence on hope is predicated upon the belief that God is omni-powerful, that his intentions and plans are mysterious and non-transparent to us, and that at any point in our lives, he may decide to intervene on our behalf, which means that the objective, rational, actual state of affairs may in fact mean very little in terms of the outcome of any struggle or difficulty we may be involved in.

Hope empowers the person internally and allows even the ultimate defeat to be carried with dignity and with a degree of optimistic outlook on life or afterlife. Ernst Bloch thus wrote that even the person condemned to death walks to the gallows only owing to a hope, however small or glimmer it might be, that something incredible will happen and save them. Hope is an "esoteric" practice in the strictly rational sense because, rationally speaking, hope should arise from an estimation of the state of affairs we are in and the rationally foreseeable probability of changes in that state of affairs. The problem with this latter thinking is that our calculations of probability, when they are rational, tend to be based only on a limited amount and a singular kind of knowledge which has little to do with the vast ocean of the unconscious which our rational faculties cannot reach: "Scholarliness alone is not enough; there is a knowledge of the heart that gives deeper insight" (Jung, 1989: 233).

In his *Answer to Job*, Jung connects this call of the deep, the spirit of the deep, with the Holy Spirit, and mentions that the indwelling of the Holy Spirit makes us more like Christ (Jung, 1953–1983, 11: paragraph 758). For

Jung, the Holy Spirit is the most mystical of the three faces of God; it appears that he experienced his own spiritual callings as the religious experiences of a Christian, which is likely something many Christians would be surprised by. Jung's preoccupation was the practical application of the inspirations and insights revealed by the Spirit (the Holy Spirit) in making key life decisions, the same decisions that he dwelled upon in his introspective research and in his therapeutic practice.

One wonders what the practical significance of this distinction between the rational and the esoteric is for psychotherapy and for our everyday life, namely what is it that "the spirit of the deep," as Jung calls it, leads us to, which we would miss if we stuck to the "spirit of this world," namely the rational, the conventional, scientific, or, as psychologists often term it today, "the psychology based on evidence."

There is hardly a more miserable self-denigration of psychology than its contemporary self-definition as being "evidence-based" alone. The practical significance of being open to esoteric, in fact somatic, intuitive and imagination-driven knowledge is, as Jung says, "living our lives to the full," and this means "living what we have not lived, in ways which we have not tried, living in the ways which we have left to others to live" (paraphrase of Jung, 1989: 233).

There is a value to change regardless of whether a change is necessary. The psyche of people who often change themselves and their circumstances is different from that of people who are caught up in their patterns which, while serving them well every day, deprive them of insights into what their lives could be like should they have lived them significantly differently. The way we *feel* determines the level of our internal mobilization and ability to attain different modal worlds. To jump from one modal world that is the actual state of affairs to another, one must *first depart* from the actual, current world: one must be willing to *abandon* one's pattern of thought and behavior in order to welcome a new reality. Thus, a degree of wondering, of exploring the seemingly unthinkable, or testing the limits and daring to break some of the conventional social rules, is a part of being led by the "spirit of the deep."

The therapeutic value of change in itself is well known, primarily in its capacity to strengthen the person's confidence in their own ability to alter the modal worlds that define their life: good decision-makers are individuals who constantly make decisions and are confident that they can do it effectively; good strategists are individuals who are regularly involved in designing strategies for various endeavors and, consequently, have confidence that they can win in most situations. Good practitioners of a particular skill or craft are people who regularly practice the skill and know how to apply it, not only when it is necessary, but whenever they have a reasonable opportunity. A karate master does not apply their craft only when one's life is at stake: they train every day and use the principles of karate in life outside of physical combat: they are thus able to slow their breathing under stressful situations, to lower their heart rate, to relax before going to sleep and to burst into action with full concentration due to their practice of the "*kime*," or "contraction." Similarly, a good decision-maker and a life strategist will change things, shift their modal worlds by making everyday decisions, not only when the circumstances demand a decision, but whenever they have a reasonable opportunity to change something. They will seek alternative life experiences not in order to drown their depression in new encounters or new activities, but because they are driven by intuition and a curiosity to explore the knowledge that comes with those experiences.

Esoteric practices and thinking are a form of well-recognized essentialism in philosophy, namely the view that we truly know things not through their superficial appearances, but through seeking to penetrate into their "essence," into what makes them specifically the things that they are, and this often involves events and knowledge which, on a superficial level, seem unrelated to the phenomenon that we are trying to understand. When writing about essentialism, Kazimierz Ajdukiewicz writes that the very modern meaning of ontology has been shaped by phenomenologists, who believe that the essence of "what is," namely the current modal world, the actual "reality" is grasped only through the *intuition of essences* (Ajdukiewicz, 1973: 76). He describes how Edmund Husserl sees the intuition of essences based on a Platonic vision of ideas which represent the ideal forms of things, the ideal sets of attributes that the pure concept of a certain event or experience ought to possess, and how he proceeds to discuss the application of these ideal attributes to our understanding of phenomena (Ajdukiewicz, 1973: 42–43). There are both similarities and differences between the phenomenological understanding of essences and intuition that Ajdukiewicz describes and Jung's (and my) view of esoteric knowledge here.

The similarities lie in the phenomenologists' understanding that what makes some experience what it essentially is does not actually exist in space in time, which means that it is not part of an actual state of affairs. Only by delving into that ideal, which exists on a level different from the existence of the specific circumstances in which we find ourselves, can we grasp the "essence" of the experience. This almost conforms to the very notion of esoteric. However, on the other hand, the phenomenological, and particularly Husserl's, concept of "idea" is very Platonic and does not adequately correspond to my notions of idea here, where an idea is a project, a strategy, an inroad into solving a difficult situation, or a way to shift between modal worlds, a way to call into actual existence another, possible world or state of affairs. Ideas for Husserl are merely concepts, whereas ideas in the sense relevant to a modal logic-informed way of therapy and decision-making alike are more active—they are endowed with intention and a drive—Lacan would say with *jouissance*, to succeed, to contract the reality and produce a different form and content of it.

A change in modal worlds is part of exploring life, and Jung connects it to the concept of epistemically oriented suffering. He writes that, from a Christian perspective, nobody can avoid suffering the fate of Christ himself, going through humiliation, pain, and deprivation for the sake of uniting with the spirit of the depth, after which experience one is mocked by those devoted to the spirit of this world.

The esoteric, the faith, the symbolic interpretation of what, for most, is unknowable, causes one to become subject to public scorn; however, the privilege to attain deeper knowledge is always paid for by being disparaged by the majority, and Jung describes this on his own example of being mocked (Jung, 1989: 234). One subjects oneself to experiences that lead to a rejection by the mainstream scientific, social, or religious community in order to ensure privileged access to knowledge that is deeper and perhaps more practically useful than what is either obvious or can be arrived at through mere rational argument. The structure of an idea in this context is a projection from one modal world to another, arising from the depths of the subconscious, from somatic intuitions, while elaborated and accompanied by rational considerations that operationalize the intuitions in light of the specific challenges and problems to solve. As Jung puts it, "it was easy for them to laugh, since I had to do strange things" (Jung, 1989: 234).

The experiment with the unconscious that so profoundly characterizes psychoanalysis, and especially Jungian psychoanalysis, which strongly relies on introspection and self-analysis, is an example of the esoteric use of modal logic. The individual subconscious and the collective unconscious are sets of modal worlds ready to be called into actuality (or reality) by being drawn into the conscious moment, by becoming our conscious "reality." This may be as simple as choosing to decide based on intuition or on a dream, which Jung considered more reliable as a guide for action than waking arguments and reasons. Such a decision will lead to both a different experience of the action and likely a different outcome, which will, both on the procedural and value-level in deciding, and on the level of the resulting state of affairs, actualize a modal world that would otherwise not be "real."

In the Tarot card "The Sun," the child holds the red flag of victory, of joy and optimism. The archetypal meaning is that of good developments, of fulfillment of hopes. The "Sun" card suggests belief, reliance on a deeper calling into the future, into new decisions which will change us. Jung describes his hesitation to follow this calling of the Holy Spirit by asking whether God expects him not only to go on "swaying bridges" and "into the mist," but also to "do without meaning" (Jung, 1989: 235). This is a particularly important remark because Jung here describes a degree of self-coercion to follow calls from the subconscious, or calls by the Holy Spirit, and the resistance offered by his scientific, rational self, embedded in twentieth-century European society. He then describes the steps of inner calling that he almost forces himself to follow, but can't really manage to do so, by the words: "I limp after you on crutches of understanding. I am a man and you stride like a God. [...] I follow, but it terrifies me [...] I cannot follow, since your meaning is a supreme meaning and your steps are the steps of a God" (Jung, 1989: 235).

Figure 2.1 The Tarot card "The Sun."

The supreme meaning, as Jung describes it, is a conglomerate of the understandable and the impossible to understand, a mixture of the logical and the paradoxical, all of the ingredients in that mixture connected by the terrifying faith in the "spirit of the deep," which appears to linguistically evolve in Jung's narrative into the Holy Spirit of Christianity. The paradoxes are logical nightmares when looked upon from the point of view of the binary logic of our everydayness; however, they are at the same time beautiful symbols of a future when they are looked upon as aesthetic pronunciations of deeper, mystical truths. It is thus no wonder that most of the archetypal meanings discussed by Jung are visual: the *I Ching*'s hexagrams capture graphically the paradoxes of the Yin and Yang, the female and male, the flowing and the strong and resistant; the Tarot images such as that of "The Sun" capture the powerful symbols of the subconscious that help us interpret the present, such as the image of a cheerful child on a white horse.

The "supreme meaning" is difficult to articulate in the scientific language of Jung the psychiatrist, and it is difficult to articulate and justify to the bourgeois European society, fascinated by science, when the actions required to attain that meaning are so unconventional ("it is not difficult for them to laugh, since I must do strange things"). Knowledge offered by the Holy Spirit comes through dreams and visions, through symbols of which one can be certain that they bear clear universal meanings (such as the white horse, the naked child, the red flag, and the powerful sun above on the card depicted here), yet one cannot present these symbols as scientific findings.

It would appear, on this reading of esotericism, that every worthwhile idea as a vector stemming from the present, actual modal world, and pointing toward a different modal world which can be brought into actuality, is initially esoteric, as the inspiration for it usually comes from the deep, rather than from our rational reasoning. It is true that some of the scientific ideas have arisen from research previously intended to produce quite different results, and this is described at length in Kuhn's infamous *Structure of the Scientific Revolutions* (Kuhn, 2012). However, the truly innovative ideas, born from a suffering in seemingly insoluble life situations, such as the situations which make individuals "stuck" and bring them to therapy, almost always appear as coming from nowhere, or are reached exactly through these strange sources: dreams, daydreaming, as sudden bursts of inspiration amid seemingly unrelated activities, or as visions.

The idea as a projection of will and wisdom into a current modal world at the same time calls into actuality a different modal world and embodies the esoteric nature of all creative knowledge. Just as a painter, when acting on inspiration, would not hesitate for a moment to say that his ideas come from his subconscious, or that his brush or his anticipation of sound and melody are led by a "spirit of the deep," so shouldn't a psychologist and a philosopher: the sources of new ideas and novel conceptual perspectives, just like the sources of art and aesthetic innovation through artistic creations, come from the deep, they are led by the spirit, and only subsequently become subject to rational interpretation, including that which elaborates the presence of archetypes in them.

A key moment to completing this somewhat unusual discussion of modal logic without equations and formal definitions is to mention the fear of modal thinking. Jung describes a fearful disposition toward the truth, although the mystical, the subconscious, is what he ultimately seeks, and what he feels he in fact returns to, for it is him, it is his soul. However, he is fearful because it is different, it is subject to different laws of modality, where anything is possible, not just on an abstract level, but in a very real, immediate sense: another modal world can be called into existence within minutes if an attitude is changed and decisions are made that had hitherto been considered inconceivable by the same person. This is how we change; it is how our lives change, and it is how we grow as persons—making changes which sometimes look irrational to the point of being self-defeating. Fear is a part of the awareness of the modality of our decision-making: the same person that makes a predictable, safe decision at one moment may, suddenly and seemingly without reason, make the most irrational, yet deeply satisfying decision leading to a direction of self-realization which may be shocking both to the person, the agent, and to the other people who are impacted by the agent's decisions.

A simple example is a situation where one wonders whether to risk one's present circumstances and situation in favor of a different career, different partner, wife or husband, and a different country. The desire to change circumstances might not be motivated by an acute crisis or deprivation, but simply by a *calling to make a change*, to develop in a new direction and to seek satisfactions not typical of the life one leads. This situation is common in counseling: people arrive for therapy asking whether they should leave their present partners, their families, their jobs and their countries and move somewhere completely different, with a new person, or alone, and start a new life. Sometimes they see this as a completely unrealistic desire because "they have everything they need" at present, they are considered "realized" or fulfilled as men or women, as professionals, or as friends, family members, parents, or leaders of groups.

Sometimes the individuals who face such tectonic decisions are managers and executives in companies or institutions who hold considerable responsibility, and their desires involve giving up on the lives they live. When questioned about the rational reasons for their desire to engage in major change, they can give none. Yet, the dissatisfaction and longing are there, undeniable and impossible to suppress without them bursting out somewhere else in the person's life.

The drive to change, the longing for the missing object, is an example of what Jung describes as a desire from the deep, a message from the deep that threatens the destruction of the person's Persona, or public face: one's career, social status, family.

The logical situation here corresponds to the subconscious desire, which is the actual driver of the agony of the person's situation, on the one hand, as one modal world, and to the conscious reasons *not to* depart from the present circumstances, which appear safe and sufficiently satisfying to offset the risk for something the benefits of which are not even rationally comprehensible. One of the two worlds, the actual circumstances, are more real in the sense that they are the actual state of affairs; however, the possibility that everything might change into a completely different actuality is so strong that just one decision, one temporary mood, one desire that the person indulges in, might completely dismiss the actual modal world into potentiality and call a completely different modal world into actuality.

What would an adviser or counselor do in the described situation? This very much depends on how seriously the counselor takes the esoteric reasons arising from the unconscious, how creative he or she is in understanding the importance and the idea as a spark, an arrow flying from the unconscious depths into the everyday, conscious realm. A person might lose everything one presently has—things one considers definitive of one's very identity—if that person ventures after their subconscious desires. It is impossible to say where the person will end up, what kind of a modal world this will be. However, the modal world that draws the person to a radical change undermines their current state of affairs, their currently actual modal world. If the desired modal world is neglected, ignored, it will likely erode the currently actual modal world. If the person does not indulge the subconscious desire, the entire modal world will likely be corrupted to the extent that the person will feel broken and unfulfilled.

The subconscious individually, and the unconscious collectively, are the source of all esoteric practices, and yet they are the bedrock of the most "classic" psychotherapeutic theory in the Western world, psychoanalysis. The counselor thus must be aware that people can change in an instant, that those they work with may simply decide to jump out of one style of modality, which defines their current patterns, into a completely different style, where choices and decisions that nobody would expect of them might become the norm of their new self. It is for the counselor to factor these aspects of modality into their own self-understanding, for this same modality applies *to the counselor*: the less predictable we are, and the more radically we are able to change the direction of our decision-making based on our understanding of modality and what it can offer us may well indicate just how free as human beings we are and to what extent we have developed a capacity to innovate in our own lives.

It is often difficult for the counselors to work with clients who are able to change so abruptly and so extensively in a short time, even in situations where it was the counselor who initially encourages rapid change in the client; similarly, it is difficult for counselors to face their own changes in seeing and understanding one and the same client. It appears that the very modality of reality, its inevitable esotericism and the manner of revelation of its insights, which is often frightening and sudden, coming from unexpected sources, is the source of unrest both for the therapists and for the client, and at the same time perhaps the pivotal source of hope in the achievement of the ultimate desire with which people approach therapy: to change as completely as they can, and live a life which, as Jung says, they had hitherto left to someone else to live.

Jung explains the above idea by comparing his vision of his soul to a desert, barren and desolate, asking himself how he has allowed his soul to become so forgotten: "Have I lived too much outside of myself in men and events? Why did I avoid myself? Was I not dear to myself?" (Jung, 1989: 235–236). These are the questions all of us may ask ourselves at points in our lives when we feel stuck, which is when we are candidates for counseling. When a person arrives for counseling, they are already likely to ask themselves these questions, or are at least experiencing them indirectly, in a non-manifest way. When the questions break out into the open, the sudden and often radical shifting of modal worlds becomes a very real possibility.

References

Ajdukiewicz, Kazimierz (1973). *Problems & theories of philosophy.* Cambridge: Cambridge University Press.

Freud, Sigmund (2010). *The interpretation of dreams.* Translated by James Strachey. New York: Basic Books.

Jung, C. G. (1953–1983). *The collected works of C. G. Jung.* Edited by Sir Herbert Read, Michael Fordham, and Gerhard Adler. Princeton: Princeton University Press.

Jung, C. G. (1989). *The Red Book.* Edited by Sonu Shamdasani. Translated by Mark Kyburz, John Peck, and Sonu Shamdasani. New York: W. W. Norton & Company.

Kuhn, Thomas (first edition 1962, fifth edition 2012). *The structure of scientific revolutions.* Chicago: Chicago University Press.

Lacan, Jacques (1998). *The seminar of Jacques Lacan, Book 11: The four fundamental concepts of psychoanalysis.* Rio de Janeiro: Jorge Zahar.

Marinoff, Lou (2009). "Synchronicities, serpents and something else-ness." *Philosophical Practice,* Vol. 4, No. 3: 519–534.

Petković, Gordana (2021). "Otvoreno pismo Vučiću: Oliver Ivanović i Vladimir Cvijan su vaš Adnan Kašogi." Nova.Rs, August 3. https://nova.rs/vesti/politika/otvoreno-pismo-vucicu-vladimir-cvijan-i-oliver-ivanovic-su-vas-adnan-kasogi/.

Shusterman, Richard (2008). *Body consciousness: A philosophy of mindfulness and somaesthetics.* Cambridge: Cambridge University Press.

Shusterman, Richard (2012). *Thinking through the body: Essays in somaesthetics.* Cambridge: Cambridge University Press.

Chapter 3

KEY CONCEPTS IN THE MODERN PHILOSOPHY OF PSYCHIATRY AND PSYCHOTHERAPY

On the one hand, the idea that language is the universe of psychotherapy is trivial because any kind of "talk therapy" obviously depends on the competent and creative use of language in order to be effective. However, the reality hides more than it seems at first sight. Language is not only the instrument of psychotherapy (as it is of any communication); it is also the conceptual context of health and pathology, healing and seeking, and establishing organic bonds with the therapist and others in a quest for a good life. Perhaps most importantly, language and what Ludwig Wittgenstein called "language games" is a beacon of identity. Observing, intervening in, and changing the language a person uses (language in the broad sense, bordering with the person's general mannerism) can change not only the person's psychotherapeutic status ("heal" them) but also the person as a whole. Thus, the language games we play, in a sense, are ourselves: the role of language in psychotherapy extends over all psychotherapeutic interventions and all relevant relationships. Moreover, psychotherapeutic change is a change in language and can be tracked, measured, and assessed in terms of the language the person uses in relating to the world.

The above idea is probably why John Searle equated language with consciousness (Searle, 1983). If in psychotherapy we work with consciousness, then perceiving consciousness as language allows us greater precision and ability to be more specific in our interventions. Furthermore, perceiving personal identities in society as linguistic identities, or communication portals through which the person accesses other persons and their social world, renders psychotherapeutic interventions even more concrete and focused on communication.

One particular feature of language games applies to all games, but is particularly deceitful with regard to language and communication more generally: it is the feature of games to "suck in" the players and the observers, to absorb them in the game itself to the extent that their contextual world diminishes dramatically, and the normativity of their views and reactions is constrained by the boundaries of the game. An awareness of this feature of language games is a key element that distinguishes therapeutic discourse from the everyday neurotic discourse. In the psychoanalytic tradition, there is a widespread view that all our regular interactions are in some way neurotic, because they are based on the quest of what psychoanalysts call "the missing object." Thus, language games are often structured along the various views and pursuits of a missing object, where friends, family members, colleagues, and other relevant partners in dialogue will tend to join the interlocutor in the pursuit of the missing object. When people discuss the lack that they encounter at work, in private life, or on holidays, they project an expectation of the interlocutor to identify with their situation and focus the discourse on the propositions of the initial statements made by the interlocutor: if someone starts a discussion about marital issues, or about a political problem, or about a health issue, it is considered a matter of good manners to "stick to the topic," namely to join the language game along the initially proposed terms. This type of contextual normativity allows the language game to run in a fairly strict form, and makes the ordinary discourse fundamentally neurotic, because it tends to be predicated on an irremediable lack. The "problem" is the proposition of the discourse: this problem cannot be solved and the lack cannot be filled because otherwise the whole point of the conversation, including the emotional exchange involved in it, would be lost. This is why a frequent problem in interpersonal relationships arises when one person voices a concern or a worry and the other person, rather than empathically listening to the first's narrative, immediately tries to propose solutions. Such a discussion often leads to problems to the extent that married couples, for example, end up in counseling, because the narrative predicated on a missing object is fundamentally neurotic and it does not seek to fill the lack; rather it expects to be received by the interlocutor with the lack preserved. The lack is the substance and the pretext of the communication. If it could be removed, another lack would have to be found in order for the underlying emotional exchange to be able to take place under the same conventional terms.

The therapeutic discourse is different from the ordinary neurotic language game because it is a meta-discourse: it primarily depends on the therapist's ability to observe the structure of the interlocutor's language game, to discern the rules and the "scoring system" of the game, and to influence the nature of the game in a direction that will heal the most important issues seen in the client's narrative. It could be argued that the acquisition of this meta-perspective is the whole goal of psychotherapeutic training and building of therapeutic experience. Thus, the therapist does not join the client in an effort to attain the (fundamentally unattainable) missing object: rather, the therapist steers the discussion in the direction where the client will be able to benefit from insights without focusing too much on the missing object. In the most advanced interventions, the therapist is actually able to elucidate to the client that without the missing object the client would be even more unhappy and incomplete and would inevitably find another missing object to worry about, as this is the nature of our psychic life. Such elucidations might then lead to transformative changes in one's approach to everyday experience. Ancient philosophers would call such transformative views "the attainment of wisdom" and the resulting changes in practical decisions—the ability to live "a good life." The entire process has been fundamentally philosophical from the outset.

The observation of language games is key to understanding not only the internal dynamics of a psychotherapeutic encounter and the necessary interventions in its course, it also allows the assessment of the overall dimensions of the process, its perspectives, and the deciding on when it should, or will, end. The therapist's ability to maintain a vision that reaches above and over the language game of the client allows him to see when the client will suddenly feel that her issues have been "resolved," even though in terms of the explicit "complaint" or details of the case not much has been done and no real progress has been made. I recently had a situation that perfectly illustrates this principle with a female client in counseling. Andronella, a 40-year-old university lecturer, arrived for counseling with a complaint of burnout: she explained that her boss basically mobbed her intensely, that she was so pressured by administrative tasks that she could not do her own research and was therefore unable to either fulfill the conditions for academic promotion or to even defend herself from everyday abuse. She explained that her boss expected her to give her lifts in her car to and from work, to work from home, even from the hospital, after surgery, and that she (the boss) had insisted that the funds payable to the boss be channeled through the client's private bank account, which bordered on criminality. A part of her initial narrative was that she also had no support from her parents, that she had just emerged from a difficult emotional breakup, and that neither her mother nor her father could offer her emotional support. She described the emotionality of her mother as "that of a fridge." This was almost an identical case to that of Paula, described in the Introduction.

The initial interventions in the subsequent course of counseling focused on addressing the burnout. Andronella took sick leave from her job for two months, during which time she recuperated and completed a crucial paper for publication, which was required for her promotion. After sick leave, her relationship with her boss underwent major changes: as instructed in therapy, she gradually changed the mannerism of her communication with her boss and established firmer boundaries that allowed her more maneuvering space to limit what she was required to do as part of her job. She even established new alliances with powerful individuals in her faculty, allowing her additional avenues to work toward promotion. Andronella showed a limited commitment to completing her research agenda. Intelligent and discerning, she was able to keep to a minimum of agreed commitments during therapy in order not to alienate her therapist, while at the same time gradually developing a different, more in-depth narrative, which focused on her very different relationships with her father and her mother.

It turned out that Andronella was extremely attached to her mother—twice a cancer survivor—despite her description of her mother as emotionally insensitive and with an extremely low level of communication skills. At the same time, she started to show increasing coldness and animosity toward her father, a retired university professor whom she described as extremely demanding of her time and care, a person whom she did not in fact love, and who had denied her fatherly love at her most tender age. She explained to me that when she was 15, her father had told her that "he had much more important things to worry about than her," and that "in the subsequent 25 years he had done everything to assure her that this was indeed the case." She was tidy and regular with appointments; however, when the discussion came to her relationship with her father, at one stage she warned me that she worried whether I would stop seeing her as her last therapist did if she said to me what she really thought of her father. When I mentioned that I would like to know what her view of her father was, she stated that she thought it would be best for everyone if her father died.

Like most clients in therapy, Andronella played two different language games at the same time. One was the explicit narrative that made up the "complaint" with which she arrived for counseling. This narrative was not "fake": she really was burned out and suffered at her workplace, and during the therapeutic interventions, a lot of which were directive and included coaching to achieve her goals, Andronella addressed this narrative successfully. One could say that on this level the therapy was a success. However, the other language game played by Andronella was more important and deeper than the first one. This was the initially untold narrative of her problematic relationship with her father, which remained unsolved. It seemed to me that Andronella hated her father. She cared for him; however, she gave the impression that she felt trapped in being his daughter, and that she feared that he would disown her and leave her without inheritance if she did not offer him help in his old age. Andronella had a fiancé with whom she was trying to become pregnant at the time she underwent counseling, and they were preparing to start living together in an apartment owned by her father. She repeatedly voiced an anxiety that her father might "spoil it for her finally" if he were to sell that apartment "while he was still alive." The undercurrent of Andronella's second language game was that she desired the death of her father as a solution to their troubled relationship. I understood that this was the ethical reason for her previous therapist stopping working with her: it was just too offensive for him to be part of the process where Andronella saw the very existence of her (seemingly rather benevolent) father as a source of her problems. Her father was hardly responsible for her difficult breakup in her previous relationship. He had left her property, supported her in her early academic career, and seemed a moderately difficult older man who had no history of violence or any kind of serious abuse toward his family. I thus understood why Andronella's previous therapist was repulsed by her attitude toward her father.

At one stage, Andronella's father became seriously ill, collapsed, and ended up in the hospital. Andronella seemed worried that he would be released and that she would need to care for him. I could see that, if her father died, Andronella would likely quit further therapy as the process seemed to serve her to attain a degree of control over her destructive feelings for her father while he was still alive. At the time, my own holiday was approaching, and I was preparing clients for a month-long break in our sessions (always a sensitive and demanding process). Andronella turned up energized with news of her father's death. She accepted a break in our sessions cheerfully and changed her tone in subsequent communication about her first language game (I had tried to help her fulfill some of the benchmarks for promotion as I was also an academic, and some of these actions had to continue regardless of the counseling sessions). At the time of writing this description of her case, I am confident that Andronella will not continue her therapy, although none of the flashpoints in her narrative that she identified as requiring a resolution have been addressed, other than her father's death.

What, then, does Andronella's language game tell us?

It seems that Andronella's primary need in life is simplification. She has deficient emotional relationships with her parents: she is extremely attached to her mother, although she has never received emotional support from her mother, whose emotional intelligence is apparently quite low. On the other hand, she spends most of her life so far without being able to truly feel anything substantial for her father: to her, he was merely a source of complexity. She felt that she needed to worry about many potential problems her father could cause her—as it turns out, he has not caused any of these problems to the point of his death. Despite his benevolent presence in her life, his lack of emotional skills and—this should not be underestimated—her lack of genuine love for him and her inability to overcome the obstacles in communication created by his personal style, have led the two of them into a situation where she could hardly wait for her father to die. This is an ethically challenging situation for any therapist. The reason I stayed in the counseling process was that I did not see how my leaving Andronella would help this situation in any way. I was thus able to witness her problems being subjectively "resolved" for her by her father's passing away. This has simplified Andronella's life. She now owns her father's apartment that she plans to live in, and the seaside weekend house that she loves so much. No further care is required for her father, and she senses, at some level, that her mother and she are now "free." She is now able to enjoy her life and her plans with the resources owned by her father that she had felt insecure about, and without the pressures associated with her father's "demanding" communication style. Andronella is, however, likely to face relatively serious identity issues later when she realizes just how much of the content of her unresolved personal issues she has placed in her relationship with her father, and just how much her father was the psychological scapegoat for her own dysfunctions. She will likely find herself even more dysfunctional now that she is no longer able to resort to blaming the "negative influence" of her father. With all of her father's property, and all of the time that she will no longer need to dedicate to caring for him, Andronella will likely be no more effective in fulfilling the requirements for her career promotion than before, and she may face more of the same problems in her emotional life of the same sort as she did while her father was alive. If her own personal circumstances and dispositions do not change dramatically (and this is highly unlikely), she will come full circle to ask herself questions about what the cause of her difficulties was really and why she had decided to deposit all of those sources of her problems in the personality of her father. She will, in other words, come to realize that the father was in fact the scapegoat of the family, and that he had been scapegoated by her and her mother. It is then that Andronella's language game will likely implode, and she will compensate for this implosion either by mental illness or by personal unhappiness (family dysfunctionality, difficult interpersonal relationships, depression, even potential hospitalization). The two language games which Andronella presented in therapy until the transformative moment of her father's death, which she now sees as a solution and therapeutic outcome at this stage of her life, have remained largely intact. She has placed the first language game (career) partly under control, but the second, deeper language game is now allowed to unfold unconsciously, without therapy, under the guise of a putative "resolution" through her father's death. The sense of relief triggered by the father's death will cause her to neglect the first language game as well (she is already failing to complete the tasks she has been helped with in order to achieve an exit from her career stalemate through academic promotion). When the second language game (difficult personal issues projected into the relationship with her late father) escalates without a deep solution and without therapy to keep the tension under control, the first language game will deteriorate due to neglect. A year or two from now, Andronella will emerge with two more difficult language games than they were when she first showed up for therapy. This will be epistemically productive, because her crisis will bring her deeper and closer to the core issues that cause her unrest and unhappiness; however, in terms of her suffering and quality of life, this will present her therapy as unsuccessful, despite her current sense that the therapy has been a success and that it coincided with her father's death as a resolution of all of the "external" causes of her inner conflicts. Her father's death has not solved anything for Andronella: it has merely removed a compensatory pretense that used to keep both of her language games in some kind of check. Without that break, the two language games will now roll down the slope of Andronella's unexpecting mindscape with full force.

Sometimes, therapy must be unsuccessful in the way it has been with Andronella, especially when the client does not see their language games clearly and is convinced that therapy has been a success. In such situations, the therapist's view of the overall shape of the client's language games might allow him to predict the end of therapy and the resulting escalation of the client's language games later. Just like listening in on a broken language that gradually deteriorates allows the linguistically competent observer to predict when a communication breakdown will occur, the observation of broader language games played by clients allows the therapist to determine when the counseling will be terminated and how this language game, or games (as in Andronella's case) will develop in the foreseeable future.

The Language of Joy in Psychotherapy: Ancient and Modern Considerations[1]

When psychotherapy is seen as a language game, the fact that this allows the overall shape of the game to be visible to the therapist, this vision also reveals the particular value-foundation upon which every game is built. The substantive philosophical aspect of psychotherapy consists primarily of values, while the structural and methodological aspect is revealed in the linguistic and gaming aspect of the process. These two paradigms: that of language

1 This section is based on the article by Aleksandar Fatić (2014). Thanks are due to the American Humanist Association, the owner of the journal, for permission to use material from this article here.

games, and that of values that found the rules of the language game, offer a rudimentary structure upon which to view psychotherapy from a philosophical point of view.

It is clear from the above example with Andronella as the main character that values that found the client's language games not only determine the dynamics and the eventual outcome of the games, but can also dismay the therapist, as was the case with Andronella's former therapist, who refused to continue to work with her once he learned about her values that governed her relationship with her father. We establish relationships with our clients that are largely determined by the client's and our own values. The two groups of values do not necessarily have to coincide, or to be reconcilable in all their aspects: sometimes, as in my relationship with Andronella, although our values in terms of fatherly relationships and what we consider proper and healthy in such relationships were clearly very different, there were also other values at play, on my side, that caused me to continue to work with Andronella where her former psychotherapist had chosen not to. These values included my belief that both Andronella and her father might fare even worse off in the late stage of their relationship if Andronella was left without therapeutic support. This was a consequentialist value of seeking to avoid greater harm that motivated me to stay in the therapeutic relationship with Andronella. Her former therapist had, likely, also perceived the need to avoid causing greater harm, but he saw a way of avoiding this in refusing to continue to work with Andronella. This might have been the case because he perceived working with a client as necessarily supporting and strengthening the client—something that I do not believe in, nor do I practice in this way. Sometimes, one avoids greater harm by preventing the client from achieving her goals, in cases where attaining such goals would harm others. There are differences in the particular counselors' views of what counseling should or does include: Andronella's former therapist's and my views on this are likely different. However, what matters here is that Andronella's language game was predicated upon a particular set of values. This is characteristic of every game. As any game is normative—it depends on rules, otherwise it would not be able to be played—it is always an articulation of the person's value system. Similarly, the language of the inter-relationship between the therapist and the client within the psychotherapeutic process is also a game. This game is predicated upon an interaction of the values of the client and those of the therapist; that is why not every client is appropriate for every therapist, and vice versa. However, one of the most universal and useful ways of understanding the nature of the psychotherapeutic language game is that which analyzes it in terms of pleasure and pain.

One of the most uncontroversial ways in which clients tend to describe their goals in psychotherapy is ancient: it is to maximize and minimize pain in solving a particular life issue. The way in which pain and pleasure balance, however, is not simple: rather than maximizing pleasure and minimizing pain directly, people tend to seek sustainable balances of pleasure over pain. This requires threading carefully through the turbulent waters of moral and existential dilemmas that clients bring to counseling. More often than not, the actual counseling process resembles the ancient Epicurean forms of philosophical practice, where a certain minimalism, close to asceticism, was applied to the measures of pleasure sought in resolving life dilemmas, because the small amounts of pleasure and life satisfaction were considered to be sustainable, as opposed to extreme pleasure, which, as a rule, invited painful consequences. This simple logic of ancient philosophical counseling has gradually become one of the standard pillars of psychotherapeutic work with existential pain. Balancing pain with pleasure seems to be the most general value structure that is at once sufficiently practical for counseling work with clients who are not accomplished philosophers, and sufficiently precise to address a number of value issues involved in any language game. Assuming that experiences and life strategies that affirm an important value held by the person produce pleasant emotions, and that experiences that militate against important values generate unpleasant emotions, the language game based on pleasure and pain is able to therapeutically operationalize the values that make up the person's identity and that, at the same time, determine the normative content of one's life issues. Often, the substance of the dilemmas people bring to counseling is ethical: the pain that they feel as a result of deviating from the values they hold dear under the pressure of external circumstances can obliterate much of their overall life satisfaction: in such cases, the identification of values and of the person's actual language game can make the difference between emotional survival and emotional downfall for the person. This means that the counseling language game must be sufficiently practical (and, by extension, simple), and sufficiently precise to address values with a high degree of leverage. The therapeutic philosophy that focuses on pleasure and pain seems to have proven one of the simplest and most effective conceptualizations of the language game that takes place in psychotherapy and counseling.

In this section, we discuss the pleasure and pain language game in counseling in terms of Epicurean ethics, as it seems to us that the Epicurean tradition is the proper philosophical ground on which this type of conceptualization of therapy has been founded. This section thus explores the extent to which Epicurean ethics as a general philosophy of life can be integrated in a practical approach to philosophical counseling.

Epicureanism emerged in a historical era that was very different from modern times and addressed a different philosophical ethos of the time. This alone makes it difficult for Epicureanism to satisfy all the normative criteria for modern ethics. In this section, we address aspects of the modern "external"—duty- and demand-driven ethics that may contribute to the emergence of some of the main issues for modern philosophical counseling. We point out aspects of Epicurean ethics that are potentially powerful tools to address the issues of mood and meaning in philosophical counseling and thus serve as a contemporary complement to a complex duty-bound, yet pragmatist view of ethics. We further argue that ethics is at the very heart of philosophical counseling and psychotherapy alike (in fact, we see philosophical counseling as an overarching framework for all kinds of psychotherapy and point to the fundamentally philosophical foundations of psychotherapy throughout this book).

Philosophical Practice and Mass Neurosis

The return to philosophical practice in the modern age has met various responses from the counseling and consulting professions, most notably from psychology and psychiatry. While the more philosophically educated psychologists and psychiatrists have tended to support applied philosophy as a counseling method, and some have even joined in the philosophical exercise, those threatened by philosophy have initiated, in some countries, what is in effect a "turf war" with practicing philosophers. War rages mainly around the terminology used. One of the strategic strongholds of the medical and paramedical professions in counseling is the concept of "therapy," which is widely frowned upon when used by philosophers. While "therapy" in the modern sense has admittedly been appropriated by medicine, generically it is as philosophical as it is medical:

> Empty is that philosopher's discourse which offers therapy for no human passion. Just as there is no use in medical expertise if it does not expel the sickness of bodies, so there is no use in philosophy if it does not expel the passions of the soul. (Bailey, 1926: 31)

Since Antiquity the task of practical philosophy has been seen to "expel passions of the soul" by providing precepts for a balanced, happy life (*eudaimonia*). Such a life has been thought to include moderate pleasures and a wisdom that allows virtue to flourish and thus conscience to rest at ease. Perhaps the best formulation of this perception of ethics was Epicurus' 5th Principal Doctrine (or Sovran Doctrine), which reads:

> It is impossible to live a pleasant life without living wisely and honorably and justly, and it is impossible to live wisely and honorably and justly without living pleasantly. Whenever any one of these is lacking, when, for instance, the man is not able to live wisely, though he lives honorably and justly, it is impossible for him to live a pleasant life.

This simple principle translates into much of modern counseling practice by relating neurosis with the separation of life pleasure from virtue. So many cases in counseling include dilemmas that are induced in individuals by cultural pressures, where fundamental convergencies between ethical values and personal pleasure are violated. Such are situations where individuals come to philosophical counseling after cheating on their spouses with existential dilemmas that are in fact simple violations of the principle of convergence of virtue and pleasure, such as: "to what extent I owe it to myself to be happy, even if that means leaving my wife (husband) and kids for another woman (man)"? When such clients are asked by therapists what they think their proposed cause of action is likely to yield in the final outcome, they typically identify suffering, a sense of guilt, an uncertain new relationship, and potential disproportionate loss of children and trust by family members and peers, often a loss of self-esteem. When asked why, then, they are contemplating a decision that they anticipate will bring them disproportionate pain for short-term (dubious) pleasure, the frequent response is: "I have been in psychotherapy and have been told that I have the right to be happy now."

The problem with much politically correct psychotherapy is that it is philosophically poorly founded. Practical ethics is conservative by nature because it derives from logic and from the long accumulation of experience, all of which yields general truths that tend to corroborate the Epicurean principle of convergence between ethical propriety and sustainable pleasure. The superficial and, frankly speaking, unintelligent idea that is commonplace in modern psychotherapy that "a good divorce is better than a bad marriage" and that "one has a duty to oneself to be happy now," in situations such as the described one, leads people into unwise decisions that are uninformed by philosophical principles. Following such advice, or therapeutic suggestion (which need not be explicit, but is effective enough to cause catastrophic consequences), leads people into subsequent situations where we work to remedy enormous existential losses, such as the loss of contact with children, loneliness and depression, substance abuse, low sense of self-worth and, sometimes, suicide attempts. Pleasure and pain as categories for the assessment of psychotherapeutic success seem simple, but they require a nuanced context of consideration: the balancing of pleasure and pain requires careful consideration of long-term consequences; thus the Epicurean ascetic idea that small pleasures, which converge with virtuous choices, lead to a happy life because they are sustainable in the long term and do not invite painful aftermaths.

The practice of philosophical counsel is firmly embedded in an appropriate philosophical context for each individual client. In terms of the language games, both therapeutic and general ones in life, the Epicurean logic of pleasure and pain is a sound and fairly general foundation on which to build an essentially pragmatist approach to counseling. The argument rests on the idea that many of the cognitive, emotional, and volitional problems for which people seek counseling today are caused, or at least exacerbated, by the dominant duty-bound culture and by a corresponding "external," duty-driven morality that has long been accepted as dominant. While Epicureanism is not capable of replacing external morality in the sense of providing precepts for what is morally right and wrong (nor does it purport to do this), it is practically useful for helping clients find a balance between external pressures and "hedonistic" duties to themselves.

Epicurean ethics treats hedonistic duties to oneself as equal with any external duties to others: an aspect of ethics as philosophy of life that has long been forgotten. The absence of this "internal" element of "duty of indulgence" may account for the normative perspectives in which it appears perfectly consistent to claim that a person can be highly moral, and highly valued by her community, yet utterly unhappy. The idea that one can be a morally perfect agent and yet commit suicide out of misery is one that should not be so easily accepted. On a theoretical level, it is consistent with duty-bound morality. On a psychological level, the division between the idea of moral propriety as duty-driven and pleasure as "something else-ness" compared to moral normativity is a cause of neurosis. The two types of mutually contradictory expectations—one arising from duty-bound morality (what one ought to do regardless of how one feels about it) and one associated with the socially induced requirement to be "happy" (how one ought to attain satisfaction in life despite the duty-bound morality) are the normative source of internal tensions that render us neurotic at every stage of decision-making in life. Contrariwise, the ancient way of looking at ethics and happiness as complementary and mutually convergent values avoids the neurotic structure from the start: one seeks happiness through virtue, counting on the approval by the community in the process. The former view of ethics is piecemeal and restrictive; the latter is inclusive and allows the quest for sustainable pleasure as the goal of psychotherapy to be attained alongside the moral requirements adopted by society. On this view, being unhappy and living a depraved life would be immoral because it would suggest a negligence of the moral duty to seek satisfaction and moderate pleasure arising from a virtuous life.

The language games exemplified by such value structures are dynamically radically different. One is a game of antagonistic balancing between mutually irreconcilable values; the other is a harmonious process of factoring various complementary values in a patchwork of satisfying decisions making up one's everydayness. A large part of psychotherapeutic interventions in fact consists of trying to reconcile the neurotic polarities of ethics seen as one type of normativity and happiness seen as a different type of values, inherently disposed to militate against ethics, if allowed to be pursued in an uncontrolled way.

The Epicurean *Tetrapharmakos* (the four key doctrines that serve as mnemonic devices for everyday rehearsal) suggests:

1. Do not fear gods; they do not care about human affairs.
2. Do not fear death, because it is merely a disappearance from being, and as such it does not bring any new threatening experience.
3. Know that all things necessary for happiness (in the minimalist sense of absence of pain and want (*aponia*) and of anxiety (*ataraxia*)) are easy to procure.
4. Be aware that all inevitable pains tend to be outweighed by pleasures. If one swaps "fear of gods" with "fear of life," "anxiety," or "uncertainty," one gets fairly contemporary advice on the approach to take to addressing the mass neurosis of today. Part of the neurosis is caused by the rampant fabrication of needs that are increasingly difficult to satisfy, yet: "Insatiable is not the stomach, as the many say, but false opinion about the stomach's boundless need to be filled" (Bailey, 1926: 39).

In any situation where subjective feelings of deprivation are caused by the unavailability of something that we perceive as necessary, a "false opinion" is likely at work. Epicureans believed that philosophy's therapeutic task was primarily to dispel false opinions and liberate the "student" (client) from subjective deprivation, usually not by procuring what was missing, but by removing the conviction that what was missing was necessary. Wherever intense seriousness is present in those natural desires which do not lead to pain if they are unfulfilled, these come about because of empty opinion; and it is not because of their own nature that they are not relaxed, but because of the "empty opinion" of the person (Bailey, 1926: 30).

It is easy to see how these Epicurean views negate the currently prevalent, originally Marxist, idea that "a man's richness is a richness of needs" and its industrial perversion through the marketing of happiness through consumption (Marx, 2007). The concept of richness of needs has even entered modern left-wing criminology as that of "relative deprivation" (Webber, 2007). Relative deprivation is a subjective sense of lack that is predicated upon socially induced expectations: thus, in a poor neighborhood, having enough food to put on the table is considered opulence; however, in a rich one, not having a swimming pool in the backyard is seen as relative deprivation, because all the neighbors have one. The sense of relative deprivation generates unhappiness just as real deprivation might. The concept of relative deprivation thus illustrates the framing and conceptualization of the lack or missing object that define one's life satisfaction: rather than seeking to build a pool, the client in quality counseling will reconceptualize the need for a pool considering one's overall life priorities.

Relative deprivation, furthermore, carries a trap than any hysterical situation where one seeks to attain a missing object generates: by seeking to remedy a lack, one tends to create more lack on the other side, sometimes far more perilous ones, and this brings us into the realm of the language games of pleasure and pain in public and industrial policy. Consider the automotive industry. Not so long ago, in Western societies, most cars were more or less the same. They consisted of an internal combustion engine, a fairly basic interior and controls that allowed simple monitoring of the engine and other functions. People basically covered the same distances as they do today by using those old cars, which had no electronics, no battery-powered engines, no air conditioning (windows and ventilators were considered sufficient for the job while the car was moving), and no sophisticated mechanical additions to a basic construction. Riding in those cars was less comfortable than in modern cars with lots of additional equipment; however, the sense of freedom was greater. When an old-fashioned car broke down on the road, if it was a trivial mechanical defect, the driver could often repair the car by himself. Changing spark plugs was easy and quick, as in old engines they were easily accessible and required only one special tool to be removed: a tool that was inexpensive and easy to carry. The same was the case with the air filter, which could be taken out from the top of the engine using only bare hands. Light bulbs could be replaced simply by unscrewing a couple of easy screws. All cars had a spare wheel; most of these wheels were relatively small and they could be replaced at the side of the road even by small individuals without much strength in their arms. Today's cars, on the other hand, offer far more comfort: they are equipped with lots of electronics and complicated mechanical structures; however, they make the driver completely dependent on garages and road assistance. Most modern cars do not have a spare wheel, which means that in case of a tire puncture drivers must either improvise with various forms, which at best can get them to the nearest tire shop, or they must call road assistance and wait for the tow truck. One cannot access the spark plugs without specialized tools required to remove the massive engine cover, and to change a light bulb one must often remove an entire bumper, which sometimes weighs 50 or more kilograms, and dismantle parts of the car body. In other words, the driver faces many more "lacks" and "missing objects" in the driving experience than was the case with older cars, although the entire development of the new cars has been predicated upon addressing the perceived "lacks" of the old cars.

Similar dialectics of the lack and the associated deficit of pleasure (or active pain, if it is attached to a "lack") apply to social engineering. Consider the evolution of sexual "rights." The emancipation of sexes through specific forms of identity politics has been motivated by the perceived need to remedy a lack of equality, free will in sexual relations, unfair distribution of labor in families, or whatever other concerns might have been prevalent in the evolution of the feminist movement. While these "lacks" have arguably been addressed by feminist politics, new cleavages arose in the areas of key emotional needs of both sexes: people are increasingly alone, marriages are divorced at an alarming proportion (in some countries over 50 percent of all marriages), this generates an enormous set of problems for children, people find it increasingly difficult to court and establish new emotional relationships, and the discourse of "rights" increasingly militates against the older discourse of emotional needs and the importance of family as the elementary social unit.

Epicureanism, like Stoicism, suggests that the cure for the ills arising from inauthentic needs, induced by society, which cause anxiety and feelings of deprivation because they are difficult to satisfy, is the development of *self-discipline*. Much of our distress, both individually and collectively, is not amenable to medical intervention, and time does not appear to heal *all* wounds or solve all problems (unless, of course, all problems are, as Stalin quipped, solved by death [...]). When we do not know our own minds and proclivities, we may be unable to discover why sleep does not come easily, or why a career no longer seems fulfilling, or why the general sense of dissatisfaction will not lift, or anxiety will not pass into peace and calm. The Stoic sage does not make demands on the external world but instead develops self-discipline so as to deal reasonably with the world as it presents itself (Ferraiolo, 2010: 629–630).

However, Epicureanism sees this self-discipline in a slightly different light than Stoicism. Stoic counsel is almost exclusively *rationalist*. The rational explanation of the need to develop self-discipline sufficient to deal with the world as it presents itself, while making no demands on that world, is theoretically coherent: it can support any type of rational self-discipline from that of a hermit to that of a business owner wisely refraining from expanding too much. However, the Stoic does not effectively address the affective side of the deprivation arising from self-denial: for him the forfeiture of satisfaction for the sake of peace and calm is sufficient for a wise life, and the quest for positive pleasure is not necessary for the balance such life requires. Acting wisely by accepting the external limitations and resigning oneself to restrictive circumstances ought to lead to as much happiness as can reasonably be expected in life. For many people today, this is insufficient, as the element of positive affect is missing. At least on the surface of things, the "Stoic sage" of today could fit in the common clinical picture of depression.

Again, the explanation of this seeming paradox is in the different language games played at different times in society. In ancient times, for which therapy longs so much today, the dominant language game was that tasked with finding a proper "recipe" for a good life, with just the right amounts of the various ingredients, including excitement, contentment, friendship, benign conversations, walks in nature, competition, professional achievement, and so on. The modern language game is based on a preconceived idea of the good life that includes social "success": to have such success, one must move fast, through many social interactions, and must actively seek satisfactions every day. The Stoic (or Epicurean, which, interestingly, is very similar) sage would instead seek minimalist pleasures and a reduction of needs to avoid pain. The language game of pleasure and pain in ancient times is what therapists are trying to teach their clients in the therapy rooms of modern times, because the dominant language game is pathologizing and predicated upon a quest for excitement and pleasure that, due to their intensity, inevitably leads to the opposite, to suffering, deprivation, and infliction of pain on self and others. Being "depressed" as a Stoic or Epicurean today seems a healthy alternative to the lost balance between the smallness and sustainability of attainments and pleasurable experiences.

The Stoic call for a rejection of passion in a world where virtually nothing can be achieved without passion is a difficult proposition, to say the least. The original form of Stoicism emerged in a world where, for example, most "free" Greeks and Romans did not have to work. Theirs was a very different world from the present one, where work is often equal to social identity and industriousness is equal to the individual's value for the community. Again, it is often the case in counseling that pathology is identified as associated with the idea that constant engagement, constant work, implies personal worth and self-respect, while idleness and what the ancients would consider invaluable opportunity for reflection and self-improvement are associated with social marginalization, even moral delinquency. Modern psychotherapy and counseling are thus so often a replacement for constructive idleness. The latter is almost disallowed by society, and thus an excuse of illness, or therapy, seems required for the person to be able to reflect on one's difficulties and opportunities for self-development.

A part of this constructive idleness that often hides behind psychotherapy is the need to develop a life plan. It is a part of the ancient way of thinking about the good life that a plan must exist where certain habits and values are inculcated in a way that promises the wisest decisions being made in most circumstances. This rational aspect of planning one's life is often disregarded in modern psychotherapy, even when it serves as an umbrella for reflection and self-examination.

Most psychotherapeutic approaches focus predominantly on the *affective* side and on the resulting suffering of the client, without sufficiently addressing the rational side of the need to devise a life plan that is based on one's authentic *values*. Often such psychotherapy collapses into a strategy of "supporting the client" rather uncritically, and, as a result, develops into quasi-friendships, misplaced commiseration and the taking of the client's side in concrete life situations. This is usually damaging to the client in the long term, as what the client seeks in psychotherapy, in most ordinary cases, is not for the therapist to take her side and support her pathology, or partiality, or immaturity, but to encourage her to change and grow to reach the standard of adulthood and personal responsibility that will allow her to build quality relationships with others. For the therapist to be able to do this, he must understand that sometimes he should not support the client and that often, he must remind the client of her responsibility to others, especially to vulnerable third-party individuals, such as children or dependents. All of this was self-understandable in ancient therapeutic schools (they were called therapeutic schools, and in their writings the teachers used concepts such as "medicine" to address precepts of wisdom that were considered the foundation of counseling within the schools). Modern psychotherapeutic schools are reminiscent of the ancient schools of practical ethics in the way they conceptualize relationships in philosophical terms; however, the modern psychotherapeutic practice is partly a business, and this impacts the way in which it treats its clients. The ideologies of taking the client's side and "empowering" the client uncritically arise from the business mentality of modern psychotherapy and are potentially highly damaging. If the client is destructive to the vulnerable persons in her vicinity, one does not "empower" the client or support them; rather, one seeks to contain and change the client in the direction of facilitating a more harmonious community including both the client and those the client impacts in her everyday interactions.

Sometimes the exaggerated emphasis on the affective and uncritically supportive side results in protracted therapy, with no clear structure based on a foreseen outcome or "exit strategy." This involves a high cost for the client over time, tends to cause the counselee's long-term dependency on the counselor, and usually exacerbates the client's lack of self-confidence in decision-making. Psychotherapists who fall into this trap are difficult to detect because they can be very popular and they often come highly recommended by other clients, whom they have similarly "empowered" to the detriment of the connected and vulnerable persons. Few questions are usually asked about therapists who have had many of the same clients for years, although this should raise issues about the methodology, aims, and effectiveness of the counseling that they provide.

Epicurean counsel appears to integrate the rational and affective side in talk therapy by essentially agreeing with the Stoic understanding of minimalism, which Epicureans understand as the safest way to avoid disturbance. When a Stoic suggests that one ought to "return to the small place one belongs to" as a general strategy of self-denial that is "in accordance with nature," an Epicurean would agree, not necessarily because this is a way of nature, but because it is a way least likely to cause disturbance in the future (Aurelius, 2002). Disturbance is a form of pain, which, by definition, is evil. Epicureanism goes a step further and suggests that virtue, rather than being "an end in itself"—a moral standard, is merely a means to attain the maximum safe level of pleasure.

In the ancient language game of pain and pleasure, in the context of counseling, living wisely means maximizing pleasure while minimizing pain, including that pain which is caused by certain pleasures, in which case one must abstain from such pleasures. Consequently, the most innocent pleasures, those that involve peace and quiet, such as conversations with friends, intellectual work, and moderate care for one's body, are preferred. Unlike the Stoics, who placed an emphasis on reducing one's needs and becoming resilient to treacherous pleasures, Epicureans insisted on practice aimed at developing a sensibility to enjoy safe, often minimalist, and in any case benign and sustainable pleasures. They sought to develop the skill to turn such small pleasures into a distinct sense of satisfaction and joy, even if the pleasures themselves arose from little more than the absence of pain. This is where Epicureanism provides a potent tool for philosophical counseling for anxiety, guilt, and the pervasive issues with self-fulfillment that dominate many clients' problems. It is where the language game of pleasure and pain becomes both simple and explanatorily powerful in generating therapeutic transformations and reconceptualizations of principles, values, and everyday experience.

How the Language of Pleasure and Pain Becomes the Pragmatist Language of Counseling

The complexity of many situations in modern society requires philosophical counseling to address an array of issues simultaneously, and some arise from multi-level internal questions, such as moral dilemmas relating to responsibilities, learned responses to failure, or feelings of guilt. Unlike in earlier organic communities, life in modern society makes it increasingly important for ordinary people to have a moral yardstick that is sufficiently rational and socially elaborate and tested, which they will use in making decisions amid a multitude of variables, potential outcomes, and numerous involved parties' concerns. This is the context of ethics in the modern sense that lies at the heart of modern philosophical counseling. In this context, ethics is far more specific and more restrictive than the ancient philosophy of life.

In his pragmatist proposal for a model of counseling focused on ethics, John K. Alexander proposes that the most practically useful questions to be asked in the modern context, ones capable of integrating many different concerns, are those relating to *the type of person one wishes to be or to become*: What kind of person should I be? How should I live my life? These are important practical questions because we find ourselves situated in a world not of our choosing, but one where we try to develop the knowledge and skills necessary for leading lives that we find interesting and worthwhile, or, to paraphrase William James, living a life that we find significant (Alexander, 2011: 777).

The quest of a "life one finds significant" goes back to Socrates' idea that a life not properly understood, not philosophically interpreted and directed, "the unexamined life," is not worth living. Such a life is victim to chance, source of constant disappointments, and is a continuous struggle linking one day of fear and toil to another. Only a life endowed with meaning, realistic goals and a rational perspective on chance and disappointment is potentially enjoyable in the long term. This is the point of Epicurus' idea that one ought to follow pleasure subject to what modern philosophy would call a utilitarian calculus of potential effects, within the limits of the externalities imposed by circumstances one cannot control. According to Epicureans, within such a perspective, regardless of how much actual pleasure one might be able to obtain, one's life could be considered a good life—one based on a strategy or life plan that is sound, natural, and based on seemingly indubitable inclinations of human nature: to seek pleasure and avoid pain.

The more complex the circumstances, the more difficult it is to orient one's life plan between the various claims and counterclaims of moral justification, social acceptability, others' rights and interests, and one's direct and indirect responsibilities. In such complex social circumstances, the question of "what kind of a person do I want to be" appears to integrate the natural inclinations and social concerns in what seems as a projection of one's ego among the values and choices that make up the mindscape of any decision we make. Alexander spells out three sub-questions that constitute this general question of what type of person one wants to be, namely:

1. Can one live with the consequences of what one contemplates doing (or does one like the type of person one appears to be if one does what one contemplates)?
2. Is one able and willing to defend one's actions before one's peers?
3. If everybody performed the same action in the same circumstances, what type of society would this lead to, good or bad (Alexander, 2011: 782).

Alexander suggests that each question entails the employment of a distinct methodology of ethical reasoning.

The first one lends itself to virtue ethics, namely to the exploration of what virtues one considers the most important and would therefore wish to have dominated one's actions.

The second one is suitably answered by utilitarian reasoning; by examining the consequences the action is likely to reach within the realistic limitations that apply to the decision. One might, thus, justify one's actions by pointing to their direct consequences, and to the potential (less favorable) consequences for oneself and others of acting otherwise.

The third question is best answered through the deontological ethical model: the action is justified deontologically if it is subject to universalization, namely if one could wish others to act in the same way in similar circumstances, where one would be exposed to the consequences of such action as a member of the same community.

"*Can one like the type of person one becomes by acting in a certain way?*"

The first question deals with self-value; it suggests directions for the development of virtue, but not happiness or satisfaction. One might "live with the consequences of one's actions" in numerous situations where the actions make everybody happy but the actor. The onus of the first question is on what Freud called "super-ego," namely on one's own and the community's expectations of the individual, more or less regardless of the individual's wishes or choices of what is pleasurable.

One may decide to donate an organ to save another although one likes sports and outdoor living, and giving up an organ would mean living a sedentary lifestyle for the rest of one's life. The sacrifice would be noble and would by all means receive social praise, but at the same time it would make one's life totally unhappy. One would certainly be able to like the sort of person one would appear to be after giving away an organ; however, this question is not necessarily synonymous with whether one would be able to live with one's decision from the point of view of one's own desires and needs in the future. One could consistently give away an organ and thus change one's life forever and be able to like the type of person one (socially) appears to be by doing so (thus satisfying the deontic criterion of universalization), only to commit suicide several years later out of dissatisfaction with life.

From a realistic point of view, the first question seems defective, because the essentially duty- and virtue-driven view of ethics that the question is couched in appears to omit the perspective of *necessary pleasure* to make life worth living.

"Is one able to defend one's actions before others?"

The second question is subject to similar critique. Acting altruistically and selflessly means being able to easily explain one's actions to others; at the same time, however, it fundamentally neglects the need to honor one's own desires to the extent necessary for a happy life.

A person with exceptionally strong sexual desires may be unable to satisfy such desires with one person and may embark on sexual experimentation with multiple partners. In a conservative community, such behavior might be very difficult to justify, especially in a consequentialist manner: if one had acted differently, arguably no serious consequences would have arisen for one's physical and mental well-being, while perhaps many beneficial consequences would have been made possible for others. One's sexual promiscuity or extreme sexual behavior could hurt, socially compromise, or morally confuse others. It is unclear how values such as "necessary pleasure" or "optimum quality of life" would be convincingly expressed in such a situation. Here again, the concept of morality taken by the pragmatist approach is the modern restrictive morality, rather than the philosophy of life model of ethics characteristic of the ancient philosophical schools. This appears to be the greatest problem of modern normative ethics in a practical context because it is socially focused and leaves the individual and her needs "out in the cold" if the external (social) expectations are fulfilled.

"If everybody acted the same, would this lead to a good society?"

The third question is more argumentatively challenging than the first two. At first sight, it appears to be a classical Kantian question arising from an ethics of duty: the good society, by these lights, is one where one's duties to others and to one's own "noumenal," rational nature are adequately represented. According to Kantian morality, the justifying aspect of decision-making is duty as the external link between motivation and expectations. This clearly means that a society of selfless individuals would be morally desirable.

To take the above to the extreme, the ethics of duty would be able to portray a society of unhappy selfless people as morally preferable to a society of happy selfish people who habitually encroach on the needs of others. For example, the latter community could be happy because they would rather have what they want when they want it than control their desires in exchange for others' controlling their potentially expansive and threatening desires.

The latter society would embody a kind of extremist mentality in the pursuit of immediate desires that implies accepting the risk of being victimized by the same behavior in others.

Epicurean ethics avoids advocating the latter option. However, it does not shy away from that option on principle, but contingently: any pleasure is good, and any pain is bad. Experientially (contingently) Epicureans believed that extreme pursuits of desires tend to cause more pain than pleasure in the long term, hence they argued that moderation is the most conducive to pleasure not visited by subsequent pain. However, if it was possible to pursue pleasure recklessly without having to endure painful consequences in the future, such extremism of desire would be *in principle* entirely compatible with Epicureanism.

The quest of *eudaimonia* naturally yields contingent precepts: circumstance and experience largely dictate what actions are likely to support a good life plan. At the same time, deontological moral norms based on principled visions of a morally right society often stand in contrast with experiential conclusions about what is likely to lead to *eudaimonia* for particular people. In the case of Epicurean ethics, there is no such apparent contrast. The types of pleasures recommended by Epicureans arise from moderation; they do not jeopardize the needs and pursuits of others and are thus compatible with most visions of a good society, founded on general interest and the mutual respect of rights and interests. Epicureans advised those pursuing a happy life to withdraw from public affairs, live in a community of friends who share the same values (brought to life in the Epicurean "Society of the Garden"), not be involved in politics, and generally, live a "life unknown" (Algra et al., 2005: 669–674).

It is hard to resist drawing a parallel between the Society of the Garden as it is described in Epicurean fragments and the modern concept of a psychotherapeutic community, assuming that the dominant operational language game in therapy is that of pleasure and pain, by now clearly refined by the filters of sustainability and cautious inclusion in the "recipe" for a good life. We often conclude that what truly makes a difference in the psychotherapeutic process is the therapeutic relationship, the strength, warmth, and dedication of that interaction and attachment between the client and the therapists, rather than any particular therapeutic "techniques" or "interventions." The strong, lasting relationship between client and therapist can get the client through turbulent and extremely taxing periods in life, while allowing her to preserve many of her personal resources. The sense of belonging to a relationship, a sense of shared values and the participation in and ownership of a particular "language" (or language game) with the therapist can make a difference between resilience in the face of adversity and suicide. This aspect of psychotherapy is a direct legacy of the Hellenistic "therapeutic" philosophical schools such as the Epicurean and Stoic ones.

The above-described lifestyle of the Epicurean Garden and similar Hellenistic schools, the spirit of which enthuses modern psychotherapeutic schools, does not militate against the rights and interests of others who are not members of the same value community and do not partake in the same language game predicated upon the values that make up that value community.

Even the hedonistic language game so minimalistically conceived as in the above description is not likely acceptable for an absolutist view of the good society such as that characteristic of Kant's rationalist ethics and the prevalent duty-impregnated modern views of moral and social propriety. Such absolutist duty ethics characterizes the culture of most modern liberal societies and is part of the problem mentioned at the beginning of this section, when the divergent views of pleasure and morality cause a division in the subject and set the stage for structural neurosis that we seek to address in counseling and psychotherapy. This problem is thus political and cultural, and not merely individual. It is thus not containable within a strictly ethical and psychotherapeutic discourse and must be addressed at the interface between such discourses and the political discourse, which is what we attempt in the next section of this chapter, when we discuss the divided political subject in modern society and the language of division and lack that articulates a neurotic culture and neurotic society.

The prevalence of deontic, absolutist duty ethics in liberal culture carries with it some methodological peculiarities that impact the relationship between pleasure and moral propriety. On the one hand, the deontic claim of *universalizability* is logically capable of sustaining moderate Epicurean hedonism: if everybody lived a withdrawn life of moderate pleasures, such a society would be sustainable and low in conflict potential, with everybody's rights able to be optimally protected. On the other hand, the *absolutist* side of deontological ethics in its Kantian form arises from a claim of morally rational human nature that permeates Kantian ethics (Fishkin, 1984). Such a claim, when pursued to its final consequences, paints the "good society" in extreme duty-bound terms that potentially militate against any intuitive concept of a good life. It is almost as though suffering is more noble than pleasure, that the forfeiture of personal satisfactions increases one's moral worth, and that, even when the moral duty coincides with personal spontaneity and thus can bring pleasure to the actor, the very presence of pleasure is morally suspect. The grand idea of "human dignity," which is associated with a kind of fanatical adherence to duty and a condescending view of pleasure, seems to absorb any principled possibility of convergence between morally sublime action and pleasure of the good life. Perhaps the most illustrative and drastic example of this general tendency of deontic ethics is deontologists' typically retributive views of justice and punishment, where "just desert" is seen as the sole criterion for the meting out of penalties, and the actual execution of punishments a rational moral duty of government. Thus, Kant argues that "punishment by a court (*poena forensis*) can never be inflicted merely as a means to promote some other good for the criminal himself or for civil society." The principle of punishment, for Kant, is a categorical imperative, in that, once one "deserves" to be punished, it is a matter for the society of fulfillment of his noumenal "right" to be punished. Forgiveness is an affront to human dignity, on this reading (Kant, *Metaphysics of morals,* 6:331a). Punishment, for Kant, is a physical evil that is imparted for moral badness, and any intervention or rationalization of this almost immediate conceptual connection between a moral transgression and physical retribution compromises the very categorical moral imperative (Kant, 1997, 27: 552–553).

Finally, and quite close to our point here, Kant makes it very clear what he means by categorical retribution: "Woe unto him who crawls through the windings of eudaimonism in order to discover something that releases the criminal from punishment" (Kant, 1966, 6: 331a). In other words, no amount of pleasure, either for society or for those immediately concerned by a moral transgression (which Kant equates with a crime) should be allowed to taint the pure logic of just desert. This includes forgiveness, restorative justice, and all other kinds of alternative dispute resolution, intended to limit or modulate the infliction of physical and psychological pain as means of the fulfillment of justice (Fatić, 1995).

Clearly the absolutist morality that makes up the "hard" version of deontological ethics sees the good society in terms embedded in a metaphysically very strong and committed concept of morality: man's moral identity, arising from categorical moral axioms, is constitutive of his nature; the good society is a realization of the moral threads in human nature and is not subject to consequentialist considerations. While this "hard" type of deontology certainly satisfies the criterion that, should everybody act the same (in accordance with the Kantian precepts), this would lead to a good society in the described sense, it is by no means the only or necessarily the most intuitive view of the good society.

Contingently and experientially, it is doubtful to what extent a Kantian morally absolutist society would be "good" from the point of view of practical life, or how conducive it would be for the design of productive life plans. A good society that allows the possibility of all the morally good members living miserable lives is of little value from the point of view of the good life, and thus also of philosophical counseling and psychotherapy generally.

The pain–pleasure language game as a context for the articulation of a good life, of which Epicureanism is arguably the clearest and simplest historical example in the Western tradition, does seem capable of supporting the virtue-based and consequentialist perspectives of an eclectic, pragmatist understanding of the good life as the goal of counseling. These are the perspectives embodied in the first two questions discussed earlier in this section, proposed by Alexander. As far as the third, deontological moral perspective is concerned, the pleasure–pain paradigm in ethics—and in counseling—is compatible with the requirement of universalization that is characteristic of the deontological ethical methodology; however, it does not support the stronger, "absolutist" version of deontic morality, which requires the execution of metaphysically conceived moral duties regardless of the circumstances.

The fact that the pleasure–pain paradigm does not function considering the last normative context discussed in this section, to our mind, does not make it less attractive for philosophical counseling, not least because the absolutist deontological context for ethics is of little use for counseling.

From the point of view of applied philosophy, there appears something fundamentally defective with moral doctrines that allow the unhappiness of most to constitute a morally desirable social environment if external duties and formally defined expectations are fulfilled. The assumption that this is part of a "rational human nature" appears little more convincing here than the equally plausible Epicurean claim that "humans naturally desire pleasure and avoid pain." The practical value of Alexander's model is in its pragmatic side: moral expectations (though expressed in the duty-bound terms of a restrictive morality) are seen as guiding lights for adaptation in challenging circumstances and thus ultimately have a functionalist role: the moral justifiability of actions helps the agent make better practical choices without the attendant negative phenomena such as guilt or reproach by others. It is this aspect of the pragmatist model of ethics that supports the pleasure–pain language game in therapy that we turn to next and place it in a specific Epicurean context.

The Pragmatist Sense of Duty-Bound Morality in the Context of Counseling

The eclectic model of restrictive ethics proposed by Alexander, when it is understood in its decidedly pragmatic context, as a means to orient one's decisions in circumstances that are challenging for adaptation of behavior (in complex modern societies), while very Spartan in its emphasis on external expectations and very limited room accorded to pleasures or happiness, still plays an important soothing role compared to the conceptualizations of ethics that sharply separate it from the quality of life and contrast it with pleasure. The duty-driven moral zombie that inhabits the rationalist mindscape of absolutist ethics suffers from chronic guilt because of his very need for pleasure in situations where categorical moral precepts require self-denial and sacrifice. While the proactive pragmatic directions offered by the three questions proposed by Alexander leave no room for the pursuit of "selfish pleasure," they do address *the fear of guilt*. These are simple directions, three manageable moral tests that lead to a "way of life [...] respected and admired: or at least the minimum features of a respect worthy way of life [...]" (Hampshire, 1978: 11). Such a respectful way of life is free of blame, and thus of internalized and learned guilt. In ultimate consequence, sticking to the three questions that summarize the traditional virtue-based, consequentialist and deontic formulations of repressive morality practically liberates the agent from fear of guilt.

It is appropriate to remember here that Epicureans also considered fear of reproach arising from transgressions of socially imposed values ("fear of gods," as it was expressed at the time) one of the main reasons for unhappiness, and that they ardently argued to dispel fear of gods and fear of death. The pragmatist context for duty-bound morality emphasizes its instrumental value: unlike classical deontological ethics, which starts from claims about the rational aspects of human nature that require the recognition and abidance by certain more or less "categorical" moral duties, duty-bound morality in the pragmatist context does not serve any such fundamentalist goals: it is a means to satisfy social expectations and alleviate the threat of internal sanction or fear of guilt, while searching for an adequate adaptation strategy in complex circumstances. This means that repressive morality has only a conditional claim on the regulation of human behavior in the pragmatist context: if it can be proven to be ultimately dysfunctional, it can be rejected consistently with the pragmatist philosophy. This is a point of its sharp contrast with a genuine deontic morality, which is not sensitive to the functionalist criteria of assessment. Thus, the three eclectic moral questions proposed by Alexander need to be treated much more charitably than the duty-bound morality *sui generis*; this is warranted by the mere positioning of the three moral questions in a pragmatist context that he makes explicit.

One may note that as early as in Hellenism the external ethics of virtue (arising from the fulfillment of moral expectations of the community), or *arête*, preceded the Epicurean ethics of the good life (*eudaimonia*). Epicurus in fact argued in favor of seeking a good life filled with moderate pleasures *in opposition* to the already dominant external ethics that placed pressure on the individual arising from moral expectations. The wheel seems to have turned once again since then, and the dominant modern ethics is again an external ethics of demands on the individual. They are not always phrased in the context of virtue, but as Alexander rightly points out, the three dominant forms this pressure takes include the conceptualization of virtue, the deontologically conceived moral duty, and/or expectations arising from a prudent utilitarian calculus of predictable consequences. None of these three criteria for moral goodness are essentially related to, or necessarily conducive to, leading a good life, or enjoying *eudaimonia*. Conversely, all three can produce morally justified lives that are deprived of *eudaimonia*.

Casting the external moral demands in a pragmatist light, in the sense of interpreting their fulfillment as a means for addressing guilt is an essential strategy in counseling. This strategy is fully complementary with the introduction of an Epicurean view of *eudaimonia* as a quest for moderate pleasure. A combination of these two strategies is a particularly effective approach to addressing the modern neurosis of guilt in the counseling process.

A key aspect of pragmatist philosophy that inculcates the pleasure–pain paradigm as the foundation for counseling is its conceptual capacity to transcend the traditional methodological distinctions between deontic, consequentialist, and virtue ethics through an integrative approach that becomes a counseling project. Thus, the pragmatist counsel particularly readily lends itself to narrative conceptualizations of personal and collective identity and the good society, all of which can integrate the traditional Epicurean concept of the good life in what is at once an integrative approach to ethics and an effective method of philosophical counseling. The pragmatics of the language of joy and pain, or pleasure and pain, in psychotherapy are inextricably linked with ethics: the neurosis associated with the division of duty on the one hand and pleasure on the other is a fundamentally ethical neurosis. Much of the distress individuals bring to counseling is ethical distress: their moral dilemmas reduce their quality of life and their psychological and social functionality. Philippe Pinel's idea that psychotherapy is always a work aimed at achieving moral ends (or "moral reformation," as he put it) may be broader than meets the eye (Woods and Carlson, 1961). Rather than suggesting that individuals in counseling ought to be morally re-educated into following externally imposed moral standards, the point of a moral dimension of psychotherapy may well be that a broader, more ancient, and more inclusive form of understanding ethics needs to be induced through the counseling process, where the inevitable motivational structure of pleasure and pain would again be factored in the constitution of and strategies to achieve a good life, alongside the ethical precepts that encourage rather than disparage personal happiness and a quest for joy.

The Political Language of Neurosis: The Divided Political Subject[2]

The generally accepted principle that in psychotherapy what we deal with is primarily sociality, and only secondarily pathology, has clear political and cultural ramifications. Individual experience is shaped, among other things, by social normativity. Depending on the social "lenses" through which one perceives the world, one's experience of life will differ significantly from one society to another. Thus, a lot of the moral confusion and inner torn-ness that people experience when they arrive for counseling is a reflection of the divided political subjecthood in a given culture. We constantly seek to self-identify in the eyes of another, and one of the primary references of this determining otherness is our society. In this context, it makes sense to suggest that individual pathology tends to be induced by social pathology. Perhaps the most obvious example of this principle is the so-called divided subject, or neurotic, or hysterical subject, as it has been variously called in the different traditions of psychoanalysis.

It appears that divisions of the subject induced by political culture are one of the key strategies of governance and control, where social expectations are used in contradictory and divisive ways so that the internal resources of the person are fragmented and misdirected. Various cultural and political processes attest to this assumption. The language the society uses when it addresses its constituents, or subjects, conveys value messages that set up the rules of the language game played by virtually everybody in society. Such language is partly repressive, partly seductive, partly manipulative, and at its most malignant it suggests that any deviation from the commonplace and the widely acquiesced in prejudices and value assumptions is somehow dangerous, delinquent, and even subversive. We see this in the political correctness of various social eras, where disagreement and discontent are portrayed as criminal and treacherous for the vital interests of the community, and we see it in the counseling room, with virtually all our clients, who arrive with "complaints" that they have carefully prepared for presentation in the first session. These complaints are almost always socially acceptable; they are based on an alleged discomfort with one's own choices and beliefs that one feels society would disapprove of, and, as a rule, this initial narrative of social conventionality hides a different, divergent and divided, sometimes torn up, narrative

2 The remainder of this chapter is adapted from a keynote lecture delivered by Aleksandar Fatić (2021) to the University of Latvia's 3rd Riga Readings in Social Sciences on November 14, 2019. I am grateful to the Editor of *IRCEP*, Dr. Vasile Haţegan, for permission to use the material from that article in a part of this chapter.

of what really goes on within the person's psyche. Experienced therapists thus tend to regard the initial narrative (which is not directly false—it simply describes a level of trouble or dysfunctionality that, while perhaps requiring assistance, is not the core problem that brings the person to counseling, as was illustrated in the previous section, in the example of Andronella) merely as an introduction to real diagnostics, which is to take place once the initial discussion of the getting-to-know-you narrative is exhausted. Andronella's initial narrative was that of a burnout at work and mobbing by her boss: this was likely a true narrative, but not one that really brought Andronella to counseling, nor one that she would not have been able to untangle herself, had she really tried. Instead, the narrative was a useful entrance strategy to counseling, where she was hoping to address the less socially acceptable and deeper psychic controversy, namely her desire for the death of her father. The former, initial narrative is socially acceptable: it is somehow "all right" to be mobbed by a boss and to suffer a burnout (this means that one works excessively and thus "contributes" to society). This type of complaint is both legitimate and deserving of collective empathy; its articulation helps the person to preserve self-esteem. However, the latter narrative (desire for the death of one's father) is not socially acceptable—this was why Andronella's former therapist abandoned her as a client. To get to that narrative, one must establish an appropriate transfer with the therapist, build a strong therapeutic relationship, and use that relationship to work through the former narrative as an introduction to what really matters. The divided subject of the client thus corresponds to the divisive influences of the community culture, where, superficially, one is expected to seek help for one's problems and to be truthful to oneself and to the therapists about the nature of those problems, while at the same time some of the problems are considered less legitimate than others if they militate against important social norms. Desiring the death of one's father is considered bad socialization. Suffering in the hands of an abusive boss is not. The contradictory messages set up contradictory normative structures that articulate our personalities as structurally divided subjects. Any unification of subjecthood is considered as "uncritical" self-acceptance and a potential danger to the prevalent culture of doubt and self-doubt. It is a question that bothers us with the psychology of leadership that we cannot develop here, and where those relatively rare individuals who are able to reduce self-doubt tend to emerge as political and social leaders.

Andronella's example is stereotypical for the principle of dividedness that is omnipresent not only in counseling, but in life more generally. The divided subject is, however, more obvious and more interesting when it is considered on the level of collective subjecthood, in politics. One of the most interesting manifestations of the dialectic of divided political subjecthood was exhibited with the British leaving the European Union (Brexit), in January 2020.

The Language and Divided Subjecthood in Brexit

The beginning of the civil war in Syria and the involvement of the great powers on the opposite sides of the conflict precipitated the beginning of a sequence of waves of migration from the Middle East to Europe. People with small children, desperate to flee the fighting, did basically anything possible to arrive to countries that, on a declarative level, advocated human rights, inclusion, and democratization of the Middle East. Thus, thousands boarded boats to cross the Mediterranean, some flocked to rafts, and others paid their last savings to human smugglers to be hidden in the cargo space of trucks entering Britain through the port of Dover or to be driven to illegal forest border crossings with European countries. The European advocates of democracy and human rights (including the supporters of one of the sides in conflict in Syria) responded by introducing immigration restrictions, by trying to distribute the refugees involuntarily between the European countries, and, in some cases, as with Hungary or Slovenia, by erecting barbed wire fences and allowing informal anti-immigration citizen groups to take up arms and "patrol in search of the migrants." The language of human rights suddenly transformed into a language of "collective security" and "border protection." Italian politicians were seen banning ships with migrants from docking, which left the boats without food and medical supplies stranded in high seas. The years 2019 and 2020 showed yet another crisis of European identity: just as Europe has demonstrated its inability to act in unison to stop the bloodshed in the civil wars in the disintegrating former Yugoslavia in the early 1990s, it demonstrated its inability to live up to its own values and language game of human rights and democratization of the Middle East some two decades later.

The same years, 2019 and 2020, were marked by arguably the strongest crisis of European identity from the inside: the Brexit EU-departure negotiations by the UK and the subsequent departure from the Union of its militarily and economically most powerful country. It turned out that large sections of the British population (the majority, in fact) saw themselves as "stuck" in the European Union with its relentless bureaucracy and tendencies to standardization and control, while at the same time being unable to defend and implement the putative values on which it was founded. The ordinary Britons saw the EU as a context of decay and dilution of the collective interests and values that they perceived as vital to their identity and survival. Thus, the decision to leave, despite enormous funding and primarily leftist campaigning to the opposite (for "the remain" cause), was not a surprise. Not even the threats issued by European bureaucrats after the results of the referendum had been announced (threats relating to funding, market relations, etc.) were able to slow the Brexit process. In late January 2020, the EU had one very important member country less.

Both challenges emphasized different aspects of neurosis built into the very conception of European identity. The migration crisis forced European countries to ask themselves who they were in terms of religion and culture, and their responses were quite different: on the one hand, Germany responded with a tolerant view of the influx of migrants, partly because of its gaping needs for additional workforce, primarily for manual labor. The new European countries, championed by Hungary and its colorful president, Viktor Orbán, declined to obey the European regulations on quotas assigned to individual countries to accept the respective numbers of migrants, and exclaimed that "Hungary was a Christian country," with no place for Muslims, explaining, further, that there were few mosques in the country, and thus inadequate conditions for potential new residents to practice their religion. On the seafront, countries such as Italy and Spain struggled with sinking rafts packed with desperate refugees, pushing for quotas within the European institutions to at least partially relieve the load on their economies and societies imposed by the immediate pressure of mass arrivals across the sea.

The described developments led to a rise of the political right, challenges to the authority of the then German chancellor, Angela Merkel, and helped shape the mood in the United Kingdom to leave the EU. As this book is being written, in 2023, the problems remain largely unaddressed effectively: migrants are still arriving, although in smaller numbers and with far less sensationalist reporting, and the response by the countries of first arrival is becoming increasingly restrictive. A revival of the political right at European elections (including the return of the right to power in Italy) shows a revisiting of the collective identities. With the UK's departure from the EU, it seems the rest of the Union's members need to reconsider their own values and their own language game both between themselves and toward the challenges they face from the outside. One of the silliest formulations of this confused view of a European identity has been the statement by the head of European diplomacy, Josep Borrell, that Europe is "a garden surrounded by a jungle" (Liboreiro, 2022). The speech, which Borrell subsequently defended, although he apologized for the metaphor of the garden and jungle, focused on the idea that Europe is invaded by the rest of the world as a safe place compared to crises elsewhere, in a poorly disguised reference to the crisis in the Middle East and the migration pressure on the EU amid the Brexit process. Borrell's comments drew barrages of criticism from different parts of the world, suggesting that what Borrell described as a "garden" was in fact the result of a mass colonial plunder of what he referred to as "the jungle," and that European meddling in the internal affairs of Middle Eastern countries had largely precipitated the wars and mass displacement that had caused the mass influx of refugees. In addition, it was unclear how major rifts within the countries of the "garden" and the departure of the most powerful and affluent member of the club, combined with barbed wire and camps for the mass housing of refugees represented a "garden," rather than a scene of chaos and gradual value and symbolic disintegration of the bloc.

Borrell's unfortunate statement was a clear symptom of identity issues. Someone who really presides over a harmonious garden has no need to refer to a jungle; to the contrary, such a statement seemed like obvious compensation for fear and uncertainty with regard to Europe's identity and future, especially in the face of Brexit. The language Borrell used was a language of "the initial narrative," comparable to that of Andronella in our counseling sessions; just like with Andronella, one can only speculate what core narrative would emerge should the analysis of the language game Borrell touched upon by his statement have proceeded more deeply. This is where the question of the European crisis today touches psychoanalysis and may benefit from a slight play with psychoanalytic concepts and techniques. There are significant parallels within the divided identities reflected in the European fear of "the jungle" and the individual struggles and panic that tend to be associated with internal normative divisions and insecurities about who one is, who one wants to be, and what kind of identity one would be prepared to defend before others and under what conditions, to paraphrase Alexander's questions discussed in the previous section.

Facing Others and Facing Oneself

I propose that the issues faced by Europe as an aspired-to community (toward the end of this section, I will argue that Europe is in fact not a community and that this is the main problem with its facing other identities) are identical, or at least analogous, to problems which individual persons face in encountering others, especially those who challenge their self-perceptions. Our unconscious self-perceptions shape our attitudes to others whose identities militate against these views of ourselves. Encounters with such others, although usually unpleasant, are invaluable as triggers of self-examination and enhancers of self-knowledge. They highlight our prejudices, implicit values, commitments, and life narratives which live just underneath our conscious existence, hidden behind our deep fears and our deeply buried desires and our secretly cherished dreams. Just as a person faced with a brutal individual whom one generally "dislikes" is forced to face one's own neurotic "other," the primitive self which is kept under control by the civilized "ego," Europe has been forced to face an immediacy of undeniable human suffering in a context which directly tested its humanity.

The migration crisis faced Europe with the truth of its values and ideals as a democratic supranational society that takes it upon itself to preach values and human rights policies to the less fortunate parts of the world. This test of values for Europe came in a way for which it was completely unprepared. It proved that Europe was in fact not a society (for the various countries showed such disparate values that no "social" response to the migration crisis was possible across the board of European politics). Symbolically, the migration crisis faced Europe with its deepest frustrations from the recent past: it saw the erection of barbed wire to contain human beings, once again after World War II. Likewise, Europe saw the recruitment of "civil militias" to "hunt migrants." Once again, Europe saw its own nightmare within itself: trains in Hungary and in Austria guarded by uniformed personnel and escorted to special "camps" or "alternative stations" where "care" could be offered to the passengers who were there involuntarily, cannot avoid but cause reminiscences of the trains in WWII that took people involuntarily to places of suffering. The refugee crisis triggered the built-in neurosis of the European identity in a way for which nobody was prepared and shook the foundations of a sense of community to which European policies appealed as their value-ground for decades.

The neurotic response, with armed militias and prison trains, is a language just like any language in psychotherapy: it is a language that tells the observer (or, in psychotherapy, the therapist) what the group or individual thinks of themselves, what deep self-condemnation gave rise to such actions, and how terrible the opinion these groups and individuals have of themselves is. Those who erected barbed wire and armed their own national thugs to "hunt" unfortunate human beings trying to escape war most likely think of themselves as fundamentally being the same as their ancestors in the mid-twentieth century. Modern individuals are, of course, not the same as their ancestors. The vast majority of them would not even contemplate committing the atrocities of Nazi Germany and its allies. However, they tend to think worse of themselves. This is a familiar principle in psychoanalysis: it is what we believe we are capable of that defines our reactions, not what we are really capable of. It is what we are ashamed of that motivates our actions, not the reality of whether we ought to be ashamed of something we have nothing to do with personally. This is the definition of neurosis: it is a projection of internal tension in external action that shows just how heelish the internal world of an individual or group is. This is what occurred to Europe with the migrations of the twenty-first century and the war in Syria: it became clear what some Europeans thought of themselves. This was extremely frightening, a dark picture in the mirror.

In Britain, the challenge to neurotic identity was different, and again reminiscent of the not-so-distant past. Leaving "the mess of Europe" across the English Channel proved to be the top priority: the refugee camps on the French coast with migrants desperately trying to get to the UK hidden in trucks and repeatedly pushed back by the British border guards was a graphic illustration of how Britain saw itself, again, in relation to continental Europe. Eventually the refugee camps were demolished and migrants resettled, thus signaling the abandonment of a hope, both on the part of the migrants and on the part of the French authorities, that a significant number of them might eventually find refuge in the UK.

Leaving the EU by London was a natural consequence of this self-perception of being different, and of being constrained by continental Europe. It was a deeply rooted process, and the political commentary that portrayed the British referendum as a "victory by a small margin" of those who are less well educated, less visionary, and intellectually inferior to the "remainers" is nothing but a symptom of denial. However small the actual statistical majority that swayed the referendum vote might have been, it was still a massive proportion of the British population and, more importantly, it consisted mostly of those who most spontaneously shared a sense of common identity, namely the working class.

The reaction to Brexit by Brussels has been even more neurotic: it was to make it as difficult as possible to negotiate an exit agreement, using Ireland and Scotland as chips in the game, and to humiliate the Brexiteers as much as possible on the domestic political front.

The language game of Europe was, however, divided: while it exclaimed that Britain "needed to say clearly what it wanted" in terms of when and how it wanted to exit, simultaneously it involved an institutional play seeking to delay the exit, impose conditions that challenged Britain's sense of sovereignty, and flout speculative, prohibitive financial obligations as a "price" of departure from the Union. All of this has led to a weakening of the democratic and social credentials both of the UK government at the time, which was unable to deliver on its promise of leaving the EU by October 31, 2019, and of Brussels, which portrayed itself as a supranational structure with largely non-transparent corporate interests and agendas not immediately answerable and controllable by the member countries. Only when the British prime minister, through his mouthpieces in Downing Street, threatened to obstruct the new European budget was a deal quickly agreed and signed; however, it was too late to address the cleavages that had meanwhile arisen in British domestic politics. It seemed, to outside observers at least, that the EU's behavior toward the UK, once the referendum was over and the decision by London to leave the Union final, actually confirmed the sentiments that had been voiced during the "leave" campaign by the Brexiteers. The language used and the values flouted in the aftermath of the referendum were anything but those the EU had previously argued kept the Union together. It was a neurotic, aggressive, dislikable language of threats and spitefulness that revealed deep-seated fears of the EU's own future. The parallel with personal neuroticism here is striking, of course.

The described type of contradictory language and confusing norms in one's behavior characterizes what Freud called "the divided neurotic subject," namely one that, at the same time, desires and disavows the same thing. On the one hand, Europe's language was one of "our" Europe, the self-approving view of our own tolerance, inclusiveness, and respect for the sovereign rights of the constituent nations to either voluntarily belong to our club or to voluntarily leave it. On the other hand, the same language was full of judgment and condemnation of the allegedly unpredictable situation that Europe was put into (in fact, there was nothing unpredictable about the referendum; it had been long announced, and the only thing that made the decision difficult to accept was Brussels' conviction that the result would go the other way). Europe's language also depicted most of the "leave" voters as "poorly educated," "deprived of vision," "working class," "misinformed," and all of these terms were used in an openly derogatory way. What came out as the message from Europe's handling of Brexit was that, for Brussels, it was one thing to formally possess a right and quite another to wish to exercise that right. The neurotic European identity encourages the former but disavows the latter.

The same structural situation of a divided subject was and remains reflected in the Middle Eastern refugee's issue. On the one hand, the exact position these refugees find themselves in embodies the claims of human rights entitlements that, by European standards, everybody should have. On the other hand, the refugees are in principle unwelcome within Europe (exceptions granted in situations where there are workforce shortages). This suggests that the idea of entitlements and rights is in fact a colonizing idea; other countries should institute European standards because Europe knows them to be exemplary; however, individual people, who are the primary bearers of the rights and entitlements, are no longer entitled to those claims once they show up at Europe's doorstep. The divided subject likes to preach, but it dislikes acting on the messages of the sermon. It likes to present itself to others as a desirable object, but it dislikes the troubling in-depth encounter with the Other. This is almost precisely the description of Freud's understanding of neurosis, and very much the psychological picture of Europe's reaction to Brexit.

Language as a Simplifying Concept

There are numerous ways in which to explain identity, ranging from values, social practices, rituals of membership in a community, special actions that affirm the mission and nature of a particular community, and so on. However, we would argue that language includes all of those: the play of language in the broad sense, and especially what Lacan called the spilling of the unconscious in the language. To consider the evolution of the European identity in language games, as Wittgenstein called the play of language, it is useful to consider the successive structural progression of the language games of European unity.

The first language game of identity was very specific: it was about preventing a future war between Germany and France and Germany (the European Coal and Steel Community). It was hoped that, by placing the production of coal and steel as key strategic assets under joint control, the possibility of a new Franco-German war would be averted.

The second language game was that of the single market: the facilitation of free movement of goods, people, and capital (the Maastricht Treaty on the European Union).

Both language games were easily testable because they were simple in structure and verifiable in practice; both were successful in the long-term and generated benefits for the European citizens. The fostering of a self-perception of common identity and interests by European citizens and states led to lower transaction costs, easier transportation, employability across borders, and an increased attention on commonness rather than on mutual differences.

However, the situation with the third stage in the evolution of the language game of European identity has proven both less successful than the previous two and critical in terms of the very survival of the EU. It has been the game of creation of a *common society*, with shared key values.

This third language game has proven far more complex to play and execute, far less testable for success, and, in everyday experience, highly perilous for the EU. It has faced Europe with its internal divisions in cultural and social terms, with its inner conflicts regarding alleged European values, and with its ultimate lack of capacity to implement its own putative ethical standards in reality.

One of the reasons Europe has been unable to live its values with regard to the challenges it has faced with the refugee crisis and Brexit, namely the values of tolerance, respect for the liberty and sovereignty of member countries and their citizens, and the proclaimed culture of inclusiveness, has been the divided subjecthood of Europe, resulting in a dichotomous, neurotic identity: desiring one type of values and at the same time detesting the actual presence of those values and their consequences in Europeans' everyday lives. This neurotic, divided identity has led to contradictory policies and, as a result, contradictory identity profiles of various European countries vis-à-vis the same, key challenges to European identity. Such challenges are psychological in nature because they test the limits of understanding Europe and the ability to accept messages received from the environment.

The language game of Europe is disturbed by tests such as Brexit or the refugee influx from Syria because the rules of the game are strained. The questions that constitute the strain are of the sort: Does Europe function at the level of values only if it is wealthy? If it has high employment? If it is tidy and clean? If it is not marred by thousands of desolate Syrians camping in its streets, "taking jobs from its citizens"? Does it function at the level of values only if it is complete and fully operational, with no countries exercising their right to depart from the Union, like Britain did? If Europe's values are useful only in optimal conditions, then such values have a low resilience and are unlikely to withstand future situational tests, including political, security, migration, ecological, economic, and other crises. A low level of value integrity makes Europe highly susceptible to internal political shifts and, ultimately, to political disintegration, which was arguably started by Brexit.

This political linguistic game is in fact psychologically the same as individual language games that neurotic individuals play. Consider Andronella: a person carefully concerned to appear as considerate and at the service of her elderly parents; in fact, she almost desired the death of her father and the ability to take his place in her family structure. Her proclaimed values are very different from her real values, and this is the case with most neurotic individuals. Our political behavior reflects our internal neuroticism, and it deserves to be treated in the same way as our individual neuroticism is if the structural causes of political illogicalities are to be adequately addressed.

Is European Identity a Neurotic One?

Freud considered neurosis to be based on two simultaneous yet opposed attitudes toward the same subject: desire and disavowal. The desired subject is at the same time the detested and feared subject: this is the root of a deep-seated ambivalence which, when understood properly, can lead to insights about the nature of our identity and to developing tools to address identity and value deficiencies (Verhaeghe, 2008).

While Freud believed that neurosis, grounded as it is in a divided subject, could be cured by bringing up to the conscious realm the repressed content from the unconscious, or subconscious, Lacan radicalized the idea of a divided subject, arguing that all subjects are divided, neurotic subjects, and that the fundamental ambivalence, or division, can in no therapeutic way be addressed successfully. We are all divided, and in and of ourselves we cannot overcome this division (Verhaeghe, 2008). However, there is reason to believe that one way to practically heal the divided subject is by immersing it in a strongly interconnected, organic community. An independent, relatively solitary, individualistic subject is unavoidably divided and neurotic; however, a well-integrated, insufficient by itself, but assisted-by-others subject, who belongs to an integrative, inclusive community with strong mutual bonds, can overcome one's neurosis, at least most of the time in one's life. This idea is strongly supported by observational evidence and statistics of longevity among people who change countries and cultures individually, and those who move together with their organic communities (Chopra, 1993: 53–55).

The overall implication of the social remedies to neurosis is that the nature of neurosis itself, as well as most identity-related issues, is social, rather than medical or physiological. If this is so, it has implications for collective and political identities as well: issues arising from divided group identities might be able to be addressed by increasing the cohesiveness of the group, on the one hand, and by immersing the group in a broader, inclusive and integrative group which will give it meaning and a sense of purpose and thus address its sense of incompleteness—another aspect of neurosis is that this sense of incompetence accompanies neurosis both in individuals and in collectives. It is the fear of one's own incompetence to deal with a crisis situation (or with crisis situations in the future) that causes overemphasized neurotic reactions. Thus, in the context of the political neurosis triggered by Brexit, a logical question to ask would be whether the European neurosis would have been milder, or avoided altogether, had Europe been able to generate a social bonding and cross-identification which would have addressed the divisions in its subjecthood. As it stood, Europe, divided in identities and in self-perceptions, and unified only on the level of proclamations and on paper, reacted hysterically to Britain's taking a decision to leave. Just like in a bad marriage, a person fearful of one's own emotional incompetence and sticking to the commitments on paper, reacts fearfully and aggressively to the other person deciding to leave. This is a situation too common to even need detailed clarification here.

Our proposition as to why effective community creation had not been a success in pre-Brexit Europe (and is even less likely to be so post-Brexit) is the language game of the seemingly liberal values, which translate into very illiberal practices, which lies at the foundation of European democracies. Much has been written about the deficiencies of liberalism in generating common identities and a strong sense of community belonging, and this is not the place to repeat the same arguments (Fatić, 2016). What must be said as part of our argument here is that a change of both ideology and the conceptualization of political leadership is necessary to save Europe both as a supranational institutional entity and as an attempted value community. This is what Freud would likely suggest as a general cure for neurotic persons who have difficulties compensating for their internal coping deficits in the face of life difficulties. We would propose that a thorough re-examination of the main concerns of the European citizens across the various countries, followed by a public policy geared to address the grievances and dissatisfactions—not by providing what people specifically desire or need, but by bringing them closer together in their needs—is called for. On a psychoanalytic level, this is the same as the immersion in a broader community of support and mutuality. It is one thing to offer better working conditions to railway workers in Romania or to miners in France, and quite another to *bring the overall concerns* of those workers *together* with the views of railway workers in Germany or miners in Poland. Being able to express common concerns (all of which, most likely, cannot be fully addressed by any national government or by European authorities) and cross-identify between each other as members of the same value community would facilitate a bonding and strengthening of the sense of common identity, which would make workers, miners, and others more resilient to the particular hardships they face anywhere they live. This is not a proletarian idea of the unification of the working class worldwide, but a communitarian idea of empathetic strengthening of mutual links and emotional, rather than political, bonding on a broader scale which would psychologically strengthen everyone. On a psychotherapeutic level, this is known as the idea of a therapeutic community. There is reason to believe that, as Epicurus quipped, no community that is not therapeutic serves any purpose, and this applies to political communities as well. That is where Europe failed before and after Brexit. It was a community of interest, but not a therapeutic, real community for its people and for others wishing to join its values. Its language game was false, insincere, and deeply hysterical, because the immediate language game and the meta-language game were so incongruent. The high level of neuroticism thus reflected caused the high level of antagonism on the surface, in concrete political actions taken by Brussels.

By achieving the psychological effect arising from a therapeutic community (an organic, cohesive and supportive one), the policies of community creation would immediately increase the quality of life of everybody concerned. Quality of life is a strange concept: on the one hand it appears to lend itself easily to an economic interpretation: the better the standard of living, the better, in a sense at least, the quality of life. However, on the other hand, the existential experience of one's quality of life is not necessarily related to economics, or even to democracy: one can have a high or low quality of life both when living in a society with an exceptionally high standard of living and a flourishing democracy, and in an authoritarian and poor society, if one's emotional experiences generate a high level of satisfaction. Individuals see their own happiness as a function of various subjective, in addition to objective factors, where both can be factors of what the Harvard Index of Happiness calls "flourishing" (Harvard University Human Flourishing Program, 2023). Now, of course, the sense of flourishing can also be healthy or neurotic. One group of individuals must see themselves as flourishing in conditions where they have all the jobs and a high standard of living, while preaching democracy and equality to those less objectively fortunate. Another group might see their flourishing in a community with those less fortunate, and with those with different types of culture, skills, traditions, and sensibilities. Depending on how flourishing is seen, and taught to people to see it, individuals will react and behave differently and will exhibit different signs of subjective happiness (Fatić, 2016).

On the level of subjective satisfaction, which is a key element of happiness, very simply speaking, a person who is in love will have a high quality of life even in politically suboptimal conditions, while a person who is frightened, depressed, or bored will have a low quality of life even in the wealthiest and most democratic society. The subjective aspects of quality of life always take precedence over objective aspects in one's life experience; in fact, the objective aspects (living standard, benefits, free time, etc.) are only relevant insofar as they can translate into the subjective aspects (the actual sense of satisfaction). Whether one has free time makes a difference in one's quality of life only if one enjoys free time. Someone who is addicted to work cannot enjoy free time, and thus it is not a resource, but a burden for him. The kinds of individuals we create in our societies will determine what kinds of life capital or social capital will matter in defining happiness or quality of life. Arguably the sense of satisfaction depends more on the fulfillment achieved through quality interpersonal relationships than on external factors (Chopra, 1993). Thus, any community building must rely more on internal, subjective, than on external, objective factors, and must focus on principles developed in psychotherapy to increase the quality of life in the most direct and effective, rather than the indirect, meandering, institutional ways.

One inevitable way to do the above is to circumvent an exclusive focus on institutionality insofar as it obscures access to information about what really matters to individuals. To be sure, institutional efficiency does matter to most people, and getting the appropriate services and protecting one's rights and social and legal entitlements through the institutions undeniably contributes to heightening one's quality of life. However, on the other hand, in most cases, an overwhelming focus on institutionality clouds the leaders' vision of the internal factors that make up the substance of a relatively high quality of life. This particularly applies to procedures as a part of institutionality. Procedural correctness is generally considered necessary for the correctness of the substantive outcomes of the respective procedures; however, the costs of procedures should not be underestimated. Procedures often involve administrative evil, namely the focus of institutions on following the law and the rules of the procedures themselves to the extent of trampling on the obvious concerns of the citizens the law and the rules were designed to address in the first place. Examples of this are legion, however, perhaps the most obvious is bureaucracy. Instead of being taken as a tool for the provision of services that may or may not be necessary, bureaucratic procedures are standardized, with the end result that individual judgment is drastically circumscribed, and procedures are applied both where they are and where they are not necessary, even when they are openly destructive to the otherwise easily attainable satisfactory outcome of a solution to a particular situation. Not every client of bureaucratic institutions is the same, and judgment is necessary in providing any kind of institutional service or performing any kind of social action. In a society oriented to individual and collective happiness and flourishing, individuals must be held accountable for their professional judgment, rather than simply assigned procedural standards that help them to avoid making a personal call whenever possible and thus also avoid facing any kind of accountability for judgment. It is in the absence of this kind of individual normativity and responsibility for the substance of decisions regarding the flourishing of other members of the community that administrative evil sets in and procedures start to detract from community welfare rather than increasing and streamlining it.

Bureaucracy is a well-known problem as a part of European institutionality, both for individual citizens and for member countries. In collective and political psychology, the language game of bureaucracy plays the role of a symptom, which stabilizes a deeply set neurosis associated with a lack of authority. A lacking authority figure destabilizes the person, just as the lack of a master subject destabilizes a political collective. In Lacanian psychoanalysis, the best and most standard example of the lacking subject is the Oedipus complex: a child lacks insight into one's needs and drives, which appear as part of her sexuality, and to address that lack, she turns to the father (Master signifier S1) to provide the relevant direction (knowledge, S2) (Verhaeghe, 2008: 48). In political psychology, the absence of a hierarchical structure that gives stability to the community, specifically the hierarchy of substantive values that define a value community, a true society, is compensated by procedures that simulate the society. Where membership in a political community can be articulated in the language of bureaucracy such as citizenship, various types of residency, refugee status, and so on, this bureaucratic "speak" is merely a language game that masques the lack of a substantive value community, where individuals would be accepted depending on their values and life situation, and not on artificially created bureaucratic criteria of "admissibility." The very language of bureaucracy reflects the absence of a community: one is admitted to a hospital or confined to a prison, not to an organic community. A society, or a valued community, accepts and protects those who harbor the same values.

The Authority Figure in Neurosis

A key stabilizing factor in the formation of an identity, whether it is an individual or group identity, is the socializing influence that is typically exercised by an authority figure. Traditionally, in Western societies this role has been played by the father in the family and by father-like figures in the corporate world and the world of institutional governance. Lacan thus calls the socializing function "Name of the Father." According to Lacanian psychoanalysis, the successful execution of the role of Name of the Father builds a person's resilience to psychosis and disorganization of identity under pressure. For him, socialization is a large part of the concept of "normalization" or establishing normalcy, and any disturbance in the structure of socialization increases the risk of psychopathology later in life. Thus, if the function of Name of the Father is blocked, this may lead to neurosis. Such blockage happens when the legislator, the norm-giver and socializer, typically the father, does not perform his function effectively, for example, because one is not sufficiently active, interested as a father, or one is inept at exercising the normative functions expected of a father. If, however, the function Name of the Father is absent, this predisposes a person to manifest psychosis later in life, if the life experience contains triggers which confront the person too closely with an unbearable "Real." The function Name of the Father is absent if the person who plays that function (again, typically, but not exclusively, the father) is physically inaccessible, because he has died, left the family, or is otherwise unavailable (ill, in prison, etc.). Such situations maximize the risk of psychosis because they deprive the child of key orientational influences which allow her to build sufficient and high-quality responses to stressors later in life (Lacan, 1993).

There are various ways to establish an authority figure that will anchor one's hierarchy of values. One is to bestow that role upon a person or institution. This is the way most people in established democracies function: they believe in their institutions and politicians and trust that their state is fundamentally benevolent. They are willing to learn from their state and accept the values it suggests. Others set role models and try to orient their values the same way the role model does or is thought to do. Others still follow ideological principles and movements and derive the normativity and structure of their decisions and, indeed, a sense of meaning in their lives from those movements. After all, belonging is a powerful source of meaning where other meanings are absent. Someone without a family, or without a close circle of friends, or a strong sense of professional or vocational identity will likely immerse herself in an ideology or political movement to avoid that sense of inner void that Karl Jaspers so powerfully wrote about as the contact with nothingness in "borderline situations" (Mundt, 2014). This contact with nothingness, with non-being, which has marked an entire tradition of existential psychotherapy and existential philosophy, largely corresponds to the traditional psychiatric idea of total decompensation: in the psychoanalytic tradition, especially in Lacanian psychoanalysis, the idea behind therapy is the establishment of a structure that allows the person (or the healthy part of any person) to hold on to something while inevitably sliding into an inner abyss when faced with what Lacan described as the "unbearable Real," with the unacceptable and impossible to metabolize experiences that life throws at us. Not incidentally, Heidegger used the concept of our "thrown-ness" into the world, where we are basically helpless and subject to the whim of forces far beyond our strength and control (Heidegger, 1996). Almost invariably, this situation of being fundamentally helpless in life suggests one's existential condition of confronting a potential internal disorganization or decompensation: madness. Lacanian psychoanalysis sees structure, a relationship, the ability to rely on others and develop a normative relationship with them, specifically one's ability to cling to an authority structure in one's life experience, as a fundamental precondition for avoiding (the otherwise inevitable) decompensation. The language one uses in this process both reflects the structure one partakes of (whether there is a hierarchy of values and whether there is Name of the Father as the authority figure that will save us from our "borderlineness" and our "thrown-ness" or not. Analyzing the language as the horizon that delineates the limits of our sane existence, or our ability to develop a hierarchy of authority, like a ladder that we can climb while hanging in the black abyss of the threat of unbearable Real, allows largely the same conclusions for individuals and for groups and political structures.

Our discussion toward the end of this chapter included one example of a political borderline situation for a familiar political structure (the EU); an example that is at once contemporary, familiar to most readers, and avoids the overexploited examples of pathologies in social dynamics such as that of the Nazis in WWII. There are many lower-level pathologies in political dynamics in our current societies that reflect neurotic structures and reactions in the same way as individuals exhibit those structures. Brexit was a particularly clear example. There is thus something to be said for a parallel between the application of the concept of therapeutic community and the use of language as a tool to create and measure the influence of that community on individuals and groups in standard psychotherapy and in the psychotherapeutic analysis of politics. It appears that the models of reaction described here are largely the same in individual and in political decision-making. Lacan and his tradition of psychoanalysts believed that neurosis doggedly follows us in every step we make in life while pursuing the chimera of our "missing object," equally on all levels of our social functioning, and, contrary to Freud, who believed that to bring out the unconscious compensations and attempts to establish some kind of internal order at the price of everyday functioning, when faced with fear of the nothingness, or madness, or "thrown-ness," or "borderline-ness," Lacan argued that all that unconscious is spilled right there in front of us—in our language (Hook, 2013).

The discourse of the patient, client, or a political community reveals the structure of neurosis or psychosis in much the same way independently of who the actors are. It is one of the advantages of a psychotherapeutic vantage on this discourse that, by focusing on structure, on the relationship that underlies the discourse, and on the lack, or the missing object, that the discourse articulates, or masques, it is able to derive conclusions about the structural issues underlying that discourse irrespective of whether it is the discourse of Andronella, who masques hatred of her father and, likely, of her desire to be her father, or the discourse of the EU when facing the pain of Brexit, or the discourse of a private person being faced with the loss of a structure of family support on which one used to pin one's own personal stability and sanity, leading him or her to decompensation, depression, or crime. The psychological content compressed in the language and structured through the language games that the therapist observes both in the therapy room and in public policy is what makes language not just a tool for psychotherapy (it is a tool for politics, and for most other human endeavors, as well), but a particular epistemic horizon that, if treated properly, as a repository of psychic content that is "spilled out in the language," yields psychodiagnostics and, if appropriate, psychotherapeutic insights across the board of human life that is mediated, structured, and sometimes psychologically compensated by language itself.

References

Alexander, John K. (2011). "An outline of a pragmatic method for deciding what to do." *Philosophical Practice*, Vol. 6, No. 2: 777–784.

Algra, Keimpe, Barnes, Jonathan, Mansfeld, Jaap, and Schofield, Malcolm (eds.) (2005). *The Cambridge history of Hellenistic philosophy*. Cambridge: Cambridge University Press.

Aurelius, Marcus (2002). *Meditations.* Edited by Gregory Hays. New York: Random House.

Bailey, Cyril (1926). *Epicurus: The extant remains.* Oxford: Clarendon Press.

Chopra, Deepak (1993). *Ageless body, timeless mind.* New York: Random House.

Fatić, Aleksandar (1995). *Punishment and restorative crime-handling. A social theory of trust.* Aldershot: Ashgate.

Fatić, Aleksandar (2014). "Epicurean ethics in the pragmatist philosophical counsel." *Essays in the Philosophy of Humanism,* Vol. 22, No. 1: 63–77. https://doi.org/10.1558/eph.v22i1.63.

Fatić, Aleksandar (2016). *Virtue as identity: Emotions and the moral personality.* London: Rowman & Littlefield.

Fatić, Aleksandar (2021). "The language game of Europe: Politics, identity and the divided subject." *Interdisciplinary Research in Counseling, Ethics and Philosophy (IRCEP),* Vol. 1, No. 1: 9–20.

Ferraiolo, William (2010). "The IDEA method: Stoic counsel." *Philosophical Practice,* Vol. 5: 627–633.

Fishkin, James S. (1984). *Beyond subjective morality: Ethical reasoning and political philosophy.* New Haven: Yale University Press.

Hampshire, Stuart, ed. (1978). *Public and private morality.* Cambridge: Cambridge University Press.

Harvard University Human Flourishing Program (2023). "Our flourishing measure." https://hfh.fas.harvard.edu/measuring-flourishing. Accessed August 15.

Heidegger, Martin (1996). *Being and time.* Translated by Joan Stambaugh. 7th ed. Albany: SUNY Press.

Hook, Derek (2013). "Tracking the Lacanian unconscious in language." *Psychodynamic Practice,* Vol. 19, No. 1: 38–54. https://doi.org/10.1080/14753634.2013.750094.

Kant, Immanuel (1966). *The metaphysics of morals.* Translated and edited by Mary Gregor. Cambridge: Cambridge University Press [Akademie pagination 6:331a].

Kant, Immanuel (1997). *Metaphysics of morals Vigilantius (Lectures on ethics).* Edited by Peter Heath and J. B. Schneewind. Translated by Peter Heath. Cambridge: Cambridge University Press [Akademie pagination 27:552–553].

Lacan, Jacques (1993). *The psychoses.* Translated by R. Grigg. Edited by J. A. Miller within *The seminar of Jacques Lacan, Book 3: The psychoses 1955–1956.* New York: W. W. Norton & Company.

Liboreiro, Jorge (2022). "Josep Borrell apologizes for controversial 'garden vs jungle' metaphor but defends speech." *Euronews,* October 19. http://euronews.com/my-europe/2022/10/19/josep-borell-apologises-for-controversial-garden-vs-junge-metaphor-but-stands-his-ground.

Marx, Karl (2007). *Economic and philosophic manuscripts of 1844.* Translated by Martin Milligan. Mineola: Dover Publications.

Mundt, Christoph (2014). "Jaspers concept of 'limit situation': Extensions and therapeutic applications." In: Fuchs, T., Breyer, T., Mundt, C. (eds.), *Karl Jaspers' philosophy and psychopathology.* New York: Springer. https://doi.org/10.1007/978-1-4614-8878-1_11.

Searle, John (1983). *Intentionality.* Cambridge: Cambridge University Press.

Verhaeghe, Paul (2008). *On being normal and other disorders.* London: Karnac Books.

Webber, Craig (2007). "Re-evaluating relative deprivation theory." *Theoretical Criminology,* Vol. 11: 95–118. http://dx.doi.org/10.1177/1362480607072737.

Woods, E. A. and Carlson, E. T. (1961). "The psychiatry of Philippe Pinel." *Bulletin of the History of Medicine,* Vol. 35, No. 1: 14–25.

Chapter 4

FEAR, DEATH, AND LOSS: CHALLENGES TO THE GOOD LIFE AND DRIVERS OF PSYCHOTHERAPY

Vulnerability as an Underlying Existential Situation

Jessy is a painter. In her early thirties, she is exceptionally successful: she owns her own studio with several assistant painters working for her, and she exhibits her works in prestigious museums worldwide. At the same time, Jessy is a sociable, unassuming young woman who dresses in a minimalist style and easily establishes communication with most people. She has a wide circle of friends and is physically active. She jogs, bushwalks, and mountain-hikes.

Jessy's paintings are all black and white. She claims that she dislikes colors and the last time she used them was when she absolutely had to, during her studies. In her first "phase," she sketched faces, and now she only does paintings of nature: mostly barren mountains and water. Her paintings of mountains are predominantly white, representing winter scenery. Water in her paintings is never calm or reflective; it is always in turmoil. On one of her pictures of the River Thames, the water is dark, muddy, and she describes it by likening it to volcanic magma.

She never paints human interaction and insists that her painting is never based on a "narrative," but always only on impressions. There is a marked absence of sociality in her work, however it is aesthetically impressive art.

Jessy has a special method of painting where she hides the traces of her brush, approaching all lines from an angle. After her paintings have dried, she sands them so that the surface is completely even, with no trace of her hand on the painting. Most of her works are large: they are 3-, 5-, or even 7-meter canvases.

Physically, Jessy is pretty, with long, voluminous, curly hair. During the time I was in contact with her, she wore white sneakers, a jeans skirt, and a T-shirt. However, she drives a luxurious electric BMW.

Jessy claims that her life is "easy," flexible, and allows her a great deal of freedom, for which she is thankful. However, she goes to bed at 10 p.m., rises very early, and paints for several hours every day. Although she is still young, all her assistants are younger than she is. She points out that she once had an assistant who was older than her and a man, but "he had as huge an ego as I do," she says, so she had to let him go.

When speaking about lifelong commitments, she states that any kind of "life-long contract" is unnatural to her. She then vaguely mentions "marriage" to illustrate such a contract.

At one stage, in a group, Jessy suddenly volunteered to make a statement about herself that was entirely out of context of the discussion. She said: "*I am a boa constrictor.*"

I find Jessy very interesting. Her "whiteness" of style and her minimalism are almost snow-like; however, without the frost—she is a cheerful, communicative lady. Her language lacks sophistication, and she tends to use coarse language. The language, at times, is at stark odds with her general appearance and her "whiteness."

Jessy's style of painting appears to reveal a strong need for control and an apprehension of social structure—of structured human relationships: her reservations about lifelong commitments, her avoidance of pictorial representations of any social interactions in her art, and the lack of color in her work all suggest deep-seated issues with control and preventing hurt.

In her strongly controlled appearance, two aesthetic moments stand out: her buoyant hair and her luxury car. These two elements suggest a live fire of passion underneath her strictly minimalist external presentation. In conversations, she gives away signals of looking for support and comfort. The way she looks and reaches out for others in communication is almost childlike.

Two things worried me about Jessy.

One was her seemingly obsessive sanding of her paintings and her technique to hide her "hand" while painting. This suggested an abrasive approach to an aspect of herself that might be very important. I found myself unable to resist developing a psychoanalytic explanation of this moment in Jessy.

The other thing that worried me was her statement, given "out of the blue": "I am a boa constrictor." This sounded very much like a warning to all or some of those present in the group. I perceived it as a message along the following lines: "I should warn you that, if you come close to me, I will strangle and swallow you. It is up to you to decide, but you are warned." This statement was given apparently completely out of context, in a cheerful group, discussing general life issues.

In working on Jessy's profile, I found the need for control relevant on at least two levels. The first one is obvious and relates to her desire to keep as many elements of her work, appearance, and her life easily manageable: black and white is more easily managed both in everyday life and in art than a multitude of colors; a minimalist style in clothing is more easily manageable than a more elaborate one; impressionist representations of nature are more easily managed than those of complex social relationships and emotions associated with social structure.

The second level of simplicity is based on the organization of her life: her early rising, several hours of painting, insistence on keeping life simple and "easy." When she discusses famous artists, one of the first things that she notes is "he had a hard life." It seems that an "easy" life is important to Jessy. She repeatedly points out that her life is "easy," that she is lucky. Perhaps, she fears life difficulties more than would ordinarily be the case and does her utmost to keep her life "easy." This interpretation would support her reluctance to embrace "life-long contracts."

Jessy appears to have a peculiar relationship with her body. She is thin and does not "wear" her body in a way that would accentuate it; however, she tends to expose parts of her body that she is aware of as being attractive. She also allows her hair to fly around freely, in contrast to the minimalism of the rest of her appearance. There is a "black and whiteness" about this view of her body, too.

The two most problematic moments in my communication with Jessy were the abrasion of her paintings, on which she insists is "extreme," and the statement about her seeing herself as a constrictor snake.

Jessy suggested that she would allow me to see, in her studio, how she sands her paintings to the non-recognition of her hand, but there is a clear sense of hesitation and wariness. I suspect that there are secrets, and keys to her secrets, in her studio. Jessy knew this and was careful about opening that door into her identity.

The above may relate to the second worrying moment, namely Jessy's self-description as a constrictor snake. I felt that this explained a considerable amount about Jessy's vulnerability. Jessy avoids human interactions in her paintings because they are potentially a source of pain and vulnerability. She has likely suffered a relationship-induced trauma, and this trauma has probably exposed some of her vulnerabilities. As a result, she now builds a black-and-white world where nobody is allowed except as an observer of her art. She feels that if someone really did enter her inner world and untamed her real needs for intimacy, she might constrict and "devour" them by her need for closeness and belonging. Jessy perceives her needs for human intimacy as being so extreme that they can only be held in check if she completely denies them, both in her art and in her everyday life.

Her blunt statement "I am a boa constrictor" was in fact the same statement that she gives away by her reaching out in communication and seeking support. The message is that those who insist on coming too close to her must be prepared to be owned to the very extreme, or else should stay at a social distance, to "make things simple," as she says. Jessy's art and overall demeanor are a language, just as any person's creations and general mannerisms of life are a language; however, interpreting this language is often a challenge.

Jessy is surrounded by people who stay on the surface of the value and emotional messages that she broadcasts. She is likable and desirable as an acquaintance, and for most people this will suffice in terms of their relationships with her. However, no organic relationship can be established without *linking our individual vulnerabilities.* Jessy chooses to keep her life inorganic with her snowy sceneries and paintings of boiling magmatic waves which, along with the complete absence of any social structure, reflect a *longing and tension* inside, but *not an articulated desire.*

Our vulnerabilities are the hooks by which we attach ourselves to each other, and at the same time they are the portals through which we establish organic bonds, whether they are friendship, romantic love, or some other type of fellowship with strong family-type links. Thus, disguising one's vulnerabilities under a coldness, formalism, or unavailability is a *flight from organicism.* The most common reason is a lack of courage to accept one's own vulnerability and a fear of the hardship of life, including the emotional pain that is triggered when organic relationships are broken or prove unsuccessful.

Jessy's self-definition as a "boa constrictor" is in fact a step forward in relation to the most common way in which people flee organicism out of fear of failure and hurt. Unlike many who simply choose to remain silent or undecided about various proposed relationships, Jessy *stays out of reach*, but at the same time *sends a coded message about her reasons.* She thus still leaves some room open for those who wish to risk being "constricted" by her hidden, vulnerable possessiveness, and who approach her closely. The statement is in fact a warning that comes alongside a potential permission to pass through the gates of her privacy. It is this interpretation that allows a proactive approach to Jessy and a potential untangling of the secrets hidden in her behavioral language.

Jessy masks her hesitation to let people very close by a peculiar, cheerful carelessness. When I asked her whether she would send me photos of her large canvases, edging closer to her inviting me to her studio, she did not respond the entire day, and then behaved as though she had simply not seen my messages. Having considered the request and thought about it, she sent the photographs and encouraged a subsequent online group discussion about them. She also tried to water down her earlier statement about being a "boa," but when I suggested that this had puzzled me for a few days and that I thought I understood, she did not ask what it was that I thought I had understood; she just smiled. Jessy wants to be "discovered" or "deciphered" and the snake metaphor was a hint for those interested in decoding her.

Jessy's vulnerability, like the vulnerability of all of us, is a language in itself: by accessing those vulnerabilities, we are able to access each other; however, this requires considerable attention and interest in the other person, and the fast-paced life that we lead, with so many distractions, does not encourage such relationships.

An interesting point about Jessy is that, with all her masking and symbolic coding of her vulnerabilities, she is more open than most other members of the same group: they remain silent when she posts in the group chat, and when she speaks about her art and herself, others politely compliment her and withdraw. It seems that her personality threatens them, although she is unassuming. Her voicing the metaphors about her vulnerabilities *triggers their vulnerabilities*, and they erect their own "veils of Maya" to protect themselves. The group dynamic is like a dance with fan-lobes: everybody at the same time hides a part of their face and reveals another part, and the more some reveal, the more others tend to instinctively hide.

This illustrates an important role of vulnerability in our identity: on the one hand, vulnerability is a weakness in our strategies to face life, and this is the natural reason we try to hide it when addressing life difficulties; however, on the other hand, vulnerability is exactly that link which we use to "hook up" with others and to establish quality organic relationships. A dynamic of tactfully accessing others' vulnerabilities is the way of establishing true person-to-person communication and a true community, whether it is a community of just two individuals or a broader organic community of friends, fellows, a family, or a small social group.

One way in which vulnerability might be hidden is by coldness and a transformation of the need for close human connection and support into a strong organization and strategy of life. This tactic of hiding vulnerability is exemplified in highly accomplished or financially secure people who pursue their vocations out of enjoyment, and at the same time map their life strategies so that they depend on others as little as possible. They see their life path as a highway that does not tolerate the complications of an organic relationship. However, as with every living system, turning a natural, organic landscape into a highway carries a hefty price in terms of the destruction of wildlife and habitat for some species. The same is the case with the internal ecosystem of values and sentiments, which is adversely affected by strategies to hide our vulnerabilities. Our internal environment inevitably pays a price for any strategy that is aimed at masking what we truly feel and desire.

Individuals who systematically avoid recognizing and acknowledging their vulnerabilities often pursue general life strategies which, very often, include seeking a high level of professional success, simple and predictable relationships and a streamlined lifestyle governed by their ambitions (concerning life goals whose attainment they can, in large measure, control), while appearing very efficient and well-organized, even content and self-sufficient. Such individuals, in fact, build their professional exteriorizations, their buildings of emotional glass and concrete, over the messy but live organic environment of small bends in the current of their life, of unexpected creatures which emerge when the person navigates those bends with patience, and over stagnant waters potentially teeming with internal life. They build their constructions over potentially incredible encounters with people who would never wander onto their highway or into their glass-and-concrete edifices which they appear so proud of. When such individuals, with all of their psychological constructs, come for counseling, it is usually fairly late in their lives, when they feel that they have missed out on organicism so much that reconsidering all of the structure, success and reductionism which they had adopted in order to expedite their attainment of goals can no longer produce quality organic results.

Jessy's luxury car, which stands out from most other cars in her parking lot, is a statement of power and originality. Jessy wants to control the circumstances and to rise above the ordinary and the everyday. However, this very *claim of extraordinariness marks a relationship to everydayness* that reveals vulnerability and fear: being extraordinary means not being immersed in the ordinary everydayness, which is messy, dangerous, and involves numerous possibilities of hurt. Jessy seeks a way above and over the ordinariness—that is why her paintings are colorless, and her passions are reflected in the smoking clouds, foaming sea waves, magmatic, heavy river waters, and harsh but cold and calm, spectacular snow mountain canvases. In her pictures, there is no bliss, no calm, no warm beauty. There is no consolation. In Jessy's art, there is only the acceptance of the harshness of life which, when she draws faces, carves deep traces in old people's skin. Jessy is prepared against life: she is not immersed in it.

Jessy is skilled at communication, but her skills focus on control. She is very precise about the dynamics of her conversations, with proper pauses and encouragement to keep the contact alive but at the same time prevent it from becoming too familiar. Our skills convey to others much about who we are, and this is largely identical to where our vulnerabilities lie.

Mike Tyson, the best heavyweight boxer of all time, was bullied as a child. He was subjected to peer violence, and as a reaction, he became proficient in the martial art, to the extent of dominating the world of boxing.

Bruce Lee was insecure as a young man before taking up Wing Chun kung fu and then, in his late twenties, he invented a whole new style of the martial art, Jeet Kune Do, before dying at the age of 32.

It is a widely recognized fact that most psychotherapists have personal reasons for choosing the profession, and these reasons are myriad: from the most common, personal insecurity and lack of success in love and romantic relationships, to general issues of communication.

People who are particularly resilient in life have developed their skills and capacities in response to the difficulties and jeopardy they have faced in life, often in childhood. Many rich company owners remember their roots in poverty, and this applies both to legitimate businesspeople and to criminal entrepreneurs. El Chapo Guzmán, the Mexican drug baron, started in poverty and became one of the wealthiest men in the world, prior to his downfall. The founder of Microsoft, Bill Gates, started in a garage, with limited resources, and developed one of the most advanced hi-tech empires globally. Toyota, a Japanese car factory, had started as a small family-owned textile-machinery factory before World War II, and with resilience and perseverance in innovation, eventually it became the producer of one of the most reliable car brands in the world. The way Toyota operates is known in industrial theory as "Toyota kata," a routine of self-improvement that is applicable to personal development, as well as to corporate advancement, and is the fruit of long inner struggle by the Japanese people who had worked at the old Toyota (Rother, 2010).

Examples of developing personal and organizational traits and skills of various sorts out of an initial want and sense of inadequacy are innumerable. The same principle is always relevant in counseling: Jessy's exceptionally honed skills to control and manage communication and relationships may well be the result of a time of her difficulty managing or controlling important interchanges with others.

Of course, in counseling as in any human endeavor, it is possible to be mistaken in the general strategies to assess someone through their vulnerabilities. It is possible that Jessy is simply a lucky girl with talent, strong family backing, and an "easy life," as she puts it, whose skills come naturally or have been taught to her by her parents. However, there are too many coincidences in such a scenario. Jessy's art is not necessarily the art of a person with an entirely easy life: her snowy mountains, rugged scenery, her black-and-white artistic world, and her faces of old people all tell a story that is hardly a rosy and carefree one. There is reason for the general principles of therapeutic assessment of vulnerabilities, and even though such assessments can in principle be wrong, in practice they are rarely so, because we as people tend to share so much burden of life and so many of our vulnerabilities that when there are several signs that point in a singular direction, at specific vulnerabilities, more often than not they tend to lead to a correct conclusion.

Although I have not known Jessy closely, I would be fairly confident in saying that there is much to discover in terms of her vulnerabilities regarding her capacities to establish meaningful romantic relationships, for example.

Vulnerability usually manifests itself in an array of ordinary actions and, with a skilled eye, it can be relatively easily spotted. People who have trouble with being photographed usually harbor a vulnerability with regard to their appearance; those who insist on showing their intellectual superiority often mask a deep vulnerability with regard to ordinary, jolly relationships with others; and many who exhibit a wild lifestyle and tend to act recklessly, on other occasions display an unusually high sensitivity to social norms, especially to prejudice characteristic of their societies.

The described, fairly coarse way to pick out vulnerabilities is common and rests on the assumption of relative cultural uniformity: individuals who, on the one hand, break social rules of the conservative society in various ways, from engaging in hedonistic lifestyles to refusing to work in conventional jobs, often display unusually conservative views with regard to the values of their societies in other fields of their lives: they have very specific views about who their romantic partners should be (how old, with what social background, etc.), how their children ought to grow up (this especially concerns their preferred desires for career, life partnerships, or lifestyles), etc. In counseling we often meet people who are exceptionally sexually promiscuous but would not marry someone who is much older than they are, even if life brings them together naturally. We see individuals who use serious drugs extensively but can't imagine that their children would use light drugs recreationally. Others, with anarchist social views, find it repugnant that their kids might marry a person of a different race, or religion, or even nationality. There are numerous examples of value inconsistencies of this sort, and most clients try to explain the contradiction away in highly articulate and rational ways. However, studying prejudice as a symptom of vulnerability is invaluable for the proper assessment of vulnerabilities, and for determining the proper direction of intervention.

Vulnerability and Prejudice: The Disorder of Being "Too Normal"

In many ways, prejudice is a picture of one's vulnerabilities because it shows the repressive side of our socialization which, as Lacan surmised, makes up our very "normalcy." In this way, it is possible to be "too normal," and in most societies, people who suffer from prejudice are too normal. Thus, paradoxically, not receiving sufficient and adequate socialization leads to "abnormality," and at the same time, receiving too much of it leads to another extreme of abnormality, namely to "too much normalcy." Individuals who are inflexible in terms of their expectations of life, who have difficulty looking for signs in their everyday lives and making decisions with regard to those signs, all along maintaining a "strategic vision of life," often end up wasting many emotions, many opportunities for self-realization and self-improvement, and many opportunities to step forward, simply because the road that unfolds before them is not that one which they have learned to expect.

Prejudice schematically structures our life expectations, and in a way, it simplifies them. However, as with any conceptual reduction, prejudice harbors an inherent flaw in that it threatens to deprive us of much of the life experience we otherwise might be able to attain. People who have culturally induced "standard" beliefs about whom they should socialize with, whom they should marry, have kids with, and how they should strive to spend their old age often miss out on the spontaneous qualities of life that they strongly regret later, when it is too late for a second run.

One of my clients, Mary, used to date an older man, over 20 years her senior, and was infatuated not with him as a person, but with what he represented for her socially: experience, intellectual success, and leadership. However, Mary and her partner ran into problems largely because Mary refused to even consider her partner's expectations of her: she insisted that she wanted to be "equal" and to be treated accordingly; however, when he asked her to go shopping for food or to prepare meals and clean the house as much as he does, she refused. When I asked her why she behaved in such a way, she responded: "My youth is my biggest advantage with regard to him." In other words, although she thought of herself as a decent, fair young woman, she believed that, given the age difference between her and her partner (the partner she had freely chosen), she was entitled to privileges which placed the man in a seriously unequal position.

Mary expected her partner to mentor her in her postgraduate studies, to include her in his lectures at international conferences, as a younger colleague, to help her enroll in a good PhD program, and to provide her with all kinds of professional favors. She considered her partner a "star" and was proud that she was in a relationship with him. However, at the same time, she harbored a socially induced age prejudice: she believed her partner was too old for her, and thus calculated that being in a relationship with him (and, as she mentioned, having kids and being married to him) allowed her a "trade off" in terms of behaving in an unusually exploitative way in private life. She expected her partner to provide a house for both of them, which he did, but she also expected him to buy food and attend to housekeeping, while she studied.

When her partner asked her to leave his house, she felt extremely offended. Although his breaking up with her was not particularly conflictual, and he attempted to maintain an ordinary social contact with her afterward, she cut off all communications with him and portrayed him to those close to her as someone who had humiliated her by "throwing her out."

What Mary did not see from her vantage point on their relationship was that her partner had reason to view the relationship differently. He probably saw the professional favors she expected of him as stretching the limits of what is legitimate: she mentioned that he had refused to be her direct supervisor for her postgraduate thesis. However, he agreed to help her professionally in all other ways: he took her to conferences, allowed her to be a coauthor with him on some of his lectures and academic papers, and so on. When it came to their private life, however, her partner expected her to be truly equal at least in that area: to attend to her part of the household duties and to behave in a partner-like manner, not as someone who needs to be looked after.

When Mary's partner saw that she considered her very presence in their relationship as a favor to him, and had no intention of truly living up to the equality she declaratively demanded, he broke up with her. For Mary, this was unthinkable because she was so much younger, she was pretty, and she was promising to be successful. In her perspective, it was nothing short of inconceivable that her partner would "throw her out" of his life. When he did, she developed a grudge against him for what seemed like a lifetime.

In Mary's case, prejudice is a clear sign of vulnerability that relates to a disturbed sense of self-worth.

Mary associates her own value as a person with her attractive looks and her intellectual prowess: when she enters a relationship, she seeks to *trade these qualities against the qualities of her partner.* She does not perceive her worth as lying in her emotions, in her ability to offer support, to love her partner, to make a home for them, or in any other more common way; thus when the former qualities, which she sees as her key strengths in the relationship, are rejected because of the absence of the latter qualities, which Mary does not consider important, she is hurt. Her vulnerability is exacerbated through her facing of her emotional failures (she mentions that she is "unable to love anyone," that she is "an emotional invalid," etc.). Mary then runs away and cuts off communications.

The severing of communication is always a sign of vulnerability and opens the door wide to all kinds of pathology. In this case, a breakup that is not conflictual and is followed by attempts by one side at a normal resumption of communication, no longer as partners, but as friends, or as acquaintances, should not lead to major trauma. However, the breakup was still traumatic for Mary. In this case, Mary's disturbed sense of self-worth had probably led her in the first place to choose the kind of partner she did, whom she fundamentally considered less valuable as a partner than herself, because of his older age. The partner's subsequent refusal to engage in the game of affirming each other's value in terms of the prejudice Mary operated on ("he is too old for me") further threatened her sense of self-worth. It is likely that after this breakup Mary will move along another axis of the prejudice: she may find a completely different partner, a much younger one, in line with her prejudice, but then she will again try to establish her sense of self-worth in that relationship, by using the *remaining qualities that she feels put her apart* from the other women of her age group: perhaps her looks, or her intellect, or something else that she might decide to include in how she asserts her identity and her self-confidence. These qualities might have no connection with what her partner might value about her, just as they did not with her older partner.

What would be the philosophical, counseling intervention that might help Mary? Most likely, it would first critically examine her prejudice that her partner is too old for her. There are multiple reasons she might think this, and some of them seem reasonable. For example, she might argue that if they had children, her partner would likely die long before she would, and she would have to bring the kids up by herself or with a new partner. In fact, she said so in one of our sessions, but added that she was prepared to face that prospect. Alternatively, she might think that her partner might soon lose interest in various activities that remain important to her, such as travel, going out late at night, or pursuing sports. She might be worried about the future of their sex life as her partner ages. All these reasons would be "rational," but none of them are necessarily "justified" in themselves.

Many younger people die before their older counterparts. Likewise, older parents are often calmer and more constructive with children; they tend to raise their kids better. Similarly, one's interests, activity, and sex drive cannot be singularly attributed to age, as many older people are more active than many younger people. There is some reason in these general directions of potential apprehension by Mary, but none of these negative possibilities are unequivocal. Nobody knows how long somebody will live and what the future holds. However, if Mary had been concerned about any of these possibilities, this would constitute a particular decision-making situation for her: through critical discussion with a therapist, she should be able to resolve these ambivalences one way or the other.

The problem with Mary, however, was not that she authentically harbored any of these specific worries. She was aware of them, and she was able to single-handedly resolve them by taking a stance that she was prepared to raise the kids alone if her partner were to die early, that she was happy with the prospect of having an active life with him as long as possible, and so on. Her problem, quite separately from these "objective" concerns, was her prejudice that he was "too old for her" in the sense that she was taught to think that somebody 20 or more years her senior was too old to plan a life with. She was taught this by her family, her friends, her relatives, her social circle, her society. In fact, deep inside, Mary did not believe in this mantra; however, *the mantra was still a part of her.* She struggled with the dogma and resolved it by an internal "trade off": "He is too old for me, but he is a top expert in our common field of science, we could do great things together. I can become like him, and meanwhile he will not leave me, whatever I do. Young, pretty and smart as I am, I am such a great value for him that he would never forgo me, which gives me the necessary security."

Mary's calculation proved wrong, but it is the psychological state of her calculation that was devastating for her.

The very equation: "My youth equals (or exceeds) the benefits of his accomplishments and maturity" was there to compensate for the anxiety inflicted by the division between the internalized belief ("he is too old for me") and the actual value-stance Mary held close to her heart ("he may not be too old for me, depending on many circumstances"). The trade-off Mary engaged in was a way to affirm her intimate belief *against* the internalized, thus externally imposed, normative statement (he is too old for me), however, in a way that would be defensible before those who hold the external belief (parents, friends, the social circle, etc.). The trade-off could be presented as: "Indeed he is too old for me, but he has qualities which justify me making the exception, because somebody younger would not be able to offer me the value which he can, and this value is crucial to me." In fact, this is how she justified this relationship to her parents.

Mary introduced her boyfriend to her mother and father, and while her father spoke with her partner openly about his worries, accepting Mary's decision, her mother appeared unable to deal with the fact that Mary was in a relationship with "a man her (the mother's) age." At the same time, however, when meeting Mary's partner, she discussed with him ways in which he could help Mary get a job, finish her studies, and advance her career. Her mother's behavior clearly illustrated the way in which Mary herself thought about her situation: accepting both the prejudice (external belief) and the intimate belief, which was contrary to the prejudice, and linking them by an unprincipled calculation. It is not surprising, then, that this type of behavior caused doubts in Mary's boyfriend about the true motives by Mary to even enter a relationship with him. When the man ended the relationship, thus invalidating the entire imaginary trade-off, this decompensated Mary. To cope with the shock, she decided to change her way of conducting social relationships fairly drastically. She declared that her next choice for a partner would be someone "clean." When I asked her what this meant, to be "clean," she said that the new partner would have no "life baggage." Clearly Mary recompensated herself by ascribing the breakup to the partner's unresolved "baggage." I refrained from trying to argue with her about whether there is actually anybody in our world without a "baggage of the past," and whether this was in fact the reason for the failed relationship, or the reason was in the here-and-now of their actual life, because I decided that Mary could not accept a critical perspective on what had just happened to her and needed time to heal.

After Mary's breakup with her partner, she stopped coming to see me. She also left the group she was a part of, so my information about her became haphazard and indirect. I heard that she had become religious, sought guidance from her parish priest, and that she ultimately combined her academic interests in psychotherapy with an interest in religion. All this suggested that Mary underwent an internal change. When she first came to me for counseling, she was amid a quest for sexual experience and told me a very strange narrative about sleeping with virtually every man she had met, just to "make up for starting her sexual life late," which, according to her, was in her 20s. When questioned about these presumptions, why she thought that she had "started late," what she thought she would gain with her promiscuity, and what potential damage she thought she would inflict on her own future life and on others in her life, she seemed unmoved, her focus remaining solely on her body and her sexuality as an object that she wanted to "master." All our work and therapy failed to produce a major change in this blunt and resilient attitude to body and sexuality, which Mary appeared to separate from her emotional life, but this separation obviously had the potential to ruin her emotional life in the future. However, after the breakup of her relationship with the older man, she suddenly became a religious woman, most likely conforming to the rules and values of the church community, and that would, luckily, exclude her former ways of pursuing "self-awareness." It appears that the trauma of the failure of her "trade off" between prejudice and internal belief had *pushed her in a constructive and productive direction.*

Mary's primary vulnerability relates to her sense of *self-worth.* This self-appreciation stands in a complicated relationship with her sexuality, her body, and her need for social recognition. All of these vulnerabilities are poorly served by the prejudices of Mary's society and family. These prejudices happen to be very strong and very restrictive. Hence, Mary's problems that would need to be addressed by philosophically informed counseling lie in the realm of *value and prejudice.* If she were able to critically re-examine her values in a frank, safe, and elaborate way, with her counselor, she would likely be able to adopt a more practical and more principled stance toward the externally imposed value-statements that have become a part of her mental landscape and which she feels have stifled a large part of her life.

Vulnerability and Fear

One frequent misconception in counseling is that our fears are intimately connected with our vulnerabilities.

Fear and vulnerability are different things and, while fear may relate to vulnerability, we often fear things that have little to do with our vulnerabilities.

Depending on the way we approach our vulnerability, it may be a source of strength and resilience, as well as of social skills and of a drive for communication, which may benefit us and others around us.

People who are aware of their vulnerabilities can empower themselves and others who harbor similar vulnerabilities. After all, *the counselor is vulnerable to all of the life issues and challenges that most clients face.* We face ourselves regularly in the narratives of our clients, and fear of what we might find in those narratives that might enliven our own traumas is something we learn to live with. However, our self-revelation of our vulnerabilities that connect us to our clients regularly *empowers our therapeutic relationship*; rather than considering us weak and inadequate because we face the same problems in our parenting, our romantic relationships, and our political and social engagement, clients take those vulnerabilities as *points of contact*, as *portals* through which we can better approach their issues and suffering. As I mentioned earlier, the revelation and articulation of vulnerabilities is a precondition for the establishment of any organic relationship, and effective psychotherapeutic or counseling relationships are among the most organic relationships people can get into. In such relationships, we learn from our clients about their lives, their thoughts and emotions, including facts, ideas, and experiences which no other living soul knows, including their spouses, children, or parents. A philosophically informed counseling relationship is more than friendship: it is an *organic alliance for achieving the truth about ourselves.*

Contrary to vulnerability, fear is a singularly destructive emotion. I am very much at odds here with the traditional evolutionist psychology, which regards fear as part of its evolutionist ideology and suggests, accordingly, that "fear has instrumental value which has developed through our evolution, to protect us from danger." This is nonsense. Fear has never played any redemptory or life-saving role in our history. The mere observance of the effects of fear on our lives shows this convincingly.

The evolutionist explanations that "fear freeze," a situation where in dangerous situations, such as that of a battlefield, extreme fear often causes the person to "freeze" and lose control of their bodies and their psychological processes, including perception, have an evolutionary value, are nothing short of laughable. One of the proverbial examples is an imaginary situation where, when a Neanderthal is attacked by a bear or another predatory animal, freezing from fear would have saved him because the animal would have thought the Neanderthal was dead and would leave. This simplistic explanation of how fear is evolutionarily justified, referencing the idea back to Darwin, has extended in modern psychiatry to applications to explain the "utility" of anxiety disorders (Marks and Nesse, 1994).

Similar almost proverbial explanations and illustrations are attached to the famous "fight or flight" reflex, which is described as a generalized streamlining of our perceptual, muscular and neural capacities at the moment of threat to life or limb, where the individual uses the reduced physical competencies (movements of large muscle groups, while the small muscle groups are "lost," a "tunnel vision," with a loss of peripheral vision, the loss of auditory perception, etc.) to focus on either escaping the *Tyrannosaurus* who has ambushed the group while sleeping, in the dead of night, or fighting to push through and try to save oneself. Thus, streamlining our capacities in the way of removing some and leaving others is supposed to aid survival in critical situations.

It is incredible that serious psychologists quote examples like this. The pervasive narrative of "fight or flight," where fear causes the person in a critical life situation to either run for their life or fight to survive, does not explain how *fear* benefits the person in danger, when fighting or running in a calm and calculated way would allow more skills to be applied in the fight or a more effective and better planned escape.

The evolutionist argument that the perceptual reduction which occurs in fright, such as the narrowing of vision, loss of depth perception and of control of small muscle groups is the result of blood being pumped in the large muscle groups, which are responsible for running or wrestling, while reducing the perceptual content so as to increase focus on the threat, is another example of utter nonsense. The fear response to threat is regarded as the major impediment in military combat training, and soldiers and other fighters spend countless hours training to overcome fear and reduce all its physical consequences that retard their ability to fight effectively (Howe, 2005).

The loss of control of small muscle groups due to fear is a major problem for the military, because it means that using the trigger finger and coordinating the eye and hand in aiming a weapon become nearly impossible. Similarly, the narrowing of vision and the loss of hearing, both common consequences of battlefield fear, cause havoc in the soldiers' efforts to coordinate troop movement, receive and relay orders and information, and orient themselves vis-à-vis the enemy and their co-combatants. It is easily imaginable that similar problems would have applied in the earlier stages of our "evolution," where the human group fought with another group or faced a predator. There is *no positive side to fear*, and evolutionist psychology's incredible attempts to portray fear as an evolutionary benefit merely testify to the unfoundedness of that psychology and its built-in ideological need to affirm the evolutionist paradigm by using it on important aspects of our lives, largely indiscriminately.

Fear has never played any constructive part in our evolution. If anything, fear has hindered us throughout our development, and it is our task as a human society to address fear as one of the major problems for our individual and collective well-being. Freedom from fear is the ideal of any kind of psychotherapy. Fear does not serve the purpose of keeping us away from danger: we are more than capable of avoiding danger merely by judging situations that we face. We don't need the darkened and cloudy situations that fear induces in us to decide, choose, or avoid anything. All of this we can do without fear, and in most cases much better than we do it when we act out of fear. I cannot emphasize enough the need to see *fear as a pathology* of our existence.

Contrary to vulnerability, which is a part of our existential condition and which is a link we use to connect to others, fear is a projection; it is an induced mental situation that is not authentically our own. Our fears are *socially learned*, and those fears that are instinctive, such as fear of the dark, fear of heights, or fear of moving ground, are the results of *collective trauma*. Fear of the dark exists in cultures where traumatic events are associated with darkness. In maritime cultures where people spend a lot of time in or around the water, whether swimming or in boats, the fear of moving ground makes no sense and is far less common than in landlocked cultures. There is nothing "innate" about our fears: they are traces of trauma, individual or collective, and whenever there is a reaction to trauma in the form of fear, the sensible question to ask is "where is the pain" (Maté, 2021).

Fear masks pain, and vulnerability is a form of self-awareness. Pain is not a constructive experience because it leads to trauma. In many ways, we live in a culture of pain, where our maturity tends to be measured by our ability to accept and withstand pain. This has been a long-standing tradition, reaching back before Christ. In many parts of the world, young men undergo various rites to confirm their manhood and join the ranks of adult men in their society. Sometimes they are expected to face wild animals (in at least one tribe I know of, boys "become men" by swimming with sharks), engage in mutual combat, or accept some other kind of physical or psychological pain (e.g., withstanding a period of solitude in a lone cabin in the winter, climbing a perilous mountain alone, or hunting for dangerous game). Pain has become an integral part of our socialization, and—Lacan would say—of our very conceptions of normalcy. However, pain is a source of trauma, and the experience of trauma has been deeply repressed in many societies (not only Western ones).

I would propose that fear, rather than being an evolutionary valuable emotional tool for survival, is associated with trauma, and the role of trauma in human development is controversial. It is possible that a degree of trauma builds resilience, in a way analogous to that of building muscle through the repetitive infliction of small tears and bruises on the muscle through exercise. In the process of healing these micro-traumas, the muscle strengthens and grows. When a bone is bruised, sometimes it develops additional calcification and becomes stronger in the place of injury than it was before the injury. I am not entirely sure that micro-traumas are not a way for us to grow. However, major trauma is damaging in much the same way as fear is: trauma tests our personal resources in ways where it is unclear to us whether we will be able to overcome the emotional challenge, and this uncertainty leaves a scar, a trauma that influences our future life. The content of such trauma is fear.

I will later argue that trauma is in fact often used as an alibi for social dysfunction, and that Maté's views on trauma have contributed to this destructive trend. However, at this stage, in the context of fear, trauma plays a key role which, when elucidated closely, shows key features of fear and illustrates just how bizarre it is to consider fear useful and productive of quality life strategies.

Gabor Maté, in his movie *The Wisdom of Trauma*, points out that trauma is not what happens to us, but *what happens inside us because of what happens to us.* The society that teaches us to use pain as a means of socialization traumatizes us in all kinds of ways. Equally, what happens to us in modern society almost regularly traumatizes us, and the result of trauma is what others perceive as our social dysfunctionality, mental illness, violence, or otherwise problematic behavior. Maté correctly points out that what society does to rectify these "disorders" focuses on manifestations, on behavior, on symptoms. In this, he is almost in Lacanian positions: to address the causes of mental disorder, one should never focus on the symptom. If anything, the symptom might be the healthiest possible reaction to the stressor the person can muster at a particular time, and even if therapy could remove symptoms, sometimes by doing so it could inflict far more damage on the person.

Maté has another crucial point here: "So much of what we call abnormality in this culture is normal response to an abnormal culture. The abnormality does not reside in the pathology of individuals, but in the very culture that drives people into suffering and dysfunction" (Maté, 2021). The trauma results from the pain of our social experience (Lacan would call this the unbearable structural Real, where structure, as I mentioned before, is a social relationship or relationships). *The lasting content of trauma is not pain, but fear.* Trauma is inflicted through pain; however, trauma as a structural problem, as a long-standing issue which influences the overall well-being of the person and the community alike, lives through fear, not through pain.

Sometimes fear is connected to the pain in the sense that what we fear is the reliving of the original pain, either through memories, such as in traumas caused by extreme violence, genocide, displacement, or rape. However, fear may be the source of pain itself: we may fear our own fear, because the feeling of fear itself is painful, inhibiting, and degrading for us.

While vulnerability is internal to us, something we become aware of as an inroad into our intimacy that is potentially open to the world, to those whom we choose to let in, whereby the world can come close to our intimate core and hurt or heal us, equally, fear is something external; it is an invasion of our privacy and our intimacy *by concerns and threats that are foreign to us.* That is why Maté says, seemingly hermetically, that trauma *disconnects our awareness from our core*, from our "authentic self."

Although I dislike the term "authentic self," because I don't really know what it could possibly mean, and it appears too metaphysically presumptuous to me (it is possible that our "self" is nothing other than a process, rather than a fixed "authentic" or "inauthentic" identity), the distinction Maté makes between "authenticity" and "inauthenticity" appears to me to mirror the distinction between *outwardness* and *inwardness.* Our inwardness is what we are experientially, how we experience ourselves and our identity. Our outwardness is the world, what Lacan calls the Real. There is an in-built *tension* in our relationship with the world, and thus a tension between our inwardness and our outwardness. Fear comes from the Real, from the outside; it is an invasion of our inwardness from outside which, to survive, we must process symbolically—we must give it *meaning.*

Perhaps the evolutionist explanations of fear as something positive, which I have just criticized, are merely one of the ways to symbolically process this invasion of our inside psychological experience from the outside, and to give it some acceptable meaning, though it would then be a bad and unconvincing way to do so. There is thus a fundamental structural difference between vulnerability and fear: vulnerability is a feature of our inwardness which, when we become aware of it, may become a source of psychological strength. Fear, on the other hand, is one of those onslaughts of the Real that are invariably destructive: it is the stuff of bad dreams, of suffering, and of pain.

Fighting fear or creating a personal and group culture to combat fear is a top priority for counseling. An important point of counseling is to create such a personal and group culture where vulnerability, equipped with awareness, would be the primary reference in setting up organic links between people (initially between the therapist and the client), and where pain as a source of pathology and fear as its substance would be removed from the person.

Conversely, removing fear does not imply removing vulnerability: to the contrary, one's vulnerabilities, when adequately articulated and presented in communication, become one of the best ways to establish healing organic links with others. This alone illustrates that *vulnerability* does not cause fear and *can exist without fear.* On the other hand, fear causes new vulnerabilities which, infected with fear and solidified in such a conglomerate with fear through time, become a psychological scar that hinders our identity processes and makes us dysfunctional.

While working with clients who have suffered trauma, I often wondered about the very threshold of trauma—when does a hurtful experience become a "trauma": it is easy to see trauma as a result of major threatening experiences such as warfare, victimhood, displacement, severe physical and sexual violence, and so on. However, most trauma occurs at a lower threshold, and I have frequently been puzzled as to whether a dysfunctionality is the result of a trauma, whether the experience that caused it "qualifies" as trauma. The hurtful content of the trauma is mostly contained in fear, and obviously whether an experience will develop into an inhibitory trauma or will be processed and turned into a resource for future decision-making depends on the way in which one addresses the fear that makes up trauma.

The pain of the experience generates the first shape, and fear gives trauma its lasting content. Trauma is a structure that blocks our identity processes from functioning freely, but in the context of the role of the community that I have been discussing here, isn't it one of the tasks of the community to address such negative experiences and help its members process them so that they do not become trauma? Consider many cases of trauma, such as those arising from rape, from physical and emotional violence, from institutional evil, false imprisonment, discrimination, racism, and so on. Isn't it the role of the community, and the institutions, to address such hurts and actively work on turning them into experiences that their victims can adequately process? In other words, is it not one of the key tasks of the community and its institutions to address the fear that arises from that initial pain which generates trauma?

It appears that in most cases the reason the initial pain turns into lasting trauma is the fear that the institutions and the community in its informal shape have not adequately addressed. Thus, in an important sense, the source of trauma is a dysfunctional, pathological society.

There is no way to prevent hurtful experiences which arise in the course of life; however, major differences occur between the consequences such experiences leave for people who enjoy community support, ranging from that given by the family to that offered by society at large, on the one hand, and those who must deal with the hurt on their own, without the solidarity, empathy, and active assistance of important others. In the latter case, lasting trauma as an inhibitor of life plans is much more likely than in the former case. From the point of view of the community serving primarily the goal of achieving the good life for its members, it could be considered a key part of the very social contract that the community shows solidarity and empathy and helps its members weather the storms of hurt, violence, and victimization, all of which are inevitable parts of the life experience. Consequently, it could be argued that those communities that fail on those accounts of moral emotions also fail the legitimacy test in light of the social contract and lose legitimate normative power over their members.

Interventions in Fear and Trauma: The Therapeutic Leadership

The solidarity the community must show in cases of deep hurt with potential to turn into the crust of lasting trauma consists in large part in placing itself (the community) between the victim of the hurt and the source of the hurt. It is the role of the friends, compatriots, and the institutions to shield the victim, who is one of their members, from the fear that accompanies the sense of powerlessness that typically arises from victimization. Again, I would consider this simple dialectic of solidarity the very core of the social contract in the context of achieving good communal life.

If the community is represented in the hurtful situation by a therapist, then the therapist becomes an important part of the victim's world by opening emotionally to the victim and communicating with them on the level of their trauma. This is fairly taxing on the therapist, because they must take part in the hurtful experience in order to identify with the victim. In addition, to address the hurt adequately, the therapist must substitute roles to some extent: in most situations, the victims of hurtful experiences benefit the most from a correction of their traumatized view of those who have inflicted hurt on them through the therapist's taking over of an equivalent role to that of the significant others who have been the source of the hurt. For example, traumas associated with emotional relationships, which are by far the most prevalent cases in any type of counseling for trauma anywhere (just as relationship issues are by far the most prevalent of all cases overall), are often best addressed by the therapist's taking over, to some extent, the role of the emotional partner who initially inflicted the hurt, not in the sense of playing the role of the exact partner, but rather demonstrating to the victim of the hurt that a different emotional relationship equivalent to that which initially hurt them is possible without inflicting the trauma. This is a key use for transfer in therapy for partnership-induced trauma.

How does this mechanism work? The two dominant models of transfer, or projection of the roles of important others by the client onto the therapist, include the construction of a parent in the shape of the therapist and the projection of a lover through the therapist. Where trauma is inflicted in a romantic relationship, obviously the latter type of identification, or transfer, is particularly useful to allow the therapist to work on neutralizing the hurtful effects of the experience and preventing the solidification of the hurt into a lasting trauma. If the victim sees the therapist as an embodiment, or role-equivalent, of a partner who inflicted the hurt, then it is the role of the therapist to play that role and invalidate the potential conclusion that partnerships are fraught with dangers and that hurt, resulting in trauma, is a likely outcome in any partnership. This is an exceptionally demanding role for the therapist because they must parallelly play the role of a partner (symbolically, of course—not effectively) and must maintain a "birds-eye perspective" on the process. By playing the role of the partner, the therapist prevents the validation of a traumatizing meaning that the client might, and is likely to, attach to the hurt, with all the inhibitory effects of such a meaning for the person's future life. Thus, the therapist works in a sort of social laboratory with the client: the therapist shows the client, by example, what a quality relationship would involve while respecting the boundaries of the therapeutic process. These boundaries are often tested, and this is natural. If the therapist invests themselves in playing the role, then even some violations of the boundaries are justified, provided that they benefit the client and that by doing so the therapist focuses specifically on neutralizing the inhibitory consequences of the fear that relates to the hurt. Establishing trust in others in the future requires developing strong trust in the therapist, and likewise, preserving one's ability to invest emotionally in other people in the future presupposes one's ability to invest emotionally, and safely, in the therapist, following the initial hurt which, without therapy, might cause failure to reach out to others emotionally in the future. The responsibility for how far the role playing goes resides primarily with the therapist, but it seems to me that in discussions of the ethics of psychotherapy or counseling as a broader activity too much emphasis is placed on the therapist's responsibility to observe boundaries (the restrictive duty) and too little on the therapist's *proactive duty* to actually test the boundaries and to earnestly play the role suggested by the transfer. In too many cases, therapists focus on staying within the boundaries while failing the other, far more important ethical imperative, namely that to invest themselves in the client's experiences and to wrestle actively with the client's demons. This is an easier, "professional" way to conduct therapy which, expectedly, usually leads to temporary constructive results, while, after a while, for many clients the consequences of the initial hurt return and they descend back into desperation and dysfunctionality.

The therapeutic relationship that heals trauma should correct the pathological influence of society to which, as Maté points out, the personal disorder is a healthy response. Rather than seeing trauma as a pathology, we must see it as a wound inflicted on a healthy person by a pathological experience, and in most cases, the real subject of that experience is a pathological society. This brings us back to the Lacanian point of socialization: apart from helping maintain or rebuild the client's trust in others and in society after the initial hurt, the therapist also corrects the influence of the society that typically solidifies the trauma: the therapist, in addition to being a projected lover, or parent, or some other significant "Other" for the client, is also a leader in terms of representing an ideal society. The therapist's role vis-à-vis the client is one of leadership in multiple ways, including social leadership and the fostering of a vision of what true fellowship really ought to be like. For this reason, some tolerance for the breaches of the boundaries throughout the history of psychotherapy has been, and remains, inevitable.

Perhaps the most famous major breach of the therapeutic boundaries in the history of the profession has been that by Carl Gustav Jung. The situation Jung faced with Sabina Spielrein, with whom he entered a sexual relationship, was a breach of the ethics of professional conduct for psychiatrists even then, but Sigmund Freud, who was the undisputed leader of the psychoanalytic movement at the time, refused to sanction him and decided to contain his intervention to a confidential caution issued to Jung. Sabina Spielrein, on the other hand (at the time, at least), claimed that the affair with Jung had helped her overcome her difficulties (she was diagnosed with "hysteria").

Jung's relationship with Sabina was internally conflicted for him because, on the one hand, he believed in a structural framework of classic psychoanalysis, and on the other, he transgressed the methodology of Freudian psychoanalysis frequently because he sensed the need for greater organicism in therapy. Jung did not know explicitly what organicism was, nor did he consider organicism to be the "scientific" aspect of psychotherapy. In his relationship with Sabina, he frequently tried to pull back from an intensely sexual affair and desperately exclaimed to her: "But I am your physician, and we should behave accordingly." Yet, Sabina took no notice of this because, at the time, she felt that she needed Jung's attentions as a man and as a person to overcome her alienation and inhibitions. (According to some sources, Sabina later changed her mind when she was already an accomplished psychoanalyst herself and had founded the psychoanalytic movement in Russia, and claimed that Jung was a "psychopath" who had "raped her") (Sells, 2017). Sabina was later murdered by the Nazis, and her newest biography casts damning accusations not only against Jung but also against the entire psychoanalytic movement for allegedly "pillaging her heritage" as a psychoanalyst.

The question to ask here is, in fact, whether Jung would have been able to help Sabina without testing the boundaries with her? It could well be that his choice was to fulfill only one of the two sides of the ethical imperative of therapy: either preserve the boundaries, or actively engage with the patient. It turns out that the personal consequences of Jung's choice were more destructive for him than for Sabina. Following their affair, Sabina moved on with her life, married, and had a family. She proceeded to found the psychoanalytic movement in Russia. However, Jung suffered a nervous breakdown. It was Jung's wife who invited Sabina as a therapist to help Jung recover. Although it is difficult to judge complex emotional relationships, especially from a significant historical distance, it appears, at least on the surface of it, that the results of Jung's engagement with Sabina were productive for her, while Jung himself suffered the emotional fallout of the affair. I would dare to suggest that this is an example of the sort of sacrifice the counselor or therapist is sometimes obliged to make, not necessarily in terms of entering into forbidden types of relationships with clients, but more generally, in the sense of engaging with the client's world, with their "demons," in a personal, and not merely professional capacity. This is how organicism works in practice, and that is why it usually requires some type of sacrifice on behalf of the truly dedicated therapist.

I should like to extend this point of organic leadership here to human relationships generally and explore briefly the extent to which our interpersonal difficulties and wants in life satisfaction might be proportional to our inability and unwillingness to invest ourselves in others across the traditional boundaries of our relationships.

A massive proliferation of rules in modern society prevents organic relationships from unfolding spontaneously, but that is the smaller problem in terms of what causes the massive pathology of our society. The greater problem is that we are systematically discouraged by society from approaching others *across conventional limits*, and this discouragement grows in severity with time, so that today many of the organic relationships are *legally banned*. This all revolves around the axis of the liberal *public/private dichotomy*, where the tendency to protect the private and clearly delineate it from the public means that we are not entitled to approach each other privately.

For members of the community, it is far more difficult to be there for each other in their most intimate problems and traumas if the very crossing of the public/private boundary is so risky and fraught with institutional dangers. Even the most traditional and biologically necessary encounters, such as the sexual encounter between man and woman, are increasingly depersonalized and made difficult.

To develop a personal, deep relationship, two people must get to know each other, but this requires that they cross into the realm of each other's vulnerabilities and thus deep into the private realm. If they do not already know each other, *institutional society does everything to make it difficult*, sometimes impossible, for them to even get to know each other, because with so many norms of political correctness, respect for boundaries, privacy, and so on, one hardly gets any chance of becoming close with somebody else. In socially sanctioned situations, a couple might even have a sexual encounter, however, without the intimacy that arises from getting to know each other. One can have sex with another person without approaching and getting to know that person's vulnerabilities, but one cannot have an organic relationship with another without accessing their vulnerabilities.

The pathological society protects our vulnerabilities from being used for what they are best suited, namely, to invite others into organic links with us and thus address the suffering we experience in joyful and constructive ways. However, that same society does not protect us from trauma: in fact, it uses the pain that inflicts fear and thus solidifies as trauma to socialize us. In other words, society traumatizes us in order to make us conform to the standard it wants to set. This confusion between pain, trauma, fear as the content of trauma, and vulnerability marks the perimeter of our emotional lives where society often plays exceptionally damaging roles for us.

Hope and Therapeutic Engagement

One of the main dispositions that therapeutic leadership fosters is hope. However, hope is not a simple quality, nor can it be brought about by simple encouragement or by offering support to the client. To establish real hope in the client's life, it must be a hope *that relates to the therapist or includes the therapist.*

On the surface, this seems like an odd statement. It would seem logical that therapy should lead to the client's hopeful worldview and perception of their reality independently of their relationship with the therapist alone. However, this is usually not possible without the client's hope first being vested in the relationship with the therapist. To substantiate the prospect of hope, which the therapist puts before the client, *the therapist must be an actor in the scenarios the client hopes for.*

If the client needs things that one typically gets in good therapy, so much the easier for the therapist. However, again, this is rarely the case. If the client sees the therapist because they grieve over a lost relationship, marriage, or even a child, the therapy will not work if the therapist simply encourages and supports the client to see the world as worth living in, despite the loss. To establish hope, the therapist must be *a part of the hope*; they must be able to offer the client a scenario of life, an engagement, where the *therapist will play an active part*. This seemingly small requirement revolutionizes the entire traditional therapeutic methodology and the doctrine of boundaries within the paradigm of philosophically informed psychotherapy.

In a case where someone grieves a serious loss, and the therapist suggests the pursuit of activities to overcome the depression, the only way in which this will be a successful strategy is if the therapist transgresses the comfortable boundary of "professionalism" and moves in the pursuit of various activities with the client. In his *Lying on the Couch*, Irvin Yalom describes how a therapist gradually becomes involved in private relationships with clients, ends up going gambling with the "patient," goes out with him and with his wife, becomes friends, all the while conducting therapy (Yalom, 2014).

Yalom shows an ambivalent attitude to the weaknesses of his main character, loosely identified with himself. He suggests that Marshall's love of wealth and comfort pushes him outside the boundaries of proper therapy with a wealthy but demanding client. However, it would seem to me that the truth here is somewhat different. Crossing the boundaries in the described way is the only credible way of establishing hope in the client. The best way for the client to hope for friendship and love in their lives is to let them have friendship and love within their relationship with the therapist.

The psychotherapist or counselor takes a part of the client's burden; the therapist takes personal risks by entering the world of the client and becoming an active part of it, not only in the counseling room. The therapist must be willing to walk with the client, visit the client at home, if necessary, go out with the client just as Marshall does in Yalom's novel, and help the client in many of his endeavors that take place outside the counseling room. Only with this approach will the therapist be the locus of hope for the client, and then the client will be able to gradually move the focus of that hope from the therapist to other people and situations, some of whom or some of which might even have previously traumatized the client. They must first trust the therapist in order to trust the world. The client must love the therapist in order to love someone else. The client must be able to be happy with the therapist before they can be happy with someone else. This is a monumental task for the therapist.

If it is our task to try to recreate a relationship with the client where the client will restore hope through their emotions for us, this goes beyond the traditional role of transfer. The old-fashioned way of addressing transfer was to dissect it and make it inoperable, while "educating" the client in the process about their projections and false beliefs regarding the therapist. This approach has been abandoned in modern psychotherapy, which has found that transfer is the most potent, sometimes the only, tool the therapist has to influence and "pull" the client in desired directions. Transfer is thus not neutralized; to the contrary, *real therapy starts once the transfer is established.* Normally transfer comes along with a "counter-transfer," namely the therapist's own projections of their important relationships or issues onto the client. Unlike transfer, counter-transfer must be strictly controlled, and part of the supervision we go through with colleagues is to keep our awareness of our counter-transfer in check.

What I am suggesting here as the emotional content of organic psychotherapy goes considerably beyond transfer or counter-transfer: the client not only reads into their relationship with the therapist their important other relationships, or at least their aspects; the client *has* a relationship with the therapist that *actually includes* many of the aspects of their other relationships (with some boundaries in place), and through that relationship with the therapist the client restores hope and confidence in other people.

The therapist who invests themselves in the relationships with the client will not easily reject a client's request to meet outside the counseling room, at the client's home, or to go somewhere together. Such activities are risky only if the psychotherapeutic relationship is seen as a strictly professional one, which in its very core it is not. Much of what I have said so far suggests that professionalism as a general methodological paradigm of therapy should be abandoned. The relationship between the client and the psychotherapist is fundamentally private. They both must be able to own this relationship, and their mutual feelings ought to be stronger than those between friends: the "risks" that one normally thinks of when engaging in interactions with unknown others do not really come to mind when one engages in the same activities with a dear person. Our clients are dear to us, and we are often dear to them. Thus the "boundaries" of "professionalism" which apply to the doctor–patient relationship, or to the car mechanic–customer relationship by no means hold for the therapist–client relationship. This generates serious consequences for how philosophical therapy is conducted vis-à-vis traditional psychotherapy (Fatić, 2025).

In my personal experience, I have always found the line separating my "interventions" as a therapist and my "interventions" as a friend to be very thin indeed. It has seemed to me that the one quality that unites therapy and friendship in the helping sense is leadership, and that the common conclusion that leadership consists in communication talents and skills is only a part of the story.

What leadership really requires, in its core, is a deep interest in other people and a fundamental love, or liking, of the other human being. If we love, or like, someone, we will be willing and able to invest more of ourselves in our relationship with them, and our ability to help them in any regard will be greater. Thus, to me, the idea that psychotherapy or counseling are "professional" has always seemed not only counterproductive, but absurd. I have found that even as a university professor, I could only be relatively "professional" in, for example, marking students' exams, in times of the global pandemic, such as in 2020 and 2021, when all the teaching was conducted online and once the written exams were in for grading. This is a restrictive situation where one can truly be relatively "professional" by grading the exams as "objectively" as it is generally possible. I have also found that the grades I gave to students were by far the lowest when I awarded them "objectively." This means that my grading was far more benevolent when I knew the person. When one teaches in person, they know more about the capacities and knowledge of the students, even without the exam, than one can possibly know when one teaches many students online. Thus, to me at least, "professionalism" and "objectivity" are in fact fallback options under restrictive circumstances; they are not the preferred option by any lights.

Nobody comes to a therapy session with the expectation of "objectivity" by the counselor. They seek community, an alliance, and ethically informed empowerment and assistance. Above all, the clients seek benevolence. The more "objective" we are, the less benevolent we are, because there is less personal chemistry between us and other persons. When we teach online, the process is far less organic and not as similar to the therapeutic discourse as it ideally should be.

Psychotherapy is a highly organic process, which, while it is experimentally conducted online, is only properly done in person. Thus, the concepts of professionalism and objectivity are as fundamentally foreign to counseling as indifference is foreign to love and friendship. I would never willingly go for therapy to a professional and objective therapist who does not like me, and I don't expect my clients to come to me without expecting me to like them, or to be generally curious about and drawn by people. All these qualities are unnecessary in the strict perspective of professionalism and objectivity.

Having said all of the above, it follows that the fundamentals of intervention in fear and trauma consist of offering hope and security that are focused on the very relationship between the therapist and the client. In addition, an ideal therapy includes positing and striving for goals of satisfaction that the therapist is able to offer or fulfill for the client in their own relationship.

The engagement which, by definition, tests the boundaries of professionalism is reflected in numerous everyday therapeutic situations. For example, if a client seeks to re-establish communication with an estranged lover and fails repeatedly, a professional standard for the therapist is to decline direct involvement in the relationship. From a more philosophically sensitive point of view, this is a highly suspect standard, primarily from an ethical point of view. How can I possibly advise someone to seek communication with a loved one and then refuse to reasonably take part in it when the success of the strategy is tested on the level of the client's own efforts, because of some imaginary "professionalism"? Would such a refusal not be truly motivated by my desire to preserve my own comfort and my unwillingness to really "go out on a limb" for my client? Is that not the real normative content of much professionalism in the helping professions? We need to earnestly ask these questions of ourselves when considering whether discourse therapy can even be regarded as a profession. To adopt the paradigm of a profession would mean making the same mistake as conventional psychotherapy and, prior to that, the attempts by psychology to establish itself as a "science." In a healing relationship, I must *risk* my comfort for my client, just as I feel that I am obliged to do so for a friend. Otherwise, I am neither a friend nor a therapist worth the name.

Respect of Maturity in Therapeutic Discourse

Another aspect of intervention in fear and trauma is respect for the maturity of the client. Many clients in counseling do not actually wish to be treated as mature, adult people. They behave childishly and want to be comforted by the therapist in much the same way as a parent protects a child. This type of comforting relationship is justified only for a brief period of therapy, if the client is highly decompensated and has reduced symbolic capacities to cope with their experiences. However, if the approach continues too long, it degrades the client as a person and directs the therapeutic relationship objectifying the client, where the only subject in therapy is the therapist. In such a format of therapy, the therapist "operates" the client, only to quickly find oneself in a situation where the therapy is directive and devoid of autonomy for the client.

One key aspect of therapy is to always understand, and acknowledge through our therapeutic stance, that the client is an adult person, that what the client says, to us, means exactly what they have said, and that we expect the client to *take seriously their own decisions*, wishes, and statements, just as they take our statements and suggestions seriously. Thus, if a client says, "I want to kill myself," this is not a statement to be taken as irrational, but as a *responsible decision*. This does not mean that the therapist should always run to an emergency phone and call the police and the ambulance to hospitalize the client and prevent them from harming themselves, but it means that we should calmly and with dignity talk to the client about the grounds and ramifications of such an intention. There is no room here for either belittling the statement (that has often been a terrible, fatal mistake, resulting in actual suicides) or panicking over it. A person who says that they wish to kill themselves obviously wants to talk about the idea. The therapist's task is to discuss what the client says just the same as they would discuss any other provocative statement. Maintaining a critical discourse over whatever the client suggests (and the idea of killing oneself is not psychotic or "deranged" in and of itself) is the main precondition for establishing control over the ideation that gives rise to emotions as dynamic factors that move the client to act in whatever direction.

The same principle applies to less provocative statements and situations. I recollect an episode with one of my former supervisors in psychotherapy, quite some years ago, when a client came to his office and, at that first meeting, while they were briefly discussing the format and expectations of therapy, declared to my supervisor (who was a psychoanalyst and philosopher at the same time): "You are my third therapist, I have had sex with the previous two, and I intend to have sex with you, too." My supervisor then responded: "I don't know why you are saying this to me, but I assure you that this will not happen."

After all the years that have passed since, I consider this response to have been suboptimal. The statement "I want to have sex with you" made by someone who sees you for the first time, and is your client, is similar to the statement "I want to kill myself," in that they invite a *discussion of the reasons* for the desire or intention—the client does not invite a rejection. Obviously, the client knows that they should not have sex with the therapist, and that they cannot do so even if they decided to break the rules unless the therapist agrees. Hence the statement "I intend to have sex with you, too" is an invitation for a discussion of why one had had sex with their other therapists, whom they subsequently abandoned, and why one continues to harbor such ideas now with the third therapist, again.

Such questions would open up a discussion of what one expects from therapy. This is a direction of exchange that might open all kinds of avenues for the client's articulation of their issues and for an array of various therapeutic interventions. Saying "No, you won't have sex with me" is restrictive and might close many of those avenues for intervention. Similarly, a person who is prepared to talk about their desire to kill themselves opens up considerable room for the therapeutic intervention that might dissuade them from fulfilling their intention. Or if they are told "not to even think of it," these avenues will be closed, and any adverse outcome becomes more likely. We must treat our clients as mature interlocutors, who have reasons for their thoughts and desires, just as we treat anyone else. Such treatment alone might cause the client to approach their own ideation more responsibly and will shape the nature of the client–therapist transfer in the optimal way, thus allowing more effective progress than would the otherwise meandering infantilization of the client disguised as care and empathy.

The same principle applies to other contexts in dealing with people who expect some kind of guidance from us. I recently spoke with a master's student who had just finished her thesis. The ambitious young woman informed me, immediately after her oral defense, that she wanted to "write a book on psychotherapy." The way to respond to such statements is not to say: "You can't write a book, it is too early for you, and the master's thesis is far from a sufficient text for a book, either maturity wise, or volume wise." To do so would be utterly wrong. Instead, I responded with interest for the title of the book, upon which question she became confused and started to offer several different titles. I then asked her about the sources she would use other than those in her thesis, which confused her further. When I asked about what kind of readership she expected and where her book would be located with regard to the state of the art in the field, she started to realize that writing a book on psychotherapy requires a much greater and longer study and thinking, a grain of creativity, and a lot of luck in terms of the topic, the opportunity, and the intellectual interest of the potential public, all concurring at a certain time. However, I did not take her statement as irresponsible. She wanted to write a book, and I took that seriously. I focused on illustrating to her what it would take to act on her ambition, and I am fairly confident that, sometime in the future, she will actually write such a book.

The context is similar to statements made by clients with fear and trauma as their dominant complaints. Obviously, when a client says that they are so traumatized that they can't handle their daily living and want to kill themselves, this tells us a lot about the client's level of suffering and their sensibility. An insensitive person rarely considers killing themselves. It is far more likely that a sophisticated personality might suffer a nervous breakdown or contemplate killing themselves.

If the statement "I want to kill myself" is treated with sufficient respect and dignity, as a rational decision which one might, under certain circumstances, make, a transfer will be created that will have intersubjective value for the client. This alone will change the client's situation with which they initially arrived to counseling. Once the transfer is established, this opens a wide room for the therapist to discuss, critically, with the client the various arguments and options alternative to the client's committing suicide, all along preserving the client's subjecthood and dignity. The client is not "sick" or "disordered" merely by virtue of considering suicide. The qualification of the intention to kill oneself depends on the reasons for the intention, just the same as with any other idea or intent. As it is not difficult for an alternative to be more attractive to the person than suicide, a respectful therapy based on the described type of transfer is usually successful.

Clients who say that they want to kill themselves in the way of initiating a discussion about the desire rarely commit suicide if the therapist takes their statement in the described way, as a normal, responsible statement by a mature adult that is subject to discussion. Similarly, a client who comes for therapy for the first time and says that they have had sex with their previous therapists and intend to do so with the present therapist as well likely wishes to tell the therapist about their pain, their misgivings about therapy or therapists—things the therapist should be curious to find out about. When one approaches another person in a pub and asks them for a lighter, they might be trying to strike up a conversation; however, if they are really asking for a lighter, responding to that request is a prerequisite for what might come afterward. One must first give the person a lighter and then perhaps have a conversation. Ignoring the explicit statement invalidates any subsequent relationship.

Clients' statements in psychotherapy or counseling should always be taken seriously, and not merely as smokescreens for something else, although they are usually simply introductions into deeper subcurrents of concern. Words are not used accidentally in therapy; they always have a personal meaning, and the way into that meaning is simply by following what the person literally says at first. Taking the client's statements seriously, however, also treating them at the same time as responsible and mature, offers the sufferers of trauma and fear additional security, but it also offers them a tool to work toward re-establishing effective communication with others and regaining self-confidence and self-respect.

Understanding organic therapy as leadership easily leads to encouraging clients to develop their own leadership skills in communication, by applying the same principles that govern organic therapy to ordinary exchanges with others. This is a simple way to strengthen the client's self-confidence and ability to address any ambiguities in everyday communication: if the person learns to focus on the literal statements others make, to take them at face value and explore, based on those statements, the reasons others have for making the statement, or holding a belief that is expressed in the statement, they will soon find out that they are able to go deeper and to explore more in their social world and their interactions with others. These simple principles are often neglected, and people who have issues in communication forget the most logical and direct way to approach others. This is partly due to the cultural pressure to understand "what people mean" largely *regardless of what they say or do*: clients in therapy always "mean" what they do, and they usually "mean" what they say; however, this is usually not enough to fully understand them. One needs to start from what they "mean" (say or do) and then go deeper into their feelings and beliefs that are expressed in the statements, including those with a subconscious dimension.

During the writing of this chapter, my daughter, who was 12 at the time, related to me an experience with a school friend that explains the described principle of respectful therapeutic communication vividly. She had met a girl her age at a language camp and had become worried about her because the child had had scars on her lower arms, which suggested that she had been regularly cutting herself. All the children had noticed this, and the girl had been so unhappy that she had stated that she wanted to kill herself. Apparently, at one stage, my daughter was close to her when she spoke to her mother on the phone. When the mother started to yell at the child for having forgotten to take something with her on the trip, the girl started to cry. My daughter's comment was that the mother had yelled "over an insignificant, small thing that I can't even remember." She asked me what I thought, whether the girl could have been helped, and what "there is to do when nobody believes you that something is wrong with you." Apparently, this girl had said to her parents that she felt she could no longer cope with the stress (obviously a large part of this stress was induced by the parents' conflictual behavior toward the child), and the parents had responded that "this is nothing, it is part of becoming a teenager." What my daughter took away from this experience was, first, that another child was obviously in trouble and hurting herself to relieve psychological stress, and second, that nobody "believed" her friend that "something was wrong with her."

I proceeded to explain to my daughter that the cutting scars on the girl's arms might have suggested that she was suffering so much that she either falsely blamed herself for her inability to communicate with her parents and was punishing herself, or that she was simply under so much stress that she was inflicting physical pain on herself to redirect her thoughts from her feelings about the causes of her stress. Ksenija (my daughter) looked at me, thought for a while, and remarked: "This is all because they don't believe her when she says that something is wrong with her. *I would help her because I would believe her.*"

This is a simple, child's way of putting into words the principle of acknowledgment that makes up for much of the leadership in communication: she instinctively feels that it would help her friend if somebody "believed" her, and she decided that she would "believe her." To make things even clearer, Ksenija ended this topic by pointing it out to me: "And as a psychotherapist, don't think that I am trying to tell you something about myself. I know that you always think about whether or not what I am saying is a message. It is not. I am not trying to say anything that I am not saying directly. I am simply saying what I mean. That's it."

I couldn't possibly put it more succinctly than Ksenija did. If she had had the opportunity to talk with her girlfriend about the friend's difficulties, I am sure that by simply showing her respect and acknowledging the validity and reasonability of the reasons the child would have given for her misery, she would have made the other child feel better.

Leadership in therapy and in communication starts with what Axel Honneth so powerfully described as the *need for recognition*. This concept, which he attributes to Hegel, is one of the cornerstones of philosophically informed psychotherapy and of the theory and practical skill of leadership (Honneth, 1995). Honneth argues for a kind of "categorical imperative" of recognition, where we need to explicitly recognize the significance and presence of others in order to restore the fundamental conditions of dignified inter-subjectivity that we have lost somewhere along the way of the change of the social conditions of our lives. If one wants to be recognized by others, one first needs to recognize others.

It is interesting to briefly consider what this means for the principle of leadership that I have put forward at the end of this chapter.

First, we need to be recognized by others if we are to influence them, either through therapy, or through friendship, or through both. In integrative psychotherapy there is no "cut-off line" between friendship and therapy: in fact, friendship is a normal aspect of long-term, deep psychotherapy, just as friendship normally accompanies a close student–teacher relationship, such as in doctoral supervisions or in various research projects or practical "clinics."

In order to be recognized, we need to recognize our clients, in the way I have described here and Ksenija so poignantly illustrated through a story about her friend with traumas and communication problems whom "nobody believes."

The recognition is at once simple and difficult to accomplish: it is *structurally simple*, because the method requires simply attentive listening and the actual self-investment to "believe," or take seriously, all statements the other person is making about themselves, because they do "mean it." After the other person has ascertained that they are recognized through our taking seriously what they say or do, conditions are there for proceeding to a further step in the relationship, and that is establishing mutual confidence. Once this is attained, a true exchange starts where deeper level information is exchanged and room is opened for therapeutic, or simply empathetic, or friendly advisory intervention which will not be brushed away. By treating our clients in this way, we simultaneously teach them to do the same with their counterparts in everyday life, and to start building their qualities of leadership which start with these exceptionally simple principles of communication. The leadership that grows from these roots in communication leads toward the skills to foster interpersonal links and relationships that resemble those of family members, groups of peers, or of friends, all of which are organic and capable of producing a powerful interpersonal impact.

References

Fatić, Aleksandar (2025). *Modal integrative psychotherapy: A logical integration of psychotherapy.* New York: Palgrave Macmillan. https://link.springer.com/book/9783031919336.

Honneth, Axel (1995). *The struggle for recognition: The moral grammar of social conflicts.* Cambridge: Polity Press.

Howe, Paul (2005). *Leadership and training for the fight.* New York: Simon and Schuster.

Marks, Isaac M. and Nesse, Randolph M. (1994). "Fear and fitness: An evolutionary analysis of anxiety disorders." *Ethology and Sociobiology*, Vol. 15: 247–261.

Maté , Gabor (2021). *The wisdom of trauma* (film). https://thewisdomoftrauma.com.

Rother, Mike (2010). *Toyota kata.* New York: McGraw Hill.

Sells, Angela (2017). *Sabina Spielrein: The woman and the myth.* New York: SUNY Press.

Yalom, Irvin (2014). *Lying on the couch.* New York: Basic Books.

Chapter 5

LIFE GOALS

Life Goals and Life Plans

A life goal is a desire that is located within the space and time of one's life situation and followed by more or less systematic action. The attainment of life goals often requires planning, but plans to attain life goals are not life plans: these are two very different categories of planning. While our culture teaches us to have goals and to "fight" to attain them, and this often requires strategic planning, the process of attainment of goals, paradoxically, can militate against the development and fulfillment of adequate life plans. In this tension between life goals and life plans, many individuals who come for counseling suffer greatly because their seeming "success" by the lights of their culture is unmatched by their deep feelings of emptiness and failure.

In this chapter I will focus on an unlikely, yet, in my opinion, priceless source for the formal structuring of a therapeutic logic of life goals and life plans, namely on Wittgenstein's *Tractatus Logico-Philosophicus*, especially on his definition of *form* and its practical application to the notion of life plans (Wittgenstein, 2021).

At one stage, Wittgenstein defines form as *"the possibility of a structure"* (Wittgenstein, 2021: 2.033).[1]

This is a concept that ties in nicely with Lacan's idea of structure as a set of social relationships, or, as John Searle would put it, as a fundamental intentional inter-subjectivity that helps define most of our mental states (Searle, 1983).

Simply put, the practical success of our lives typically depends on the soundness and detailed development and execution of our life plans. While, as with any plans, life plans do not always unfold as intended, the existence of a well-elaborated life plan does in fact lead to a better orientation in decision-making, clearer self-perception, including the perception of one's values and motives, and, as a result, to a better execution. It is naturally easier to execute a plan that is clear than to execute a vague blueprint that has not been developed in detail as one's life strategy.

Life goals, on the other hand, are specific benchmarks on the way to a full execution of a life plan. Ideally, all life goals should be parts of a life plan as a general strategy in life and should correspond to specific parts of the execution of a life plan. However, in practice, life goals emerge in ways that militate against the consistent and creative execution of a life plan, rather than contributing to it. Thus, a challenge for practical philosophy and for psychotherapy and the other related helping professions is to understand life goals, especially their origin (most of our life goals are, in fact, internalized values imposed by the broader social environment), and examine each specific life goal regarding the life plan.

There is greater autonomy in developing life plans than there is in choosing life goals, and this difference leads to serious practical consequences. While the building of a life plan typically includes a deep examination of one's values and desires, thus checking against a potential falsified "authenticity" of motivation, the setting of life goals is heavily influenced by *structural violence*, namely by social and group normativity, especially expectations. These types of norms reflect almost immediately on our internal structures of motivation. One of the clear indications of this near-immediate takeover of external normativity into our internal dynamics is our *language*.

When a person is asked what their most important goals in life are, most people will respond in a similar way: depending on the society they have been raised in, they will typically declare as their own the goals that society fosters as the embodiments of its values. Most people will deny that what they seek in life is power and control of others, because that is shunned by their society. They will say that they tend to seek common ground with others, because that is socially desirable. When asked about the profile of their ideal life partner, they will insist on the personality, and not on the looks, because that is the way their society favors them to think. If they are asked about their physique, they will say that they are concerned with it as far as it impacts their health, and not for reasons of appearance alone, because that is in line with the socially preferred value of modesty. When queried about their key life goals, they will include the goals associated with making a contribution to society and seeking peace and coexistence with others, even if in actual reality these same people are extremely competitive and believe that life is there for the taking by those brave and strong enough to pick its fruits. Most importantly, and this is particularly clear in psychotherapy, clients *do not lie* when they make such obviously untrue statements. They *actually believe* that these are their goals, and many behave as though they are. Thus, they end up in counseling, because these life goals are often simply *not* their authentic goals: they are external projections inwards, so to say; they are a personally internalized social values-structure—the Lacanian "Real" of norms, which, rather than being adequately symbolically processed, invades the client's internal worlds.

As throughout this book I use examples of clients and others to illustrate various points, it is only fair to also use my own example as a case study for more general problems that clients face in counseling with us. I have recently faced a similar situation with my own life goals, and I believe it is a common situation for many people.

Having been a victim of institutional injustice and political retribution because of my criticism of an authoritarian government in my country, I have developed a strong desire to fight the institutions, humiliate and hurt them and their representatives. This came at the price of losing various institutional battles which, in an authoritarian political system, are typically won by corruption and collusion with the institutions. Rather than looking at my issues before them in an impartial way, the institutions saw me as a threat because of my media appearances which have been strongly anti-government, and responded in kind, within their powers. On an explicit level, I continued to believe that I was a peaceful person seeking compromise with others and trying to avoid confrontation. However, my actions and emotions betrayed a different picture, which I was ultimately able to fathom only gradually: I did not want to be cooperative with the corrupt institutions, and I wanted to hurt them as much as possible, in the ways available to me, which I did through my public appearances. I thus wrote relentlessly, using the momentum in my country which seemed to invite public revolt and political change, with a clear desire to deter and intimidate those who I believed had intimidated thousands of private citizens for decades, using their illegitimate connections with the political regime.

Through acting in the described way, I derived a sense of pleasure from the fear and humiliation of those within the institutions I targeted publicly. I pursued a public campaign against corrupt judges and ministry officials whom I knew had wronged me and others for political reasons, and started to advocate radical transitional justice punishments for all those who had acted in collusion with the authoritarian political regime.

Gradually, I became more radical than the mainstream political opposition and started to have trouble placing my views even in the opposition newspapers. I thus joined with a like-minded colleague, and we started appearing frequently together on several internet portals, which quickly became a source of ardent anti-government campaigns, focused on the judiciary.

Even though I had been instrumental in the abolition of the death penalty in my country, I started to advocate the temporary reintroduction of the death penalty for political and judicial crimes against the poor citizens and opponents of the political regime in power. I wanted revenge against those whom I perceived as morally degraded below the minimum acceptable standard for a decent society, those who had sold out their holy social roles of judges and institutional lawmakers for the miserable benefit of the political regime's favor. My values exhibited themselves as being quite Nietzschean, a perspective strongly opposed to who I had believed I had been prior to this experience. The radical victimization by the institutions in my capacity as an opponent of the government helped break the crust of my belief that the socially desirable values and traits which were conciliatory and compromising were actually mine: in fact, my own views and values were quite the opposite of what I had made myself believe they had been.

This reflected on my life plans in two ways.

The initial, false beliefs that the external, socially induced values were automatically my own (a common principle for most people) had led me to devise life plans that were based on such values. My life plan was to pursue an academic life and try to preserve my relationship with my child, who had been taken away from me by the corrupt institutions. I wanted to try to survive the injustice until my daughter was old enough to overcome the estrangement they had tried to impose on her. However, this was a false, inauthentic life plan, based on false, inauthentic life goals and the underlying externally induced values.

Once I realized that I harbored a Nietzschean view of the government and institutions (that they should be actively torn down if they are corrupt), my life plan changed: increasingly I started to contemplate a political or quasi-political career, and I saw myself as increasingly publicly active, trying to influence a change in the structure of political power. I started to advocate *revolutionary justice* against the leaders of the authoritarian institutions, following the example of a neighboring country which had dealt with its dictator simply by court-martialing him and executing him within hours of the verdict. My public activity, and my substantive views on the death penalty, in this limited political context, changed to diametrically opposite positions compared to my initial views, which I had held when I had believed that the values of my society had been my own.

My life plan has always been based on the idea of enjoyment, namely it included the building of a life on two pillars: the joy of doing the job that fulfills me, and the devotion of those close to me. This formal shape of a life plan, however, as Wittgenstein says, is merely a "possibility of structure," and it could be filled with different types of structure. My general sense of the way in which my life plan might work was that of a loose, cheerful, collaborative lifestyle, which would at the same time give me a strong experience of satisfaction and contribute to the satisfaction of those I care about.

However, given the life goals that have populated my life over the years immediately preceding the writing of this book, my life plan fluctuates between the structure that I had envisaged from the start and a structure that is quite the opposite of that intention. While I continue to do the job that fulfills me, my social endeavors and activism are turning the "cheerful" and "collaborative" part of the structure of my life plan into a far less carefree and far more dangerous social engagement where I still feel a strong need to contribute to society, however, in a way that requires *confrontation* with those whom I perceive as destructive. This new life plan now requires involvement in revolutionary-style social and political battles.

As it turns out, my life goals that I started with, which were all "beach, education and collaborative discourse"-type goals, proved to be merely *internalizations* of what I had chosen from the array of goals my society offered as preferable norms. In my society, which is very sensitive to challenges to fundamentally authoritarian rule, collaborative values are strongly preferred because they are not politically challenging. The experience of victimization by institutions, however, revealed a deeper structure of my goals, namely those based on a fight against the fundamentally illicit social order. I am sure that my social appearance has also changed: once a person who fought for the abolition of the death penalty and the liberal values in society, I am now one of just a few people in my society openly calling for the reintroduction of the death penalty and a full revolutionary transitional justice against the corrupt political establishment. It appears as though, within the same form of a life plan (based on the pillars of professional enjoyment and collaborative social action) my life goals, which make up the substance of the implementation of my life plan, have changed their quality completely, especially those relating to the second pillar of my life plan).

Now, does this mean that the essence of my life plan has changed?

This, of course, depends on the way in which we conceptualize the core of a life plan. According to Wittgenstein, the essence of a proposition lies in its form, not in its content; thus, the two-pillar structure of my life plan has not changed essentially, although it has changed content-wise and experientially.[2] My social appearance has certainly changed because of the different mannerisms of public discourse that I have adopted.

If the described change in my own life goals within the general framework of my life plan is now considered in an imagined context of psychotherapy (instead of the actual life experience of victimization which, in my case, caused my life goals to transform), the practical philosopher as a consultant, or, equally, a psychotherapist, would start from a complaint with which I approach the therapeutic process. I would likely come for counseling because of my dissatisfaction with who I am and the lowered quality of my life, due to a confusion in the normative foundations of my life plan. The therapist would then explore my emotions and the norms by which I live my life and would certainly find an enormous amount of over-socialization in me: a huge repressed structure of aggression against injustice sanctioned into what Freud would call "the subconscious," and an equally major structure of socially acceptable values internalized as my conscious personality.

An analysis would show that there is a cleavage in my personality, as the life goals which I pursue do not offer me the fulfillment I crave, while the explicit valuations that I attach to the values which the philosophical practitioner or psychotherapist would rightly suspect really define my sensibility is critical and perhaps even derogatory of much of my surroundings. An observant therapist would see me as a "wolf disguised into a shepherd," ashamed of my "wolfness." My therapy would likely take the road primarily based on psychoanalysis, and I would, ideally, end up in more or less the same situation I am in now, albeit due to quality therapy rather than the vagaries of life the way it has spontaneously unfolded for me.

People who attend psychotherapy, philosophical counseling, or any other type of discursive therapy often exhibit this sense of "inauthenticity" and doubt of their value identity, and it is almost always based on the uncritical internalization or "owning up" of externally imposed life goals. This is partly inevitable because we are socialized to choose between those values that we are offered, and depending on where we are born and how we are brought up, we are not offered the same things. We can only choose from what we are actually offered, and the structural violence that defines our societies means that each society will most explicitly and immediately offer us those life goals that are the least threatening to the normative structure of that society. The experience which I have described probably reveals an "onion like" structure of my personal values, which I suspect is fairly universal among people: as a person, I have *various layers of values and identities*, which may not be entirely consistent with each other. However, as my parenthood is close to the core of my personality, it is a deeper layer of my inner self. Once it is threatened and my child is placed in jeopardy, by whoever, the outer layers of the onion of my personality will peel off more easily, and what appears might be very different from what my personality used to be like with all of the surface layers on. One of my clients, also a father, described this fairly savage structure of fatherhood in the following way: "As a father, I have a duty to protect my child at the cost of my own life. And potentially of yours, if you are in my way." This is a highly socially undesirable way of looking at fatherhood because it threatens the power of society to regulate and repressively interfere in our family affairs. Thus, society represses this way of thinking both through socialization and through institutional violence if one reverts to this deeper layer of one's identity.

However, let us consider the same problem of form and structure in life plans and life goals on a less dramatic and less "core" level of our fundamental identities, which is also more common. Consider a situation where people in their late thirties come for therapy because they have trouble entering a serious relationship, including marriage and kids. This is an extremely common case in therapy. Many of these people are exceptionally well socialized. They possess good education, have rewarding jobs, promising careers ahead of them, they are socially active and have a wide circle of good friends. They contribute to society. However, they have trouble finding a life partner.

When the life goals of many of such clients are examined, they often seem quite solid. From an early age, many excelled at school, stayed away from alcohol and drugs, achieved decent education, pursued sports and outdoor activities, looked after their health, became socially active and aware of ecology, politics and business. Goal by goal, their life goals exhibit no controversy. However, they are alone and unhappy. Their life plans have either misfired, or they do not even exist.

One of the reasons for this common situation is that socialization through the internalization and acceptance of successive socially desirable life goals may in fact militate against the development of a decent and sufficiently honest and detailed life plan. Some of the life goals that society applauds are destructive for some of the life plans that the person would authentically choose. This is primarily associated with the investment of the most limited resources, time and energy, into socially particularly desirable goals, while at the same time, unavoidably, reducing the attention and work required for the achievement of more private and personal life goals, which might well be far more intimately connected with personal life plans. Any kind of work of private goals, including establishing and nourishing a family, or working on self-development in whatever context, requires as much time and a decent part of our lives, in just the same way as the achievement of socially sanctioned goals does.

There is something to be said for the priority of life plans over life goals, and for the careful selection of life goals depending on the prior elaboration of a life plan. Only with a life strategy that has been chosen consciously can one choose their life goals rationally and productively. On the other hand, the elaboration of a life plan in time, that is, sufficiently early in adult life, requires sacrifices and a degree of pain, namely the conscious foregoing of some of the life goals that are made by society to seem extremely attractive.

I wish to make one further reference to Wittgenstein here to emphasize a key role of logic in our representations of reality and in our life plans. While it is possible to develop specific strategies instrumental to the achievement of a life goal, and the life goal itself does not necessarily have to be particularly logical in light of our life as a whole, life plans tend to require considerable logic in order to even be conceptualized. Wittgenstein states that "the facts (of life) in logical space are the world" (Wittgenstein, 2021: 1.13).

This statement strongly resembles Lacan in his understanding of our psychological reality as a symbolically processed "Real." This is why the same raw experience will not translate into the same life experience for different people, because, with their different symbolic tools and capabilities, they will process that raw "Real" into different symbolic worlds.

Our experience becomes our world only when it is placed in a logical space, namely when it is understood on the basis of the logic that we accept. I use the term "logic" here loosely, to include any system of thought which is consistent in at least remotely the same way as a formal logic is. For example, a person might lead their life based on a Buddhist belief in the "whispering universe," and might, as many hermits do, develop clues about their life decisions and life actions from seemingly insignificant and unrelated events, from the weather to natural phenomena such as floods and droughts, or to the specific "vibrations" or "taste" of their day, their relationships with others at a particular time, or the seemingly accidental small events of all kinds. This way of thinking is not in accord with formal deductive logic, because many of the premises, or rules of inference, used in such a way of thinking are not "valid" from the standpoint of formal logic. However, this is not to say that such thinking is in any way inferior to a strictly formal logical one: as long as there is a structure of that thought, it deserves to be loosely called "a life logic."

The above-described is a broad concept which I believe is reconcilable with Wittgenstein's views here, even though he approached the *Tractatus* with the idea of "trimming out" everything that did not belong to rational thought. The idea that our world consists of the *facts of our life placed in a logical space* supports *any logical space*. Every community expects a particular logical space. When members of certain professions exercise their authority over the members of the community at large (e.g., doctors in times of a pandemic, judges, or politicians), there is an expectation that they will conform to a certain socially recognized logic. If they act contrary to that logic, that rightfully incites anger in the constituents of the community because it shows that the professionals are not worthy of their role and privilege in society. However, as far as our private lives are concerned, we are free to choose any type of structure to order our thinking about our lives, and we are entitled to call this structure "logic."

One very important therapeutic technique which, in traditional psychotherapy, is called "reframing," and in philosophical practice, "symbolic conceptualization," rests on this concept that *our world only exists owing to a logical space where it finds its coordinates.* Our experience is organized as a logical structure, even logical construct, around the most salient facets of the "Real." Focusing on this logical space helps address many of the decision-making issues that arise in the course of our lives; however, it is far easier to survey the logical space of our experience if we predominantly think about our lives in terms of life plans, and *not* life goals.

A life plan provides the logical context for life goals, given the key values and logical principles that order our thinking about our own life. One way to provide a logical matrix for life goals is to embrace an ideology or religion. Another way, not necessarily exclusive to the mentioned two, is to set up narrower values which will guide our lives and derive life goals from those values. This requires a philosophy of life, however rudimentary it might be. If we believe that we should listen to the whisper of God and judge at every juncture in our decision-making whether God is on our side or not, that is a philosophy of life, and a theoretically and logically sound one. This philosophy then informs a particular selection of life goals.

If my philosophy of life is based on listening in on the blessings or the absence of blessings by God for my various choices, then I will approach my life differently than if my philosophy of life is based on the principle "Never give up" and the emancipatory values based on the belief that "man chooses his own fate." These are different principled decisions on how to conceptualize life, and they must be made in order for life plans to be developed in a sufficiently articulated way. Once a philosophy of life is elected, or devised, a life plan must ensue on what, for the particular person, a successful and fulfilling life would be like. For some people, fulfillment includes founding a family, having offspring, developing full-fledged participation and membership in a community of like-minded individuals, and the serving of values such as loyalty, commitment, and friendship. For others, fulfillment might include personal achievement, career advancement, and the ability to embrace change at the price of loneliness. Neither life plan needs to be considered superior or inferior regardless of the fundamental philosophy of life; however, *a life plan should give rise to life goals.* There are numerous examples from therapeutic practice that illustrate this point.

A person who adopts the life philosophy that having a family and belonging to a close-knit community is what governs her value system, and due to contingent circumstance ends up pursuing a demanding career and status-related self-affirmation goals, at the cost of implementing a life plan that accords with her philosophy of life, enters a realm of discord which brings her to counseling and causes a fundamental lack of fulfillment.

A rational understanding of value priorities, however, does not readily translate into action in life choices because of the dynamism of psyche which is fueled by emotions. Only an *experience* will bring about an *emotion*, which will fuel *action*: that is why we learn patterns of behavior through repetitive choices and the resulting experiences, not in lectures or through academic venues. A life plan is largely a rational construction, and it is that much more realistic and has higher value for the person if she has a better understanding of her own emotions and sensibility as a whole. However, it is possible to design a good life plan and fail to implement it if the attempts are not fueled by emotions, passion, and dedication.

A lack of emotions is largely a part of identity that constitutes modern pathology and tends to be caused by family upbringing rather than by a priori and innate factors. Clinical practice often reveals issues with emotions which uncover many of the hidden roles of emotions in pursuing a life plan.

Emotions and Life Plans

The way we develop our emotions will determine the level of motivation, the directions and strength of dynamism of our actions and choices in life. This is due to the fact that emotions provide energy for the execution of life plans and specific choices, and that affinities associated with emotions determine the substance and content of those choices and life plans. In other words, we live by our emotions, and *not by our reasons*, and the healthy way to treat our reasons is as a *support to our sensibility*, not vice versa. Thus, all of the preparation for major changes in our life plans must include a cultivation of emotions and a cultural change in the way we perceive pleasure and pain. This is a principle well known in coaching and in neuro-linguistic programming (Robbins, 1992).

During the writing of this book, I became acquainted with 34-year-old Sally. A medical doctor by profession, Sally traveled with me long distance, so we had a chance to talk extensively. During the trip, she confided to me things which she claimed "she had never said to anyone she had met for the first time." This was obviously due to her need to talk and reveal bits of herself, combined with my curiosity to listen.

Sally has grown up in a family that she describes as "cold," emotionless. She blames this type of upbringing for what she openly describes as her own "coldness," and struggles to articulate her emotions better in order to position herself more comfortably in her life. She works at a major clinic as a surgical doctor and feels threatened by her older colleagues, who sometimes question her autonomy and place pressure on her organizationally and professionally. However, Sally finds it difficult to open herself up emotionally and warns me that she has lost trust in people due to a betrayal she has suffered in a recent emotional relationship. She is very cautious with people, keeps her distance, and tends to be focused on herself. At the same time, Sally is aware that she needs companionship and the warmth of a relationship and points out that "once she has a family, she will likely abandon her career because she always tends to focus completely on a single preoccupation in life."

After our initial meeting, I tried to establish communication with Sally on a number of occasions. She was exceptionally reserved, very guarded; however, she never openly rejected communication or failed to respond to ordinary questions. I decided to make a point of trying to develop a closer connection to Sally.

Looking at Sally, I saw a fairly clear life plan, however, one that could cause difficulties in realization unless Sally found a way to overcome her guard toward new social contacts. More importantly, for this argument, however, Sally is an example of how life goals are subsumed to life plans; however, her ability to implement her life plan depends on many circumstances over which Sally, just like any other person, has little control. Her identity is defined in her life plan, and the way in which she talks about her life plan uncovers a person unwilling to be randomly immersed in temporary and seemingly attractive life goals that do not fall within her life plan. Sally does not want emotional adventures: she seems determined to wait it out until she gets an opportunity for a lifelong partnership. Sally controls her emotions very strictly, however, the effort to control them is couched in her life plan. While some of the external manifestations of the exceptionally strong control of her emotions might seem a little too rigid, the general structure of her behavior is healthy: she knows what she wants and tries to get there in as simple and direct way as possible.

A different example to Sally, in fact the opposite example, is Mirella, who I met at about the same time as Sally. Mirella is 31, suffers from a well-controlled epilepsy all her life, and finds herself, at the time when I met her, embroiled in a major life confusion with regard to her emotional relationships. Mirella had emerged from a seven-year relationship which helped form her as an adult person, but before long, she became involved in another, "impossible" relationship with a man who was already in another relationship.

Mirella agreed to a "polyamorous" emotional situation because fundamentally she felt, and continues to feel endangered by her emotions. She had been left by her first, long-term partner because, as she says, she had "disappointed him." This has likely caused a deep cleavage in her self-value and self-perception: on the one end of the psychological cliff, she "hangs out" in life with her desire to reinforce her ego and her self-love as a woman. The other end of the gorge is rejection. When we spoke, she believed that my moral neutrality and understanding would extend to an uncritical acceptance of her choices and active support for them. She described her relationship with a person who was already emotionally committed as being an instantiation of her "freedom" and her choosing to freely exercise her emotions, which were considerable. Thus, her expectation was that I would embrace this context and work with her to define her choices in an atmosphere of approval and sympathy.

However, when we focused on her life plan, it became apparent not only that there was none, but that she had trouble identifying even the most basic boundaries of her personal identity. This opened up a major space for therapy; however, Mirella's need for self-valuation was severely bent toward receiving attention as a woman, so any "professional" approach which respected the boundaries hystericized Mirella. This very phenomenology meant that the analysis was actually beginning to be effective (the phenomenon that analysis always first hystericizes the person and then helps her consolidate her experience and values is an axiom in psychoanalysis). To build a new value structure or new stances toward life, the old values and stances first need to be torn down, and this experience is invariably traumatizing or at least displeasing. Thus, my communication with Mirella was promising, but I felt that any continuation of this work was exceptionally demanding and probably transgressed my energy and abilities for two reasons that most therapists face to various extents. The first was Mirella's determination to be recognized as a woman first and specifically to be accepted as a desirable woman in the face of her eccentric love life elsewhere. This alone meant the violation of some of the boundaries which, if crossed, would likely open up a process where major damage to Mirella was at least as likely as potential benefits or as likely as any personal growth.

In other words, in the described situation there seemed to exist no other way forward but to transgress the boundaries, because she refused any alternative; however, this only way was so fraught with controversy that it was clear that I could not venture that way. Connected to this was the fact that Mirella had elicited a strong father–daughter type of counter-transfer in me. I found it very difficult not to see her as a victim of her crisis of self-esteem, and this made me desire to "save" her: one of the basic situations which suggest that one should no longer engage in the specific case. The reason is that often, when psychotherapists "save" their clients, that happens exactly by crossing the boundaries in a way which additionally disorients the client, but also places the therapist in a normative wilderness, where finding one's personal, as well as therapeutic, bearings is extremely difficult. Although I generally do now have qualms crossing some types of boundaries, in this situation, with the particular sexual type of boundaries being at stake, obviously the boundaries needed to be kept intact in every way. The result was Mirella's strong antagonization.

Unable to discuss Mirella's life plan, or even her life goals, our discourse collapsed into discussions of emotions alone, but we touched upon the values of responsibility and structural limitation arising from others' legitimate expectations of Mirella, which she perceived as breaks on her "liberty." She felt that our discussion had additionally confirmed her insufficient value as a woman and decided that she would "continue towards love" with a person who was already committed and in a situation that was obviously destined to unproductively hurt both her and potentially some other persons (the man's other partner and potentially the man himself).

It seems to me that Mirella's predicament is her cry for recognition which is so strong that it is not receptive to any rational boundaries, and this type of case in deep therapy requires a degree of recklessness, both by the client and the therapist, an inroad which might have indeed led to some equilibrium, but which I was unwilling to follow. Thus, our session was unsuccessful by Mirella's lights. I felt that it was partially successful, in the sense that both Mirella and I had come to important insights and, if we were ever to work in the future, had something to work with. However, Mirella emerged from our session with a sense of being devalued and rejected for her desire to exercise her "freedom": the same feeling that she reported experiencing from her relationship with her parents. She even remarked to me, when I saw her awake and sobbing in the middle of the night, during the first night of our planned two-day retreat: "You are the combination of my parents, which is the worst possible combination." She was definitely hystericized constructively, but, extremely agitated and unhappy, she experienced the hystericizing phase of the analysis as a traumatizing experience. I ended the session halfway, after the first night and for Mirella this meant yet another level of rejection; however, I felt that with the intensity of the transfer going for the full format which was initially planned would be beyond my energy and ability to stay focused.

Both Sally and Mirella are fundamentally unhappy women. Sally believes that having a family and children is the only thing that would fulfill her as a woman; however, in her mid-thirties she remains alone and fairly closed to relationships, or at least so it seemed in initial contact. Mirella, on the other hand, is undergoing a belated psychological "growing up" and acts from what transactional analysts call "the ego state of a child." The predominant ego state of Sally is that of a grown-up. Although Sally is superior in terms of personal maturity, she is less active and suffers less from loss than Mirella, and this is likely to push Mirella to resolve her issues sooner than Sally. Another difference is that Sally has a clear life plan; however, in her routine there is *no dynamism* that would cause her to set goals toward the achievement of that life plan. Thus, the long-term predicament of Sally, given her goals, seems gloomier than that of Mirella, even though Mirella's quality of life is lower and her level of daily agitation is higher than Sally's.

The difference lies in the principle that in order to move toward a new goal, one must feel both the attraction of the goal itself *and a level of discomfort* with one's present situation. Without discomfort in the present, change is very difficult, if not impossible.

Negative emotions are as important to achieving a life plan as positive emotions are.

One of the clearest examples where the absence of life plans due to confused and poorly articulated emotions leads to catastrophic consequences in counseling occurs in family-related issues where individuals focus on specific experiences and goals developed in particular phases of their early adult life, while forgetting that, as Mirella put it to me, "Our bodies cannot wait the way our minds can." The result is that many such individuals, focusing on specific, expected significant others in their lives, while neglecting to even observe the here-and-now of their actual new encounters and life events, remain family-less and child-less even though they state that having a family is their number one priority in life. This is a very strange situation, however, an exceptionally common one: a person claims to know exactly what the guiding value in their life is, *however their life goals do not include that value at all*, and the explanation they tend to give is that these are the "current goals," where the "real goals," the *core goals* of their life, will *come later*.

We are all prone to self-forgetting in the described way. Illogical as it is to deal with the most important things last, and with the most trivial things first—when one has the most potential, it is a rule, rather than an exception. This frequent misconception about life priorities shows just how important a well-developed life plan is. Contrary to the popular belief that plans stifle spontaneity, in fact, *plans elicit spontaneity*, because when a person is aware of a general life plan, they are able to position their goals within that plan and the activity to attain the goals is followed by a higher-level certainty that—should the goal be achieved—a solid and sound life plan, likely to lead to the person's overall satisfaction, will be solidified. This makes striving for goals more energetic and effective, and the overall enjoyment of the process greater because the person has a sense of meaning and broader context of their desires and endeavors.

An often-overlooked aspect of life plans is that they are more effective when they unfold along more dramatic scenarios, where experiences are varied and dynamic. Even the most ideal life plan, like a perfectly happy plot for a film, will likely collapse because there is not enough drive in it to motivate the person, just like a perfectly happy film will be difficult to watch to the end unless there is at least some frustration or struggle to achieve the happiness. Thus, life plans, when they are masterfully developed, include various curves on the way to the goal, adapted to the most likely life situations. One most obvious example is delays. Any complex plan of action, and thus also a life plan, tends to be temporalized, or divided into certain temporal benchmarks, where certain phases of life are dominated by specific life goals, inculcating delays and obstacles such as personal trauma, loss of loved ones, breakup of important social and emotional relationships, and so on. Such obstacles and curves in the achievement process not only make the life plan more practical, but add drama to it and make it more experientially attractive to the very actors of the life plan, to us. Many times, people have a problem dedicating themselves to a goal they are rationally fully aware is key to their future, simply because that goal is *dull.* Adding color to life plans by bringing them closer to actual life, with its pain and suffering, as well as with its joy, makes it easier to actually handle the life plan and work effectively to implement it.

I have mentioned before the concept that being unhappy with, or feeling pain with regard to, an aspect of the current life situation, is a precondition for moving on. It is very difficult to change anything if one does not feel acute pain, and this applies to different degrees to Sally and Mirella. While Sally has a "rounded up life," as she calls it, Mirella is unemployed, bursts into occasional conflicts with her parents, with whom she lives, and senses an inadequacy that moves her in different directions, meaning that she is more prone to stepping "out of her comfort zone." Thus, although Mirella is in a more precarious life situation than Sally in terms of her independence and ability to sustain herself financially, she is in a more promising psychological situation because she is searching for changes that will bring stability and security to her life. Sally, on the other hand, does not feel acute pain: she is following a well-set path both in terms of her career and in her social life; she does not sense the need to veer off that path in any way, and thus stays the course that will only take her to one potential end, or to a failure to achieve that end. Sally is not emotionally open to different options, simply because she lacks *the blessing of discomfort* with her current situation. That is how she might come to a dead end when it is too late for important changes in values and life tactics.

It is difficult to overemphasize the practical importance of a life plan in integrative counseling, in the same way in which it is difficult to overemphasize the importance of context for the meaning of any sentence or utterance. Our life goals have little practical value without the light cast on them by our life plans, and the quality and substance of our life plans and our strategies to implement them are the proper subjects of discussion in counseling. Unfortunately, very often counseling cannot focus on life plans because life goals of the moment take precedence, and this typically leads to emotional imbalances that require other types of intervention to stabilize and strengthen the person prior to even starting a proper philosophical or integrative work on clarifying the life plans.

The life plan is a form our endeavors take, considered as a system of action. It is what Wittgenstein calls "form," which he defines as "the possibility of a structure." The more structure we are able to implement in our lives, the better ordered, more predictable, and more enjoyable our life is likely to be. Contrariwise, the less structure, the more confusion and chance, the less satisfying in the long run our life will likely be: this does not mean that it will be completely devoid of temporary thrill and the excitement associated with uncertainty; however, the long-term effects of this uncertainty will degrade the quality of our life as a whole.

Structure is the *sine qua non* of a high quality of life, and while one can vary this structure, change one's priorities and life goals, amend and even completely replace one's life plan, such changes contribute to the quality of life and to our identity if they are consistently implemented within a structure of decision-making. Even if I decide to abandon my academic life and start from scratch working as a karate kata instructor in a remote part of the world, this decision may be the result of a structured process whereby I have decided to change my key values and priorities, and to embrace the life of a karate kata coach as opposed to that of a university professor. The fact that the change is drastic does not mean that it is not structured, just as any minor change might be the result of confusion, poor decision-making, and lack of structured priorities and values. To have a strong structure of beliefs and values means to have a strong identity, and the decisions made by persons with a strong identity will tend to carry a part of that strength with them; it will likely pave their way to the execution of their plans and life goals.

Given that emotions dynamize our choices and actions, that they are the fuel of our life, where rational explanations come only afterward as a sort of justification of the decisions made intuitively, through the body, and through the emotions that we also experience through the body, it appears exceptionally practically important to posit *emotions in an appropriate social context.* The traditional way of looking at emotions is as primarily individual affects: one experiences an emotion as a reaction to some type of experience, which refers in various ways to the person's important values. In some cases, emotions can be spread, through "emotional infection," to entire collectives, such as in campaigns of political radicalization; however, *sui generis* they are individual—they are personal affects.

This view does not tell us the whole story about the actual cultivation of emotions, specifically regarding the role of an organic community in developing and setting in motion different emotions between the members of a group. Closely belonging to a group greatly enhances the likelihood that the specific desired emotions between individual members of the group will develop because the group offers a guaranteeing environment that is safe and permeated with links and assumptions of trust and mutual likeness between individuals, all of which eliminate many of the otherwise common hindrances to emotions, such as mutual unfamiliarity or distrust. Individuals are able to focus on one another in light of the mutual belonging to the same community, which is characterized by a network of positive emotions; thus, they are set off on a trajectory of mutual collaboration and potential affection, without the prior meandering in the typical value- and emotional confusion that characterizes the heterogeneous and loosely connected society at large. This is why social organization in smaller, tightly knit groups of friends and associates accelerates emotional transactions and reduces the costs of such transactions, thus allowing for faster and more fulfilling interpersonal relationships.

The immersion in a community is a *catalyst for emotions*, both positive and negative. Members of the community are closer to one another than members of the society at large, and as such they are both able to experience more from one another than in the general society, and they also have the opportunity to react to one another in more direct and better-informed ways. The guaranteeing role of the community also reflects on the mutual perceptions of the identities of members of the group, as the very membership in a group partly constitutes their identity. Hence, the sentiment and ethos of group interactions carry over into the individual's one-to-one interpersonal relationships and allow for a smoother expression of personal specificities. This is the reason individuals tend to establish intimate relationships with others who belong to the same interest, profession, or social groups; however, this is also reason to consider *group membership a form of therapy* for a variety of psychological and identity disorders.

The Significance of the "Here and Now"

In modern psychotherapy, much attention is paid to the concept of "here and now," specifically with a view of making decisions and focusing on the quality of life in the present, as opposed to engaging in detailed explorations of the past or overly careful anticipations of the future consequences of our present choices. The focus on the here-and-now is thus often considered to be a healing perspective on numerous life difficulties. However, there is a philosophical and a corresponding practical side to the here-and-now that needs to be taken into account.

The here-and-now must be cast in a diachronic perspective. The synchronic perspective is one that focuses on an isolated point in time. Synchronically, I am not writing this chapter of this book. The diachronic perspective covers a longer stretch of time: diachronically, I have written this book over the course of the past two years. It is the *synchronic moment in a diachronic perspective* that gives meaning to individual decisions and choices made in that moment. The diachronic perspective does not entail that the synchronic moment will be treated as merely leading to a future, but in the form of a life plan it allows the full execution of a life goal coherent with the life plan in the synchronic moment, in the here-and-now. The meaning of the synchronic moment, of the here-and-now, is given by the overarching diachronic context; however, the main dynamism of decisions is contained in that trigger of synchronic contraction of time and experience which sparks off a move from one modal world to another, from one frame of mind, which defines the question or dilemma, to another one, which articulates the decision, the answer.

This seemingly complex temporal structure of decision-making unfolds all the time in practical counseling, where issues of meaning arise with regard to the random here-and-now. In such situations, individuals often seek spontaneous meanings associated with a sequence of events, or the potential coherences between various events, especially when they coincide in time; however, they lack the capacity to "grab" the here-and-now with or without its associated meanings and synchronicities, and to draw the synchronic here-and-now into a diachronic conceptual framework of their life plan. I should like to become briefly involved here in a logical discussion of why a life plan is necessary for a high-quality understanding of life goals in the here-and-now.

Some of the opening statements of Wittgenstein's *Tractatus* include the following:

1. The world is all that is the case.
2. What is the case, or fact, is the existence of states of affairs.
3. A logical picture of facts is a thought.
4. A proposition is a truth function of elementary propositions.

These starting principles of how we logically understand reality can be cast specifically upon our life-world in psychotherapy.

The first principle is that our own reality is what is the case for us. This means that the facts of my life determine my life, though perhaps other facts determine someone else's life, or the same facts that play a key part in my life play only a marginal or no role in someone else's life. Thus, the first task of psychotherapy is to dialogically articulate the life-world of a person: what facts, in Wittgenstein's sense of the world, are relevant for that person. In establishing those facts, the psychotherapist focuses on the here-and-now.

The synchronic situation where the contraction of the conversation occurs and churns up the key facts about the person's life-world involves not only the words exchanged in the conversation but also the behavior of the interlocutor and the language of metaphorical and tacit meanings that grow and develop between the therapist and the client. This language gradually turns into a relationship. In time, the therapist and the client develop their own taste and language for every here-and-now of their encounters. Only after such special language is built can the facts of someone's life be properly established and factored into a therapeutic approach. This is why schematic psychotherapy based on general patterns of interpretation or intervention fundamentally misses the target of the deepest values and fractures in our personalities that fundamentally cause us to seek counseling. Once the principle that our world is all that is the case in our life is stripped of its absolute validity in psychotherapy and the facts of life are fitted into some kind of "general issues," the precision and logical rigor of psychotherapy are lost.

The difference between the way we see our clients in psychotherapy and the way we see our friends whom we care about dearly is that too often, we immerse ourselves in the life-world of our friend and try to see the world through their eyes, while in psychotherapy the therapist tends to take the position of an "expert," though a friendly and unassuming one, and views the client's "issues," "symptoms," "problems," or "phenomena" in light of their own (the therapist's) learned patterns of interpretation, rather than seeing the complete states of affairs that make up the client's life-world. This is the main reason I advocate what is largely an *obliteration of the distinction between a therapist and a friend*, and the establishment of an *organic therapeutic union* between the two people who inevitably become friends in the process.

Going back to Sally, I became obsessed, though briefly, with this person who had difficulties communicating, poor social skills, and a detached perspective on her own life, almost devoid of emotions. I had no information to go with other than a very limited observation. She volunteered no testimony about her feelings. One dawn I woke up with the conclusion that Sally must be schizophrenic. This was a wild conclusion, unsupported by any serious evidence, but one that required checking. I immediately wrote to a friend who knew Sally. She had said that there were things she, as her friend, could not tell me, which Sally "needed to tell me herself." I wrote to her that I believed Sally was schizoid in her presentation of her life-world and asked whether she had ever been given the label of schizophrenia. The response was: "You put it so beautifully, her schizoid personality. Yes, and she fears judgement and rejection."

Now, diagnoses are of limited value in philosophical practice; in fact, they can be a hindrance to therapy. However, in some cases, diagnoses are useful descriptions of one's life-world, of the states of affairs in one's life, which help establish communication with the person. If the person is told that they are schizoid, they will likely take it as an alibi to continue acting in a detached and non-emotional way toward others, and sometimes, as with Sally, this will simply mean that they will focus exclusively on their own needs. Living a life where one does not care about anybody else, makes no sacrifices for others and does not see their own life, their most treasured personal values, in light of something greater than themselves—of some other person, a cause, or philosophy—is necessarily limiting and dulling.

Sally thus travels with her older friend who is also single, not too successful in her career; she spends holidays with her friend, works in private practice, and is very affluent. However, all she does concerns only one person: herself. She cannot get out of this cycle until she becomes genuinely interested in someone else and starts subsuming her needs and desires to the *desires of another.* Only thus will she become deeply relationally, structurally connected to her life-world and will start to receive an identity-based confirmation of her own personal value.

In the above sense, the here-and-now is a check of direction of the life plan. In ancient Nordic cultures, there was widespread belief that leaders of tribes and communities were qualified for their leadership positions by gods' affection. Thus, people were willing to fight and die for their leader because they believed that they would be rewarded by the gods for following their chosen leader. However, there was a here-and-now check on whether the gods were still on a leader's side. If difficulties mounted and the leader's plans fell through consistently, the community asked themselves whether the gods were still on the leader's side, or if the leader should be removed and replaced. This is a principle that applies to all life plans. We check the validity, productivity, and quality of our life plans through the here-and-now. There is, however, a big difference between using the here-and-now as a check on longer-term plans and using it as the only relevant perspective for decision-making. The here-and-now makes little sense without the context of longer-term values and plans. It is one of the dominant ways in which individual life goals, often uncritically adopted from the culture, the society, or the narrow social circle, may actually militate against high-quality life plans and cause the person to end up deadlocked in successes that don't matter, while being ultimately deprived of the values that one considers constitutive of one's own self-realization.

Another problem with life plans and the here-and-now concerns the affective content of the synchronic moment. The way in which we experience satisfaction is focused on the here-and-now. It is very easy to confuse this affective content with what is right or wrong, with what is productive or counterproductive in our life plans. Hence the common focus on "happiness" or on "feeling good" in the moment, and the equally common, yet deeply misguided, advice people receive in psychotherapy to "focus on what makes them feel good," by implication in the here-and-now, in the making of important life decisions, in reacting to important relationships or life situations which may develop into life-defining ones.

One of the more common situations of the attachment of wrong meaning to the here-and-now in terms of the value of its affective content is one where clients in psychotherapy report having received therapeutic advice to "cease communication" with other persons, in cases where the communication is stressful or unpleasant to them. While every case should be judged on its own merits, a general approach whereby individuals are encouraged to cut communications with others whenever that communication makes them feel unpleasant is doubly damaging to the client: first, it infantilizes the client, because this kind of behavior is characteristic of young children, who react to pleasure and displeasure by simply moving closer to pleasure and running away from displeasure. Such an approach to relationships makes it impossible for the person to deepen their interpersonal links and understanding of others and condemns them to a fairly superficial social existence, where dependency on the psychotherapist remains the only relatively profound relationship and becomes increasingly pronounced in the person's everyday routine.

Secondly, the above approach leads the client away from wandering about key issues in their lifelong perspective on their personal "world" in Wittgenstein's sense. By focusing excessively on the here-and-now, one can gradually create a life that has very little connection with what one would reflectively choose as one's life path. This is a very serious problem, both existentially and methodologically, in therapeutic encounters, because the continued focus on the affective content of the here-and-now absorbs large swaths of time and thus incapacitates the person to engage in pursuing life goals that become unattainable with the passage of time. Such situations can have a devastating effect on overall life satisfaction. Not acting on some life goals because to do so in the present would be unpleasant might cause a situation where once one decides to act on the same goals they are no longer reachable, such as in situations where opportunities no longer exist, or one is too old, or some other type of key condition is no longer met. If the value that defines such life goals is a core one, this could mean forfeiting key aspects of life satisfaction, even the meaning of life. This is just one of the dangers of psychotherapy that is too mellow and focused on the client's "feelings," rather than balancing the feelings with meaning.

The here-and-now is not our world by itself: it is merely a fragment of our world in the sense described by Wittgenstein's above-stated propositions. To make the here-and-now an accurate picture of our world as a whole is an art, a skill that takes considerable practice to develop; however, to merely assume, as is often the case, that the factual here-and-now is the only, or even the primary, framework for our decision-making and for our judgments of our own life situation is profoundly mistaken and can lead to the definition of a sequence of life goals that will lead us away from, rather than toward, the implementation of our life plan. Thus, we must first seek to grasp the "over-all truth" of what Wittgenstein describes as a totality of states of affairs that make up our own life-world in order to determine the relative significance of any specific here-and-now in that totality. The other name for a grasp of the totality and the process whereby we give normative meaning to that grasp is life plan.

If, logically speaking, we treat a life plan as a proposition, then Wittgenstein's above idea that "a proposition is a truth function of elementary propositions" suggests that the "truth" or validity of various life goals and the various reasonings, priorities, and existential situations which we experience in any specific here-and-now is a more elementary proposition, and that such elementary propositions receive their truthfulness or falsity, their very meaning, from a broader proposition which is the very truth function of these elementary events. In other words, whether any specific here-and-now is the truth of our lives will depend on what our life plan is. If we perceive the here-and-now in the context of our life plan, then however it turns out in the present it will be the truth with regard to that life plan.

If we meet someone who might be a potential life partner to us, then assuming that our life plan is to establish such a life partnership, treating that person and that encounter specifically in light of that life plan will fairly directly and clearly deliver the truth about whether or not the person can fit in our life plan.

Assuming that we are able to have an explicit conversation about our intentions and our life plan, it is possible that we might get a clear, explicit clarification of whether or not this person validates our here-and-now with regard to our life plan. There are other less explicit ways to establish this fact. However, if we don't approach the person from a specific point of view of our life plan, we might create perceptions that might cause the person to fit, but this fit will sooner or later prove to simply lead us *away* from our primary truth, from our life plan. The difference between the two approaches can cause considerable suffering later, a considerable loss of time and may divert our attention from other persons who might indeed be a fit to our propositional truth in our life, namely to our life plan.

There are many similar examples that equally illustrate the crucial role of a life plan in approaching the here-and-now. The role of the life plan is to illuminate the here-and-now, endow it with meaning, and facilitate a clearer vision of the decisions to be made and life goals to be articulated in the here-and-now.

One of the key problems with the present moment and our articulation of its meaning is how to establish its relationship with the broader "truth" of a life plan. Wittgenstein's understanding of the contextual proposition being the truth function of more elementary propositions (momentary situations, convictions, or attitudes) allows a holistic understanding of the validity of a life plan. Namely, the life plan is not merely a list of desires or the vision of a desired state of affairs which is sufficiently broad to span most of our life. Rather, it is an action plan that requires clear priorities, a grasp of fairly precise values, and a conceptualization of the skills required to attain those values.

The life plan is like a complex operation blueprint that envisages situations of decision-making in less-than-ideal circumstances. To articulate such a plan and implement it in detail requires constant practice, in the same way that executing a perfect military operation requires the development of a high level of skills and coordination between military personnel. Without a clear plan, most complex military operations would be doomed, and the same is the case with our lives. The main difference is that no competent military officer ever even contemplates engaging in military action without a plan, while most of us, especially in our dynamic, Western cultures, live large swaths of our lives completely without a plan, based on life goals that we routinely mistake for a proper life plan. The result is that at relatively late stages of our lives we find out that we had taken mistaken paths and ended up in a scenario and in circumstances that have little or nothing to do with our desired outcomes or values.

In all of its described meanings, the here-and-now can be seen as a kind of *laboratory* for the making of decisions: while decisions crystallize themselves in the present moment and occur almost instantaneously, their broader context is much longer than the here-and-now; thus the way we make decisions in the here-and-now illuminates the way in which we are, or the way in which we are not, aware of our own life-world—of that totality of the "states of affairs" Wittgenstein writes about.

The here-and-now is not a mystical perspective in which we are able to cut across the layers of our otherwise complicated past and anticipated future: it is an indication, a "diagnosis" of the way in which we see our world. It is thus a correct conclusion that our acting in the here-and-now is the picture of our world, of all those states of affairs which, as elementary statements, contribute to the overall truth value of our complex perceptions included in our life plan. However, the vice versa also holds: the existence, and quality, of a life plan informs and facilitates all the decisions in the here-and-now. This latter fact is often overlooked in the formulation of life goals and in the therapeutic reception of the here-and-now as "the magical moment" of self-transformation and self-development.

How Are Life Goals and Life Plans Manipulated?

Ideally, our life plans and life goals should flow from a natural order of events in our lives: our youth, middle, and old age, as well as the priorities that each of these phases of our lives brings. There is a logic associated with the natural circumstances of our existence that does not really need to be elaborated. However, society and individuals alike can manipulate the perceptions of these priorities, and thus also our life plans and life goals, with various purposes in mind, including those that can be characterized as pathological, such as the need for control. Such manipulation is very widespread and deserves to be discussed here in the context of frequent issues faced in psychotherapy in modern Western society.

One of the major problems of common psychopathology in modern societal circumstances is that of control. The ability to control events and relationships in our life projects our power, and the need for power and influence makes us feel more secure and enhances our sense of self-worth. However, when control cannot be exercised despite a pronounced need for self-confirmation, occasionally individuals, as well as political regimes and governments, will resort to manipulative strategies to exercise subconscious control over others. Such manipulations tend to be fairly complicated and, just like most other complicated maneuvers in human relationships, they become breeding grounds for pathology. Governments may use coercion to exercise control over their subjects, but a constant reliance on the use of force is difficult to sustain. "You can do many things with bayonets, but it is rather uncomfortable to sit on them" (Harari, 2015: 125). Thus arises the need for governments to produce a number of "believers" in certain values and manipulated principles, so that a culture might be established in which it would be a common expectation of all "decent people" to actually conform to the manipulated norms. Any ideology, even when it is enforced with guns, survives on its true believers: without the "soldiers" of ideology, it would collapse with the first crack in the enforcement structure which imposes it on society.

The same is the case with individual manipulation. Individuals who have a strong need to control a group of people, to be popular among friends and to be recognized as leaders in order to value themselves adequately, will develop incredible skills to connect to our conscious and unconscious life goals, needs, fears, and life plans, "hack into them," and thus control our actions, choices, and reasons.

Our belief in certain values, ideologies, or simply in other people is the strongest motivating factor that keeps us connected to a pattern of behavior. Skilled manipulators use people's belief in them to factually control the behavior, actions, and even reasoning of others. This is how sects operate: a charismatic leader, who is often seen by members of the sect as an empathetic person concerned with everybody else's welfare, is granted unconditional trust, and this allows the leader to manipulate members of the group into all kinds of controversial, even suicidal, behavior. They end up living lives secluded from the rest of society, thus avoiding the regular perceptual checks arising from a comparison with the choices and actions of other members of society. More often than not, they develop their own "special actions," or routines, which affirm their special identity and their values, which increasingly drive them away from the mainstream community. In the end, they might be prepared to go to extreme lengths to protect those values, including engaging in armed conflict with the police or in mass suicide.

The psychology of the sects is based on the well-known mechanism of "soldiers' trust." The "soldiers" of various ideologies, whether they are the soldiers of capitalism, or of democracy, or of an ideology that portrays a particular nation as chosen and special, or soldiers of any other kind of conviction, are the bedrock of any system that supports that ideology or system of beliefs.

The same principle that applies to general societal structures such as ideologies, governments, the military, or religion also applies to small informal groups. If a person is able to establish themselves as the focal point of trust by various members of a group, that person, if they are malignant, will be able to control the group and the group's interpersonal relationships. They will work carefully to establish structures of psychological and even existential dependency of individual group members on their person, their business, or their general support, and will use that influence to cause the group members to make decisions and reach choices that they had determined for those individuals.

In sects, the control over the members of the group rests with the special relationship that each group member establishes with the leader, who is at the same time the lead manipulator. Sects operate based on the manipulative leader's prerogative to control all communications, namely to possess privileged access to communications between the group's members, and to exert a normative influence on members with regard to their mutual relationships. Part of the strategy to control the sect is to ban communication between specific members of the group, namely those who, if left to communicate in an unhindered way, might question the leader's right or ability to exert control, and might develop spontaneous relationships which will challenge the leader's complete authority. Thus, individuals in a sect are allowed or disallowed by the leader to establish mutual relationships: all of their relationships are mediated by the leader.

The normative structure of the group is centered on the leader/manipulator, whereby the leader himself or herself might actually believe that they are doing good for the group; they may perceive themselves as benevolent and concerned about their constituents. The problem here is that pathological projection, fantasy, and imagination on the part of the manipulator generate the imaginary symbolic world in which all of the others unwittingly participate.

In the course of writing this book, I experienced a social situation in a group that I was leading which largely exemplified this sect-like mentality. In a group concerned with psychotherapy, which had become increasingly close as friends and collaborators, one of the members introduced her own social circle, specifically targeting the men in the group, by inviting eligible and available young women. The dynamics of the ensuing social events were such that some men became interested in some of the women, and vice versa, resulting in at least one functional relationship developing from the setting. However, in some other cases the leader/manipulator, namely the member of the group who had introduced her own group into the psychotherapy group, decided that she needed to control all of the relationships, so she assumed a superimposed position above all of the other developing interactions, accumulated exclusive information from all the participants in the exchanges, and used this monopoly of information to factually determine the development of the relationships, basically stifling all of them. This ability to first incite relationships, and then suffocate them by manipulating information, gave the manipulator a sense of power that was fundamental to her self-appreciation.

The results of this strategy by a group member were all negative. The first one was that, due to the disappointments induced by her controlling behavior, the psychotherapeutic group contracted and ejected most of the members of the other group from their social circle. This was reflected in a change in the structure of online discussion forums, which were changed so that the person inducing her friends as agents of her control of group inter-relationships was removed from administrative functions in those groups. The second outcome was a cooling of the relationships between the psychotherapeutic group members and that particular person, including her relationship with me. The third outcome was the cutting of the group member away from most group activities, after she had continued to try to incite uncertainties and enthusiasm for relationships between group members and her social group, with an obvious aim to remain "important." The ultimate result of this strategy to become important was the opposite of what the manipulator intended: she became *the least important* member of the psychotherapeutic group, and all of the other members displayed a reserved attitude toward her, ignoring her initiatives to the extent that they did not even comment on her ideas voiced online.

The described scenario applies in healthy groups when a sect mentality is attempted to be introduced in such groups. When toxicity is sensed by an otherwise functional and free group, its members will simply try to isolate and eliminate the source of toxicity. However, this requires recognition of the toxic influence from an early stage because if the infiltration of the group by manipulative relationships had been allowed to progress unchecked, the group would have been destroyed by divisions and shifting loyalties, all of which would have impacted the therapeutic and educational processes alive in the group very adversely.

The clearest way in which a healthy group will fend off manipulative strategies is by maintaining a singular vision of its goals and plans. If the group is constantly aware that its plan is to develop a community of psychotherapists who will be able to support each other and who will produce increasingly significant practical and scientific results, then the group will be able to determine when the effects of someone's manipulation militate against such a plan and such goals. The souring of the intra-group relationship is one example of such influence. A reduced ability to work and collaborate is another. The sapping of the group's energy and enthusiasm is a third one.

Manipulation of life goals and life plans occurs when a particular desire, or fantasy, is smuggled in as a life plan or life goal. The desire to establish a meaningful romantic relationship, or a fantasy about bringing together work and private fulfillment in a relationship, is offered to group members as a suitable replacement, even a synonym, for their established plans and goals within the group. Instead of focusing on their plans and goals, they start focusing on more particular pursuits with other individuals, while forgetting, or neglecting, the fact that these are not entirely spontaneous pursuits, but rather ones engineered by the manipulator. The shift in group dynamics from clear and legitimate plans and goals to more shady areas mixing the private and the public, the intimate and the professional, is seen by the manipulator as a source of satisfaction and confirmation of their power and influence. Gradually, the manipulator will move the focus of the entire group to these alternative goals and strategies, causing the group to lose its purpose. A sense of deep-seated dissatisfaction and misdirection will set in the group, causing it to dissipate. The manipulator will then "chase after" some members of the group, or some remaining relationships, attempting to reassemble them into a structure of influence. The net outcome will be a loss rather than gain: manipulation is always destined for destruction.

One of the "economic" ways to look at problematic relationships is that they are not overall beneficial: instead of creating a net gain in an imagined transaction occurring through the relationship, the particular interaction creates a loss. For example, a healthy relationship between two people who are looking to become romantic partners will result either in a partnership or in some other kind of beneficial outcome, including a friendship, an alliance, or at least a generally positive disposition toward each other. An interaction between two groups, such as the one described earlier in this section, would be healthy if it creates a positive value: if the new links between the members of the two groups contributed to their satisfaction, social capital and strength, or merely established new acquaintances which would open up new avenues of communication and exchange. However, if the interaction of the two groups creates friction, tension, suspicions, and divisions in one or both of the groups, that shows that the interaction is not healthy, that it is toxic and, in the described case, that it is the product of pathological manipulation.

The reason the person described in this section manipulated the two groups was not necessarily malignant in the sense that she was pursuing a rationally chosen destructive goal: it was pathological manipulation because it offered the manipulator a satisfaction arising from a sense of control. Clearly, such pronounced need for control arises from its opposite, from a deep-seated sense of lack of control over one's life or one's important life events; thus, the obsession with controlling others becomes a tool for the person to comfort herself for not being able to control herself and her own feelings. This is a similar situation as with hyperactivity: a hyperactive person who cannot sit still for a moment, who constantly travels, seeks thrills and engages with other people to the extent of exhaustion is usually one who is afraid of facing loneliness and her own depths. Likewise, a manipulator obsessed with control is afraid of what they feel as a fundamental lack of control in the very core of their life experience.

Obviously, one way to address manipulation in groups is to focus on the source of the pathology, namely on the manipulator, and to seek to compensate the desires that the manipulator exhibits by healthy interactions. This would mean establishing links of collaboration and healthy recognition, whereby the manipulator would be able to obtain the satisfaction of self-worth without needing to engage in controlling their social environment. One of the ways in which this could be achieved is by therapeutically explicating the life goals and life plans, and by working to help the person achieve those in a palpable, socially recognized way.

Another frequent issue with the deliberate manipulation of others in the context of their life plans and life goals is that associated with narcissistic dynamics in intimate relationships. Many clients in psychotherapy complain of having been manipulated by their partners, whereby they were forced into submissive positions where they found themselves "surviving" day after day, waiting for a promised satisfaction or happy moment to be afforded by the other partner, never knowing whether, even when that moment comes, the event or interaction will be canceled by the other. The narcissistic goal is the narcissist's control of others in order to increase a disturbed sense of the narcissist's self-worth. This sense can be damaged by a variety of life events, from an illness (especially mental illness) to a painful rejection or relationship breakup. The person then sets one's goals and uses others to increase their own sense of subjective worth, typically by causing others to suffer and to depend on her goodwill. The most typical dynamics include the narcissist's attempts to draw the victim's attention, followed by collaborative or otherwise likable behavior in order to establish a "click" or a connection with the victim. Once the victim opens up emotionally to the narcissist and becomes interested in deepening the relationship, the narcissist draws back, to provoke a reaching out. Each time the victim reaches out to the narcissist, this gratifies the narcissistic longing for self-confirmation and causes the narcissist to incite further reaching out, which they do by offering minimum encouragement before drawing back again, usually more radically than the first time. This pattern continues until it completely drains the victim of energy or sets her on a course of mental illness, because the victim is thus manipulated into a situation of inferiority and emotional dependency, where she awaits whether the narcissist will call, send a message or say something encouraging, while the narcissist appears to thrive on the suffering and submission of the victim.

Narcissistic motivation is typically both conscious and unconscious. On a conscious level, the narcissist has specific outcomes that they want to achieve by causing others to behave in a certain way. On an unconscious level, the narcissist works to satisfy their craving for self-valuation, completely oblivious, or indifferent, to the suffering of others, which is in fact the source of that satisfaction. This latter aspect of narcissistic exploitation of others is often the reason for ascribing sadistic traits to the narcissists.

During the writing of this book, I had a student by the name of Nataly, who was extremely ambitious. Nataly tried to attract my attention to her in the only way she could, given that the teaching was online due to the pandemic of Covid-19, and the technical constraints of teaching large classes online, over limited screens, imply that the lecturer does not even see all of the students who are online at the same time, but only those who speak or are otherwise active. Thus, Nataly made sure that she was active during my classes from the very first encounter and proceeded to assist me in the organization of student presentations. This gave her the opportunity to send me emails and chat messages in order to coordinate with me the presentations for each week.

At one point, I met with Nataly and some other students during face-to-face consultations, and we spent several hours together. In her mid-thirties, thin and dark-skinned, Nataly was very unusual as a person, and this made her stand out from the crowd. She openly spoke about her mental illness and her intimate relationships, about her fears and expectations, exhibiting extraordinary vulnerability, which, to all of us, was charming. Not long after this, I found myself immersed in online communications with Nataly that were increasingly private in nature, where we discussed our personal lives on a friendly basis. She had been an (unsuccessful) student of philosophy prior to completing her other degree and enrolling in postgraduate studies where I taught her, so this was another point of commonality between us, the field of philosophy. Nataly played her vulnerability to the point where I became used to our conversations, and we decided to meet for drinks during the day. However, Nataly canceled the coffee just a few hours before it was to occur. At first, I did not pay much attention to this, as I was busy at the time and I almost welcomed the cancellation; however, Nataly then stopped communicating with me for a month. Again, this was odd, but I did not see it as particularly interesting, until at one stage Nataly again tried to come close to me, followed by moving away, and repeatedly so, this time putting forward expectations that I would support her in her academic career.

At the exam, Nataly did worse than she expected, so the somewhat lower grade that she received antagonized her, and she decided that she was not going to take my course the following semester, although it was obligatory for her, and asked me to allow her an exception, which I did. However, immediately afterward, Nataly came to see me and asked me to be the supervisor of her thesis and help with papers which she needed to prepare for publication as a precondition for work on the thesis. I agreed, but then Nataly again cut off contact and became difficult to collaborate with. When I complained about this and said that I would not be able to work with her if the collaboration was so erratic, Nataly said to me: "By God, next time when we meet it will be interesting, I promise you."

That last moment was when I knew that we would never see each other again because it was going to cause problems and upheaval. I realized that she was, in fact, playing a covert emotional game with me, manipulating her vulnerability to cause me to care about her interests, only to "reject" me by cutting communication. When I would adjust to this new situation, she would immediately come back closer to me in a way that she could potentially use to exert pressure on me to advance her interests as a student illegitimately. From her exam, I knew that Nataly's ambitions were unfounded, that she was going far beyond what she was realistically capable of at that stage of her development, and I suspected that a failure to achieve the goals that were set far too high would cause either a conflict with Nataly or her regression into mental illness. Thus, I was undecided as to whether to simply distance myself completely from her or to remain in proximity in case of her dramatic psychological downfall.

Considering the situation strategically, however, it became clear to me that Nataly was trying to control me. She was acting out the typical narcissist unconscious dynamics, while at the same time seeking to achieve specific rationally set goals. Unconsciously, she sought my attention as a confirmation of her value. Consciously, she was trying to manipulate me into helping her achieve the ends which she perhaps felt she could not realistically reach by herself.

In doing so, Nataly had analyzed my own existential situation and engaged at least in some guesswork over my life plans and life goals, drawing on what she could analogously infer from my lectures. She probably decided that I would be open to the attentions of a younger woman at this stage of my life and that this was sufficient to cause me to become dependent on the somewhat unusual communication that she incited. Manipulation and control always rest on at least a rough estimate of the victim's life plans and life goals.

How does one react to the narcissistic manipulation? Most importantly, one does not feed the daemon of narcissism. I decided to be strictly objective, as much as one can be objective at all, in judging Nataly's work. I also decided that I would not show up for meetings set up with her unless she fulfilled her part, wrote all of the work we agreed on prior to the meetings, and confirmed this before each meeting. This was going to mean that Nataly would be negatively surprised by my sudden lack of response to her initiatives, but I felt that this was both necessary for the protection of the integrity of the student–teacher relationship, which is institutionally mediated, and for Nataly psychologically, because depriving the narcissist of attention might serve as a corrective factor for narcissism. The risk of this approach, of course, was that Nataly could be angered and start on a route of antagonism, initially ignited by the lower grade that she expected, which she had received from me. As I am finishing this book, it remains to be seen how the consequences of acting contrary to the narcissist's desires will play out; however, Nataly's case illustrates the model of individual manipulation of what is at least suspected to be the victim's life goals and life plans in the particular situation that interests the narcissist, where the narcissist established control in a way that it is virtually impossible for the victim to resist.

I was aware of the risks of becoming involved in Nataly's narcissistic game; however, I still found myself initially immersed in communication that it was realistically impossible for me to avoid. It started as a normal deepening of human communication through the quest for commonalities and was then skillfully manipulated into dynamics that caused me to worry because I was suddenly feeling a lack of Nataly, although I had no important personal relationship with her. This lack, which was unwarranted by the objective facts of our communication and relationship, was the sought-after outcome, the engineered part of the relationship to be used to elicit outcomes that Nataly had envisaged. The fact that this was causing me discomfort was of no concern to Nataly; to the contrary, perhaps she experienced my discomfort as a satisfaction of her self-valuation. The fact that this emotional game was additionally inappropriate given our institutional relationship and the fact that I was her professor was equally irrelevant to Nataly: the greater the risk for me, the greater the satisfaction for her narcissistic craving.

The above is an important point in working with victims of narcissistic manipulation: they should never be encouraged to self-blame for succumbing to the narcissist's advances. If it was easy to recognize and fend off such manipulation, nobody would fall prey to it, while in fact most people do become entangled quite deeply in the narcissist's torture machine of squeezing affirmations of their own self-value from the victim's deprivation of contact, of communication, of positive strokes in the sense of transactional analysis. It is only when the victim can actually recognize the narcissist manipulation, and this is never at the very beginning, because that manipulation starts as normal human kindness and only gradually transforms into openly malignant and passively aggressive behavior, that the victim can really start to fight off the narcissist. This is where the therapeutic intervention should focus.

The key in addressing control, including that exerted by the narcissist, is twofold: it includes reaffirming one's life plan and the coherent life goals which correspond to that life plan, and at the same time confronting the narcissist's expectations of affirmations of their self-worth. Typically, this involves reclaiming the victim's own self-worth: rejecting the narcissist in an exploitative framework means retaking the victim's power from the narcissist, but it also means leaving the narcissist without power. The results of this denial cannot be pleasant for the narcissist, but they are potentially transformative and healing. If the narcissistic personality reacts adversely to denial, this is a sign of internal friction and potential change. On the other hand, if the narcissist simply walks away in search of another victim, this signifies a more pessimistic therapeutic scenario. In each case, it is the conceptualization of life plans and life goals whose control is at stake. The retaking of that control from other people who wish to usurp it is a sine qua non of personal autonomy and mental well-being at the same time.

Attachment and Detachment in the Pursuit of Life Goals

A precondition for the meaningful development of interpersonal interactions which lead to a smooth and straightforward pursuit of life goals, consistent with a well-articulated life plan, is sufficient attachment. Through a healthy and strong attachment, we are able to exert mutual influence and transfer encouragement and power to each other to achieve our respective life goals. However, in some pathological cases attachment must be preceded by deliberate *detachment*, because individuals are insufficiently sensitive to constructive collaboration and are accustomed to using manipulative strategies to both interpret and address such approaches. In other words, in working to elucidate and explicate a life plan and to define good life goals within that plan, it may be necessary to expose the person to detachment, to let the person go, or to abandon them in a certain sense and to a certain degree, in order to "get their attention" for the collaborative and attachment-centered initiatives.

Situations in which detachment must occur prior to attachment are largely cultural. In certain cultures, the cutting of communication is far more accepted as a model of social behavior than in others, and psychotherapists, unfortunately, often contribute to such toxic cultures by suggesting to people, en masse, that they can, or should, cease communication with others whenever such communication is less than pleasing to them, for whatever reason.

To work with someone who manipulates others' goals in a group, one must communicate some unpleasant content, and thus a culture that encourages responding to unpleasantness by cutting communication is particularly bad for such scenarios. Especially in extremely toxic cultures for constructive communication, the ability to detach oneself from others is crucial in order to set off a way of thinking that will be more accepting of constructive exchange. In other words, *being able not to* try to help someone, or become close to someone is a precondition for actually being able to help them or develop attachment with them.

Gabor Maté describes a phenomenon where the therapist *does not want to let the client go*, or to give up, even in impossible and unmanageable situations, because the therapist believes it to be his duty to try to *fix the unfixable* (Maté, 2021). Perhaps the cultural situation where attachment is not welcomed and a prior detachment is required is one of the most impossible situations for the helper, who cannot reach out to the client without first, in a sense, "rejecting" the client. This is a very strange and damaging culture, however, one that is fairly common in modern alienated Western societies, fraught with fear of intimacy. Detachment appears to be a precondition of successful interpersonal relationships, including therapeutic relationships, and a prerequisite for the eventual development of connection and intimacy.

Part of the cultural pattern of establishing intimacy is the demand or *desire for separation* prior to growing closer with someone. Individuals who wish to become intimate, to develop a life partnership, often face the expectation between themselves that one partner (the one who has greater initiative) should first "give the other space," namely allow for the desire for separation, which will help the other person *reassert their freedom and autonomy* in choosing to enter into a relationship, and only afterward will the other person become pliable to advances by the dominant partner directed at establishing connection and intimacy.

The above can be a highly confusing dialectic that detracts from the quality of the relationship, consumes significant time, and often generates misunderstandings between the potential partners. Rather than moving closer together, it appears that people succumb to a cultural expectation, internalized psychologically, to first move away, to establish distance, almost as though they are at war with the other party, and then, upon "assessing" the situation and all the relevant aspects of the potential relationship, may they move toward their potential partner.

The desire to separate prior to establishing intimacy is the result of an imagined order of norms: perhaps this particular desire is especially illustrative of how the imagined order works, because it is so contrary to the intuitive structure of behavior once two people wish to become intimate. Rather than simply connecting, they move away, not because it makes sense technically or emotionally, but simply because it is "the way it is done," the dominant pattern of behavior which is sanctioned by the culture as facilitating "self-worth" or "self-respect."

There is a deeper current of this type of behavior, as well, namely the need to cater to one's fear of intimacy and one's other fears. Allowing ourselves time and space to consider whether to do something that we clearly want to do also gives us time to try and face our fear of losing our loneliness, to which we have perhaps become too accustomed; to challenge our self-perceptions, including that of our body, when we are intimate with the other person, or to change our relationships with our family members or our close friends, where the introduction of a new partner is sure to shift both the power structure of the relationship and its dynamics (intensity of contacts with others, the social priorities, etc.). For each of us, the list of fears is somewhat different, but I suspect it also includes some common fears. All of these fears of change, of loss, of strain to adapt, of new responsibilities, are subsumed under "fear of intimacy."

The phenomenon of fear of intimacy is the result of a symbolic order that militates against basic human needs, one of which is intimacy. Such an order generates our desires because desires are predicated upon information, upon norms, and on the standards of desirability fostered by the culture. The actual desire to separate, to remove oneself from the object of one's need, namely from intimacy, does not invalidate the conclusion that the cultural norm of separation is destructive; to the contrary, the self-destructive actual desire, namely the desire that arises from cultural norms, additionally confirms the pathology of the norm itself.

The desire to commit suicide, if it is common (as it was in some religious cults), is an actual desire arising from a cultural norm, but the fact that people kill themselves because they experience a strong desire to commit suicide does not invalidate the conclusion that such a cult culture is pathological and contrary to fundamental human needs, which do not include suicide, but to the contrary, mutual connection, the cultivation of a life instinct, and a sense of support and hope.

Our desires powerfully illustrate our cultures, and our cultures determine, to a predominant extent, the horizons of our lives. Part of the job of both practical philosophy and psychotherapy is to question our cultures and allow individuals in trouble to "reinvent themselves" as new persons, subscribing to different cultures or developing cultures for themselves that are more optimal and more constructive for their well-being.

One way to address these issues is by focusing on transcending the imagined order: the entire strength of the imagined order is in the thoughts that make it up and in the thoughts that the norms give rise to inside us.

Advancing beyond the fictitious symbolic order that requires us to remove ourselves from others means projecting a particular sentiment, value, or intention beyond the "wall" or the sanctioned perimeter of the fictitious order itself.

To establish high-quality human relationships, one must therefore transcend the fictitious order which imposes a political correctness to build human relationships by first moving in the opposite direction of warmth and mutual closeness. This is how new organic communities are created. They are usually very different in values and style of mutual inter-relationships than the mainstream communities; their identity partly derives from their different and special culture. However, to be able to project an intention or emotion beyond the customary and conventional bounds and styles of human relationships, one must first have a clear conception of the community one wishes to establish or partake in, just as one needs to first have a clear life plan in order to be able to set life goals that do not simply arise from circumstances or socially desirable values. There is thus a rational structure behind our ability to transcend the cultural limitations of group, organization, or society: this rational order of values is based on decisions made for the long term—decisions about fundamental life plans and those life goals that, along with the other *ad hoc* life goals dictated by the culture, ensure that our life plans remain on track.

The culture of detachment in intimate relationships is a degrading and destructive influence on the pursuit of organic community links with others who are potentially important to us. However, there is a different, epistemic meaning of detachment that can be useful for the articulation and adoption of life plans.

A conscious effort is required to build and sustain life plans, and this effort goes against the spontaneity of the dominant cultural norms. Individual life plans can profit from culture only if they are backed by strategy which will use elements of the culture to the advantage of the person's chosen goals. However, the opposite situation is more common: rather than taking an epistemic distance to the immediacy of the cultural norms and appreciating which aspects of the culture are useful and which ones are detrimental to our life plans, most of us simply succumb, refraining from intellectual or other conscious effort: we pursue the life goals dictated by the culture, or as Harari puts it, "we build pyramids," whether they are a fancy cottage in the countryside, a penthouse in the city, or a book that we leave behind because "leaving a mark" is the cultural norm and life goal which confirms our success and social worth, while in fact most of these goals are rarely reconcilable with rationally conceived life goals (Harari, 2015: 128–133).

We don't need cottages, travel abroad, or new books in order to fulfill quality life plans. However, the culture of legacy, of leaving a mark, makes us do things that, in fact, have little or nothing to do with our own rational projections of identity and desires.

Our desires are not irrational: they have something to do with who we authentically are, and at the same time they are connected with the cultural requirements and suggestions that make us desire certain things and experiences. It is thus the cultivation of our desires within a broader rational context of life plans, which are largely independent of our culture, that gives meaning to life goals. Establishing a healthy *epistemic distance from the immediate, overwhelming influence of cultural norms* is a prerequisite for such a rational perspective of life plans.

This emphasis on the rationality of life plans is only seemingly in discord with my earlier insistence on the role of emotions in decision-making in pursuing a quality life plan. What constitutes the actual quality of life are emotions: they are the drivers, the dynamic factors of our decisions, not our rational reasoning; however, emotions are also not entirely irrational.

Acting without a proper life plan usually results in life situations and outcomes that invite devastating emotions, such as regret, sadness, and a sense of defeat. Like engaging in a complex project or going to war without a plan, the actions and immediate goals might seem obvious, the experience might be temporarily satisfying or electrifying; however, the likely outcome will be depressing. Similarly, detaching ourselves from the misguiding immediacy of cultural expectations can save our lives both symbolically and emotionally. A large part of integrative thinking consists in these two opposing directions of the use of *attachment and detachment*: learning to ignore the norms requiring detachments as a precondition for subsequent emotional attachments, which leads to organic links and organic communities of two or more people, ranging from the family to organic society, on the one hand, and learning to exert a disciplined consciousness in detaching ourselves from the attraction and stimulation of quests of pyramids, books, unreasonable emotional conquests, or the uncritical and, in the long term, personally detrimental pursuit of career at the expense of greater and more intimate values, which will in the end determine the success or failure of our life project.

Notes

1 When referencing Wittgenstein, I depart from the general style of referencing in this book for substantive reasons. In Wittgenstein's *Tractatus*, the decimal references are crucial, and the page references in the compact printed editions where decimals are scattered are virtually useless. In the centenary edition of the *Tractatus*, the structure of the book is laid out according to Wittgenstein's intended structure, based on decimals. When referencing the *Tractatus*, I thus use the decimals to facilitate the easy use of any edition of the book, given that most readers would have the standard and not the centenary edition.

2 "The general propositional form is the essence of a proposition," Wittgenstein (2021: 5.471).

References

Harari, Yuval Noah (2015). *Sapiens: A brief history of humankind*. London: Vintage.
(2021). *The wisdom of trauma* (Film). https://thewisdomoftrauma.com.
Robbins, Anthony (1992). *Awaken the giant within*. New York: Simon and Schuster.
Searle, John (1983). *Intentionality*. Cambridge: Cambridge University Press.
Wittgenstein, Ludwig (2021). *Tractatus logico-philosophicus*. Centenary ed. London: Anthem Press.

IN THE WAY OF CONCLUSION: PSYCHOTHERAPY AS A PHILOSOPHY OF LIFE

The Social Nature of Medicalized Issues in Psychic Life

Unlike the other medical disciplines, psychiatry is a primarily socially oriented area of therapeutic intervention. Psychiatry is therefore as much a humanistic and social science discipline as it is a part of medicine; its purpose is to heal what Agamben describes as "Socialitas," the capacity and skills of individuals to maintain a healthy sociality with others, which Agamben considers a "law of nature." In the previous chapters, I have mentioned some of the reasons psychiatry and the very concept of mental health are inherently social, including not only the Lacanian tradition in psychiatry but also more recent analyses of the social causation of what is later labeled as "mental disorder," including arguments put forward by Lou Marinoff. According to Agamben, Socialitas requires that every person does their best to *cultivate and preserve sociability* (Agamben, 2013: 59). The argument implies that engaging socially, including the organic engagements with close others, part of which engagement is conflict, is a prerequisite for living in accordance with the moral norm of Socialitas. "Being nice" and "tolerant," while avoiding organic encounters and hiding behind procedurally too elaborate social norms is fundamentally antisocial because it destroys the authentic Socialitas and replicates machinery in social structure (Fatić, 2022).

I think that Agamben is very close here to the concept of an organic community. The idea that *cultivating a sense of everyday togetherness, which requires an emotional closeness, is a norm*, where organic relations are inevitably seen as constitutive of human health and wellness appears as the logical part of Socialitas. This would then require of all organized human action, especially of the helping professions, and first of all of psychiatry, to *see togetherness as health, and, conversely, to understand mutual separation and discrete individuality as at least an intrinsic risk for unwellness.* This means that psychiatry should serve Socialitas, rather than militate against it, and that it should be a force against the modern cultural subjugation of the family to an abstract idea of personal and individual liberty to pursue goals which systematically undermine Socialitas.

Psychiatry today is an area whose disciplinary location is exceptionally problematic, as its methodology and its very logic not only differ from the rest of medicine but are often directly opposed to those of medicine (Fatić, 2019). Psychiatry is a social discipline that does not address illness in the physical sense but seeks to help organize one's ways of perceiving and experiencing reality in ways that are more conducive to the person's Socialitas and thus also to the welfare of society. If psychiatry deviates from its very purpose and serves ideological goals that foster particular interests, as opposed to those that are specifically organic and social, then it has betrayed its very reason for existence and should be questioned as a discipline. Today there are all kinds of psychiatry, including the various ideologically based schools of the discipline, such as feminist psychiatry, which then, at least to a large measure, derives its "medical" conclusions from feminist ideological premises.

Arguably any kind of normative science must rest on certain theoretical assumptions, and thus also psychiatry, if it purports to be a science, must start from some kind of value normativity, or ideology. All paradigms of psychiatry throughout its fairly brief history as a science have been based on various theories of how the human mind operates and what the beacons are by which one stays normal. In this, psychiatry has traditionally depended on psychological theories, and we all know how different they are in understanding the very foundations of our psychic functioning. Thus, on the one hand, psychiatry is necessarily a practical application of a particular psychological theory. On the other hand, however, if psychiatry becomes the exteriorization and emanation in clinical practice of an antisocial theory, one that seeks to turn various identities, individual and group, into mortal enemies by describing their relationships as those of competition for power and control, of lurking violence and exploitation, while it describes the role of the organic community as a prison for otherwise free and flourishing individuals, then such psychiatry fails the imperative to serve Socialitas; it becomes a delinquent psychiatry.

One of the key problems with psychiatry from the integrative point of view is its reluctance to recognize this described role of the helping professions in serving sociality and developing organic communities. Every more or less organic form of human community is modeled upon the family, ranging from professional organizations and sport teams to the military and the police, to political parties and to countries as wholes. Thus, the modern debates over the duty of the state to "care" for its citizens derive exactly from this organic origin of the state as a community, and not as a set of institutions: a state that is indifferent to the happiness or unhappiness, or to any existential plight of its citizens, is not organically legitimate. Hence any helping profession, including psychiatry, which is also an institution, is legitimate only insofar as it serves Socialitas *by advancing the very paradigm of it, and that is the family.* The psychiatry that is predicated upon an individual, and upon a liberal ideology, fails its purpose because it then turns *against the communal interests.*

In Agamben's perspective, individual social rights (as the very concept suggests) derive from the individual's membership in a community, from his or her presumed sociality, and not from a presumed discrete and asocial identity. While political liberalism initially arose from a philosophical and practical political opposition to the state's excessive intrusion in the private lives of individual citizens and its tyrannical impulses toward individuals, liberalism, which places individual identity and individual rights before and above the communal identity and the communal sourcing of rights, when applied to the helping professions, becomes an extremely toxic and counter-intuitive ideology, which, ultimately, defeats the very meaning of these professions. Psychiatry cannot help any liberally conceived "pre-social" individual in their lonely existential condition without working for the social reconceptualization of individual desire within an organic community. In fact, the psychiatric therapeutic relationship cannot help anyone without becoming an organic community itself, and this very principle renders psychiatry a humanistic discipline. Psychiatry, as all other helping professions, is inherently communitarian, rather than liberal, and when psychiatry breaks away from its communitarian conceptual home and tries to become a "science," or a "medical discipline," including attempting to deal with "diagnoses," psychiatry sets its own course toward an inevitable failure. It truly fulfills Lacan's prophecy of necessary failure of the therapeutic "master discourse" and "discourse of the university."

Organicism in Returning to Ancient Formats of Psychotherapy

If an organic relationship requires an emphatic reaching out to the other person, then the format should reflect that characteristic of therapy. This means that traditional, ancient formats such as walking in the nature, going on joint trips, spending a few days together, either as a group or simply the person counseled and the therapist, or similar formats are much more appropriate for reaching the goals of organic therapy. All these alternative formats are included in deep psychotherapy, which I described briefly earlier on in this book.

It is not surprising that historically any close communication, ranging from personal counseling to business meetings, was conducted in baths, the sports facilities of the time, or while walking. In such settings, people are engaged in a common activity, and they face that activity together. This places them in a different mutual position than when one awaits the other in a counseling room, each ready to take their roles. The less attention is placed on the *division of roles* in counseling, and the more on the *substance* of counseling, the more organically effective that counseling is likely to be.

The format tells us about the attitude of all participants in the counseling process, and the more one is prepared to stretch one's conventional comfort zone in determining the format, the more one is able to reach out to the other person emotionally, but also cognitively. Clearly, the conventional format of counseling limits us cognitively because we cannot place ourselves "in the shoes" of the other person if we see that person as a client and do not perceive their issues from a first-person perspective. If, however, we walk, swim, travel, climb, or eat together, we are likely to integrate our perceptions of what the other person is saying with the shared experience that we are undergoing with that person, and this will likely draw the narrative of the other person into our own first-person perspective. The other person will also accept more easily the fact that we can identify with their perspective if there is a concurrent shared experience of something other than the conversation itself.

The substantive *shared experience* is like a *catalyst of conversation and bonding.* This is why the more intense the shared experience, the more strongly people tend to bond together and the more a priori trust they tend to bestow in each other in later challenging situations. It is a well-known and generally accepted principle that in developing various types of partnerships, including life partnerships, one can only reliably decide on who to partner with after one has undergone optimum common experience with that person, and has weathered, alongside them, some relatively serious difficulties together.

Without the catalytic experience which shows how we act under stress and makes our feelings and values more naked than the traditional, everyday format of conversation, it is virtually impossible to make joint life decisions.

The above principle of organicism applies to any kind of bonding, and particularly to effective psychotherapy. In order for a therapeutic relationship to be effective, it must closely resemble the family bond, where the mutual care is automatically assumed. The format of the counseling room is at stark odds with the family context of psychotherapy, just as the "alternative" (in fact, historically more traditional) formats of therapeutic discourse while walking, doing sports, traveling, or eating together naturally contribute to the organicism of the relationship and thus also to the organic effectiveness of the counseling process.

Another important issue with organicism in counseling is that it requires a *sacrifice*. In order to undergo, with the client, a common experience outside the realm of conventional counseling, the counselor must accept a risk of personal displeasure, stress, or adversity. The methodological credo of "safe environment" for the client is mistakenly extended to the assumption of a safe environment for the counselor as well. Counseling should be relatively safe for the client (although even this assumption cannot be taken for granted), but it is rarely safe for the counselor. In fact, the psychoanalytic principle that effective counseling always "hystericizes" the client suggests that before the client gets better, they will likely get worse because of the counseling, and this casts a shadow over the assumption that counseling is safe. No change in life is safe, and counseling aims at a change of the person's conceptualization and framing of values. Such a change is usually dangerous, prone to destabilizing the counselee, and, consequently, also to inflict stress on the counselor.

Only if counseling is understood as a family-like process of using and benefiting from care, where both the counselor cares for the client *and the client cares for the counselor*, the process may be effective in the long run. However, this is a process rife with sacrifices to be made by the counselor. The discomfort is an inevitable part of it, just as it is of any family-like process. The common experience of life through joint activities by the counselor and counselee, their joint pursuits, and shared interests may ameliorate the discomfort for both, and at the same time *catalyze* the attainment of greater and more beneficial outcomes. Again, this is one of the key benefits of deep psychotherapy, briefly described earlier on.

What, then, does it mean for counseling to be "family-like" in terms of format? Don't family members also talk to each other in much the same format as do the psychotherapist and the client? Where is the major difference in format between the two types of social structure or relationship?

Alex and Danny

Alex is a psychotherapist in her forties, whose husband died tragically and unexpectedly from sudden illness. She has a boy, Miles, who is one of the most talented and likable children I have had a chance to know. Miles was very attached to his father, who taught him to play guitar, spent time with him watching sports and films, and did everything in his power to make Miles' childhood a happy one. The boy faced the death of his father by mobilizing all of his internal resources to retain psychological coherence. His success at school became erratic after his father's passing, and he exhibited a generalized anxiety through the tendency to reject responsibility.

Miles' mother had to face the child's systemic illness in addition to the stress of living alone, catering for the family, and maintaining a demanding academic job. Relatively soon after her husband had died, Alex established a relationship with another man and gradually introduced her son to her new partner. By choosing her partner carefully, led by her emotions, but also by what she believed to be the best for her son, Alex accomplished an organic recreation of the family once lost, where the place of her late husband was fully preserved. The new partner is sufficiently mature not to try to take the boy's father's place and plays the role of Miles' older friend. Miles likes Danny and talks about his father with him. Danny cares for Miles and has become proficient in the treatment Miles receives for his ailment. The relationship between Alex and Danny is harmonious, and in many respects, Miles has become a happy child again. The lingering difficulties in school are the only remnant of his grieving for his father.

For Miles, his father's memory remains a *major socializing factor* for him: he speaks about his father and the experiences he had had with him, drawing parallels with his recent experiences and trying to guess what his father would have done in the situations Miles faces in the present.

Miles relies on his mother and Danny for everyday support, but at no point in their relationship is there any conflict between the role and place of Miles's father and Danny. Miles grows up in a society dominated by Western values; however, his situation, luckily, is almost the same as that of children who live in societies where the entire community takes care of them, where parents change partners but do not sever the children's links and affection for their other parent, while at the same time leaving them free to establish new loyalties with the parent's new partners. Such societies, such as that in the Caribbean (including Jamaica, which I briefly discussed above), are known to provide the most organic concept of socialization for children, with the least trauma and psychological disability arising from family disintegration. More industrialized and affluent societies in the West, however, are known to generate far greater problems for their children where families disintegrate because of the exclusive way of thinking about relationships and the ownership-dominated conceptualization of having and raising children.

Miles, Alex, and Danny are an example of how organic thinking, both affectionate and strategic at the same time, helps individuals grow within a family. It is a paradigm of how organicism operates between affectionately connected people.

How could the example of the trio be applied to other relationships? We build our relationships against the backdrop of our experience. On one level, we bring our previous experiences into a new relationship as a yardstick by which we measure the new people in our lives. However, on a different level, we build the specific "chemistry" in the new relationship based on the experiences that have marked *that relationship*. If we meet someone while rafting on a mountain river and that person attracts us by being adventurous, brave, and resilient, this is a background that will determine the way in which we will, at least initially, approach the relationship. If, on the other hand, we meet our new love in a hospital, while we are a patient and she is a doctor, and our emotions develop against the backdrop of her caring and gentle approach to us and the other patients, then this will determine our initial steps in building our relationship. Whether we have approached either of the two relationships from a history of being abused, or being cared for, or having had mostly cold and emotionless partnering affairs, will become so much less significant the more intense the experience and the identity of the others that are established through this new experience are.

Alex and Danny have shown how applying the organic principles characteristic of well-functioning families can heal even the most severe wounds inflicted by family disintegration or family tragedies. They have shown how focusing on the sensibility and interests of all members of the family in a harmonious way is a good integrative method of decision-making in key dilemmas of life. Societies such as those of Jamaica, in many other respects highly problematic, permeated with drug abuse and economic hardship, have shown, on a different level, how integrative principles save kids and protect their capacities for fruitful life despite initial childhood adversities. However, the extent to which Alex and Danny will grow together and how close they will become depends on their experiences, which will articulate and catalyze their mutual relationship. Experiences such as illness, financial hardship, abandonment by other close people, career defeats, and so on, *condense time* in a relationship. By addressing these difficult circumstances, people show their intentions, their values, and their emotions to the other person. I know Alex personally as a friend, and she has proven innumerable times just how devoted a friend she is. Not long before writing this book, I was critically ill, and her actions as a friend, including not only helping me but actually driving me while infected with Covid-19 in her car, while she was not vaccinated and had no immunity, cemented her relationship to me as a friend which would be extremely difficult, if not impossible, to shake by any smaller negative experience in the future. The magnitude of our experience is proportional to the significance and meaning of our conclusions regarding our relationships with others.

The way Alex and Danny have handled their relationship in front of Miles has not only "not harmed" Miles; it has not only helped Miles get a sense of recreated family where the place of his father is intact; furthermore, Alex's and Danny's approach has taught Miles *how to position himself constructively* in potentially similar situations in his own future life. This is an invaluable resource for him, which he has taken away from his family. Alex and Danny have managed *to turn a crisis into a resource* for Miles. This is the aim of integrative psychotherapy and of organicism in family-like human relationships overall.

Having said all this, how would the example of Alex and Danny reflect on family-friendly and family-like psychiatry? What lessons would such psychiatry be able to draw from Alex, Danny, and Miles?

The first lesson would likely be that the psychiatrist and the "patient" would need to be in a relationship not far from that between Alex and Danny in terms of frankness, mutual devotion, and sincerity. In no way should the psychiatrist try to "manipulate" or "dominate" the process. He must be able to enter deeply into a relationship and take a part of the responsibility for the future of that relationship. There are legitimate expectations by the client from the therapist, sometimes similar to those by a life partner. The client can legitimately expect that the therapist considers her rights, interests, and emotions important and does everything to advance her quality of life and that of connected persons (typically the family members). The therapist, on the other hand, has a legitimate expectation that the client is devoted to him, that she values what he does in their relationship, the way he takes care of her, and that she wishes to make his experience working with her as pleasant and as successful and as easy as possible.

Looking at these mutual expectations from aside, one quickly notices that they are almost the same as expectations by life partners of each other. When such expectations are fulfilled, the therapist and the client find themselves at uncharted terrain, where so much of what goes on between them resembles a family relationship. In such closeness between them, they sometimes slip and enter into a private, family-like, romantic relationship. This explains the relative frequency of such ethical transgressions. Not all such transgressions into romance are damaging to the client; to the contrary, they are often beneficial for them, although the very concept of trying to justify these kinds of boundary violations is considered heretical in modern psychotherapeutic schools.

The reason one must be critically aware of the methodology of counseling is primarily because counseling is not professional in the way in which most other professions are: if it is truly effective, it must be intimate and based on *mutual* care: on the care by the *therapist for the client*, and on the *care by the client for the therapist.* Both must feel good in the relationship, and both must feel that they are close and devoted to each other, that they "mean something" to each other. However, when the slipping into romance occurs, then unless there are serious consequences in terms of unwanted and damaging outcomes, this professional failure must be treated with a degree of reserve. Organic relationships are not entirely professional, and it is not by definition true that a therapist and a client who enter into a family type of relationship that is not professionally therapeutic, thereby forfeit their therapeutic relationship. At least the example of Carl Jung in the history of psychotherapy illustrates that things with boundaries in psychotherapy are not nearly as simple as the modern codes of psychotherapeutic conduct would have us believe.

Having taken on the risks of organicism, the psychotherapist must then follow the format set in my example by Alex and Danny: he must work with the client as with a friend and partner, putting her interests above those of the others in the immediate surroundings, but also placing his trust in the client that she will also take care of the sensibility and interests of the therapist.

Only if the psychiatrist allows himself to be a real person in his professional work with a client in counseling will he be able to establish an organic bond with the client. This requires the therapist to also voice some of his needs and desires, fears and expectations, not only professionally, but also personally.

Once the mutual bond of trust is established in this way, it is different from the trust characteristic of professional relationships.

I trust my car mechanic that he will service my car properly and that he will not overcharge me for it. This is professional trust. In return, my mechanic trusts me that I will show up on time when we have an appointment for the service, that I will pick up the car when agreed, that I will recommend him to my friends and other potential customers if I am happy with his services, and so on. This is a healthy professional relationship of trust. However, with a psychiatrist or a psychotherapist, I will not only trust that they will go out of their way to help me make my life more worthwhile; I will also trust them that they care for me, in much the same way as I will trust my romantic partner that she cares for me. My therapist, on the other hand, will trust me that I value his efforts, and his personality, highly, that I will do what I can to make his job easier, and that I will try to make him, or her, as happy as possible during our relationship. This is a different type of trust from that that binds me and my car mechanic.

It is unlikely that I may enter into a romantic relationship with my car mechanic based on the kind of trust we share; it is however far more likely that I, or my therapist, might be tempted to cross the boundaries of a professional relationship given the overarching kind of mutual devotion that we share in an organic therapeutic relationship. We should thus not consider such transgressions too seriously in terms of professional responsibility when they occur.

All of the mentioned aspects of organicism, exemplified in the mature partnering relationship between Alex and Danny, when applied to the therapeutic context, show why it is so difficult for psychiatrists to be good organic therapists: as *medical doctors* they are formed as *professionals*, and their focus lies within *medical logic*, which is *quite inappropriate to an organic understanding of psychotherapy*. To venture behind this logic of authority, exactness, and professional boundaries means, in a sense, to *leave psychiatry behind* and become a real "people person" in therapy. In other words, it means to engage with life as a common experience with the client and share parts of it with him or her, without necessarily seeing the client throughout the process as a sufferer, a patient, or an object of analysis.

The sense of community that resembles the family is what gives healing power to psychotherapy and its interventions. However, judging what it means to foster a family-type relationship is not always uncontroversial: in most cases what we imagine as family-like is cooperative, empathic, and supportive; however, in many cases, a true care for someone in the way a family member cares for another requires a degree of aggression, reproach, even conflict. This means that in organic psychotherapy normative neutrality can hardly exist in any significant sense. This brings us to what the example of Alex and Danny shows in terms of values.

Alex and Danny have chosen to focus on the value of family in general. Alex's late husband, Danny's ex-wife, and his son, whom he sees relatively irregularly, are absent, but Alex and Danny have decided to *recreate the family atmosphere* together, where all those members of their families who are physically absent, for various reasons, are *symbolically present*, and *their places at the family table remain preserved*. Danny occasionally brings his son along to the family, and Danny's ex-wife is recognized by the family as a part of Danny's past and present life. Similarly, the place for Miles's father remains *sanctified by the current structure of the family*. This means that all members of the family, including Danny's ex-wife and his son, *emotionally benefit* from Alex' and Danny's union, while *nobody is excluded*. This is possible because Alex and Danny have correctly assessed the manner and style of their union.

Their success depends on the *convergence of the values* they have chosen to focus on. Should they focus on different values, the union could fall apart very easily. This is a principle in all family-type relationships: *value convergence is what keeps the community together*. The same is the case in organic psychotherapy, where for the family-type relationship between the client and the therapist to flourish, there must be a significant value similarity between their choices and their self-perceptions as persons. This means that very different people, with very different sensibilities, temperaments, and value priorities will hardly be able to establish a high-quality therapeutic relationship.

Similarity is what makes for organic communities. The greater the harmony between the people's values, the more effective that community will be both in its actions as a whole and in serving the desires of its members.

Some of the problems of modern psychiatry have been pointed out by Irvin Yalom, Jonathan Redmond, and Paul Verhaeghe, namely its political tendencies to pathologize and de-pathologize various "disorders" depending on the fashions and statistical mannerism of the day (Yalom and Leszcz, 2005; Redmond, 2014; Verhaeghe, 2008). However, the problems with psychiatry associated with its fundamental lack of organicism have been sparsely addressed, and primarily by philosophers. The perspective of family-like counseling and family-type relationships as the paradigm of our overall social relationships is a fairly new one, and it seems to me that it helps practically address exactly what is missing in psychiatric methodology.

Organicism is always close to intimacy, to our inner personality: the more personal involvement and investment in a relationship, the more organic that relationship will be. Given that psychiatry sees itself as a branch of medicine, it is very difficult for it to conceptualize and professionally legislate the family-type emotional and broader personal involvement, including the personal self-examination of the psychiatrist in every specific relationship with a patient. While this is only a part of psychiatry's failure to act organically, it is a large and important one.

The psychoanalytic principle that *the truth resides in ethics*, not in facts or epistemology, not in knowledge—is closely associated with organicism in human relationships. Given that any kind of psychotherapy is based on social structure and on communication, the more organic and closer these relationships are, the more immediate and less in need of institutional mediation or rule-based governance a social structure is, the more effective the therapy will be.

The idea that, epistemically speaking, any psychotherapist is "an epistemologist of more or less private epistemologies" (Cambien, 1981: 530; Verhaeghe, 2008: 84) suggests that our individual epistemic differences may not be able to be reconciled through any kind of therapeutic process. However, the truth, which lies in the *ethics and values of our relationship*, will *integrate and transcend any epistemic differences.*

The discussion of psychotherapy in light of modal logic here elucidates, I hope, a general nature of the principles of psychotherapy considering the concept of the good life. There is nothing in psychotherapy that is not a distilled form of principles, values, and logic that make our everyday relationships better, more fulfilling, and, by extension, our life more worth living. Psychotherapy, as a discipline and as an activity, is a paradigm of the focus on the good life that has characterized practical philosophy from its inception. Psychotherapy, in other words, is the most obvious paradigm of a philosophy of life in its most practical form. This has profound implications for our understanding of both. Rather than understanding psychotherapy as a medicalized realm of correction of dysfunctionality, one might consider it a philosophy of life with its own practical interventions that are designed to seek a good life: such a quest involves both correcting the dysfunction and improving sensibility, clarifying epistemic perspectives, and examining and solidifying values.

A consequence of the above understanding of psychotherapy as a philosophy of life is that it cannot be seen as a profession, a protected, licensed, and restricted realm allegedly characterized by "expert" knowledge and a responsibility for the betterment of another's life condition that goes in any way beyond the responsibility of a philosophical interlocutor. Such a perspective has recently been called "philosophical counseling," or, more broadly, "philosophical practice." This label, while essential to highlight the practical nature of philosophy in its capacity to act as a helping discipline, is also at some level unfortunate, because it invites the introduction of all kinds of disciplinary distinctions between psychotherapy and philosophical counseling that, by my lights at least, are unwarranted and ultimately unsustainable. It seems to me that exploring the key logical, value, and epistemic aspects of our psychic difficulties reveals not primarily our pathology, but our deep human condition that has been the main subject of practical philosophy since its beginnings, at least back in the fourth-century BC, in Western tradition alone. Thus, considering logic (in this discussion, modal logic) in its fundamental role and practical consequences for psychotherapy reveals deeper facts about psychotherapy as a philosophy of life. This makes it legitimate to speak about psychotherapy as inclusive of philosophical counseling and all other types of discourse therapy. It also makes credible the view of psychotherapy as simply a philosophy of life, rather than a craft or a structured skill characteristic of social guilds. My integrative view does not "collapse" psychotherapy from a profession into merely an occupation but rather uses the interpretation of modal logic in psychotherapeutic theory and practice alike to raise and reinstate psychotherapy as a philosophy of life par excellence, founded on its reception and integration of logic, epistemology, and the interpretation of life goals within a general practical philosophical quest for a good life.

References

Agamben, Giorgio (2013). *Opus Dei. An archaeology of duty.* Translated by Adam Kotsko. Stanford: Stanford University Press.

Cambien, Jean (1981). "De (on)wetenschappelijkheid van de psychoanalyse." *Tijdschrift voor Psychiatrie*, Vol. 23, No. 4: 203–215.

Fatić, Aleksandar (2019). "Representation and pathology in philosophy and psychotherapy." *Filozofska istraživanja*, Vol. 39, No. 1: 33–47.

Fatić, Aleksandar (2022). "Why being nice is fundamentally antisocial." https://aleksandarfatic.net/why-being-nice-is-fundamentally-a-social/. Accessed January 30, 2022.

Redmond, Jonathan (2014). *Ordinary psychosis and the body*. London: Palgrave.

Verhaeghe, Paul (2008). *On being normal and other disorders*. London: Karnac Books.

Yalom, Irvin and Leszcz, Molyn (2005). *The theory and practice of group psychotherapy*. 5th ed. New York: Basic Books.

INDEX